FREE AGENT

Free Agent

The Unseen War 1941–1991

BRIAN CROZIER

![HarperCollins logo] HarperCollins*Publishers*

HarperCollins books may be purchased for educational, business, or sales
promotional use. For information, please write: Special Markets
Department, HarperCollins Publishers, Inc., 10 East 53rd Street, New York
NY 10022

FIRST EDITION

LIBRARY OF CONGRESS

ISBN 0-06-017117-0

93 94 95 96 97   10 9 8 7 6 5 4 3 2 1

This book is dedicated to those who made the 61
possible and sustained it, primarily to:

Dick (the marathon supporter), Jimmy, Rupert, Elmar,
and not forgetting Alphons and Jack; Gordon at a critical
time; Chris and Bill. And others too numerous to name
but always remembered

Contents

Author's Foreword

THIS BOOK is not about the collapse of Soviet communism: it is concerned with Western failures of will or judgment that almost enabled the Soviet side to prevail. It is the story of key episodes in the unseen war behind the Cold War, which lasted from 1941 to 1991.

By definition, this unseen or secret war was unknown to the general public, although it occasionally broke into the headlines at times of scandal, such as the unmasking of 'Kim' Philby or the humbling of the CIA after Watergate. But there was more to it than scandal headlines, much more.

There were unsung triumphs as well as hidden defeats. I have decided to tell the story as a personal contribution to the history of our troubled times, but also because, to my knowledge, nobody else was so closely involved as I was in so many aspects of the secret war.

Brian Crozier 1993

Author's Preface

THERE WAS a special touch of nastiness in Margot Honecker's pastime. She, the wife of the former East German Communist leader, used to confiscate the children of dissidents and farm them out to parents who would not let the ruling Socialist Unity Party (SED) down by contesting its right to rule.

Frau Honecker's pastime was only one of a myriad facts we in the West have learned after the partial collapse of Communism in 1989 and the 'end of the Cold War'.

In the scale of Communist horrors, though, far more terrible things have happened, from Stalin's show-trials and massacres to the crushing of the Hungarian revolt in 1956; from the slaughter of 'rich' peasants in Mao Tse-tung's China and Ho Chi Minh's Vietnam to Pol Pot's genocide in Cambodia; from Fidel Castro's torture of dissidents to Ceausescu's crushing of the Romanian people.

The toll of man-made death and destruction seems endless. And all for nothing. The 'radiant future' promised in Lenin's name simply failed to materialise. The eggs were broken, but with no omelette to show for the shells. Yet for decades the ghastly reality was camouflaged in an endless tissue of official lies, and only on 29 August 1991 in Moscow did the Soviet parliament suspend the Communist Party which had ruled over the Soviet Union since Lenin's Revolution of 1917.

The Second Revolution had then come, after a botched coup by party hard-liners. On returning from a brief house arrest in the Crimea, President Mikhail Gorbachev had reaffirmed his loyalty to the party that had betrayed him. But as he later admitted, he knew a coup was on the way but did nothing to stop it. He also admitted that the world had changed during his absence. His rival, Boris Yeltsin, President of the Russian Republic, had stood up to the coup leaders, and his courage had brought him an authority he had previously lacked.

Now, all that Gorbachev could do was acquiesce in the suspension of the Party, which was soon followed by the sealing of its buildings and the freezing of its assets. The long nightmare of Communism was over in its original home, even though it survived in China, Cuba and other places and in the deeds of terrorist gangs in Peru, the Philippines and elsewhere. The aftermath would be painful and protracted, but the threat posed by Soviet Communism to the rest of the world for more than seven decades seemed to be over.

The time, therefore, seems ripe for me to tell a story hitherto untold: the protracted war of the secret services of East and West.

I became a committed anti-Communist in 1947, but for the next dozen years I was content to write and speak about it. I was a *passivist*: a mere observer. Since I was a journalist, specialising in international affairs, this was part of my job.

In 1952 and 1953, while in Saigon and Singapore covering the first Indochina war and the Malayan Emergency for Reuters and Australian Associated Press, I made my first intelligence contacts with the British and French. Later, in London, I was able to spread my net wider. At that time, I was running a confidential bulletin for *The Economist* and broadcasting commentaries for the BBC. During this period, I saw these contacts simply as sources, useful for scoops or for confidential background to the news.

Then, in 1958, I became an activist, personally involved in the war of the secret services. At one time, I worked with the American Central Intelligence Agency and with two of Britain's secret services: the Secret Intelligence Service (SIS or MI-6) and the Information Research Department (IRD) of the Foreign Office. I write 'with' not 'for' deliberately. At all times I remained independent, executing only tasks that were in line with my own objectives. I also had dealings with the secret services of many other countries, including France, Germany, Holland, Belgium, Italy, Spain, Israel, Morocco, Iran, Argentina, Chile and Taiwan (Republic of China).

The spectacular espionage successes of Soviet intelligence, through such traitors as Philby, Blake and others, are well known. The West, too, had its successes but, with one major exception and a few smaller ones, espionage plays a relatively minor part in this story. My main concern is with the secret war for people's minds, through 'agents of influence', front organisations (on both sides of the Iron Curtain) and 'tricks' (some of them 'dirty', others relatively benign, though deceptive).

Much has been said about the damage caused to the American CIA and the Federal Bureau of Investigation or FBI, in the 1970s, in the aftermath of the Watergate affair. Much less is publicly known about the serious and largely self-inflicted damage to other Western secret services. The inside story of the closing down of the Foreign Office's IRD will be told here for the first time. So will that of the wrecking of Germany's secret intelligence service under Willy Brandt, and of General de Gaulle's decision to close down France's anti-Leninist Fifth Bureau.

Which brings me to that one 'major exception', for I will also tell the story of a secret spying operation against de Gaulle during his presidency, which I organised. Also, in 1977, in the wake of the collapse of the CIA's 'Covert Action', I set up a secret operational agency, which operated in the private sector, internationally and undetected, for ten years. This story, too, will be told for the first time.

My involvement in this secret war was, by definition, secret. I have kept silent about it until now, but today, with the Cold War over and after the extraordinary events of 1989–91, I believe that neither national nor international security will be damaged by these revelations. The public surely has a right to know what was being done, out of sight, to defend the liberties of our Western societies, which had been under attack for more than seven decades.

Whenever necessary and possible, I have supplemented my personal experience and observation by subsequent investigation. But I cannot tell the whole story. Nor can anybody else, in my view. Secret services destroy their archives, selectively and from time to time. This probably means that the full story can *never* be told. To sum up: what I say here will, I hope, be a contribution to the history of our times, but I cannot claim that it is a definitive history.

I have included many unofficial meetings and epistolary exchanges with Mrs Margaret Thatcher before and during her premiership, and similar meetings and exchanges with Ronald Reagan before and during his presidency. There was no question of publishing such exchanges while Mrs Thatcher and President Reagan were still in office. Now, I have no compunction about doing so.

Nevertheless, I have exercised self-censorship with respect to individuals, especially when they were still active while this book was being written and might be damaged or embarrassed by my revealing their identities. I have given similar consideration to protecting the families of certain people, now deceased. I have changed a number of names, and even appearances. What the people behind the fictitious names said and did is, however, not fictitious.

I make no apology for being anti-Communist. I am equally against all forms of political and religious fundamentalism, such as Nazism, Fascism, Japanese militarism and the official Islamic intolerance in, say, Iran and Saudi Arabia. Quite simply, all my adult life, I have been *for* freedom and *against* regimentation and coercion (except in emergencies such as war). That is what this unseen war was about.

I

The turning point (1941–8)

THERE MAY NEVER be a consensus among historians on the beginning of the secret war. If we are talking about the espionage war of the secret intelligence and security services, then one has to go back to the early years of Lenin's Comintern, with the creation of Communist parties in Britain, France, the US and many other countries in the 1920s and 1930s.[1]

If, however, we are referring to the secret aspects of the Cold War (the central theme of this book), then we have to select a more recent date. I am inclined to settle for 1941, when Harry Hopkins, newly recruited by Stalin's NKVD (predecessor of the KGB) first visited Moscow as President Roosevelt's personal envoy, shortly after the German invasion.

The major KGB defector Oleg Gordievsky recalls a lecture he attended early in his career, in which a senior NKVD/KGB official identified Hopkins as 'the most important of all Soviet wartime agents in the United States'.[2]

There is, however, an important gloss to be added to this key piece of information. As Christopher Andrew (the narrator of Gordievsky's revelations) puts it:

> Gordievsky, however, came gradually to the conclusion, as he discussed the Hopkins case, that Hopkins had been an unconscious rather than a conscious agent.[3]

As it happened, *Harry Hopkins was a fully recruited and therefore conscious NKVD agent.* This vitally important revelation came to me from a US high official, whose suspicion of Hopkins was confirmed from the lips of a senior KGB man, as part of the informal exchanges that developed as a result of *glasnost* and the 'end of the Cold War'.[4]

The reference to 'conscious' and 'unconscious' agents brings us straight to the heart of the secret war, which is about operations of influence. Throughout its history and many name changes, the KGB conducted such operations. It had a 'dirty tricks' department, known as 'Service A'. The 'A' stands for Active Measures (*Aktivnyye Meropriyatiya* in Russian), which included the forging of documents and the planting of false stories, known as 'disinformation'.

'Agent of influence' is an intelligence shop term for people who influence public opinion or, better still, government thinking in support of Soviet policies. (The KGB's own term for such people was 'confidential contacts'.) A 'conscious' agent, by definition, is perfectly aware of the service he or she is rendering; an 'unconscious' one is unaware that disinformation has been planted on him or her. These are *British* shop terms; the *American* versions are 'witting' and 'unwitting' respectively.

Gordievsky's revelation about Harry Hopkins was greeted with scepticism from some commentators.[5] I do not share these doubts, and the role played by Hopkins is critical if Stalin's post-war strategy is to be understood.

Harry Hopkins had been a social worker in New York in the 1920s. He was an enthusiastic supporter of Roosevelt's New Deal, the core of which was a vast federal work programme to relieve unemployment. He was, undoubtedly, an unsophisticated idealist and may well have found compatible elements in Stalin's version of socialism. As Robert Sherwood's biography (*Roosevelt and Hopkins*, 1948) makes clear, he was naturally flattered to enjoy the confidence of the two most powerful world leaders during World War II.

A paid agent cannot help being aware that he is 'doing a job' for his paymasters. But it is fair to assume, as I do, that Hopkins did the job for idealistic reasons rather than for the money. It was in the interest of the NKVD to pay him, to reduce the risk that he might feel impelled to confess. He was totally under Stalin's spell, and apprehensive about the future, should anything happen to 'Uncle Joe'. In other words he was naive.

The job he thus did 'unconsciously' (in that he did not allow for Stalin's duplicity) was simply to mislead FDR totally about Stalin's post-war intentions, and through Roosevelt, Winston Churchill. Although Churchill had

been a determined anti-Communist, from the days of the ill-fated Arch-
angel expedition of 1918, he too had fallen under Stalin's spell. To what
extent he was further influenced by Roosevelt's uncritical adulation
of Stalin, and was therefore influenced indirectly by Hopkins, is hard
to say.

Either way, the statement Churchill made to the House of Commons
on his return from the Yalta summit of February 1945 demonstrates the
depth of his misguided trust in the Soviet dictator:

> The impression I brought back from the Crimea, and from all my other con-
> tacts, is that Marshal Stalin and the Soviet leaders wish to live in honourable
> friendship and equality with the Western democracies. I feel also that their
> word is their bond. I know of no government which stands to its obligations,
> even in its own despite, more solidly than the Russian Soviet government. I
> decline absolutely to embark here on a discussion about Russian good faith.[6]

Nor was Stalin the only Communist leader who deceived Churchill.
Another was Tito of Yugoslavia, the 'resistance hero'. In his war memoirs,
Churchill records his conversation with Tito at their meeting in Naples
on 12 August 1944:

> ... Tito assured me that, as he had stated publicly, he had no desire to intro-
> duce the Communist system into Yugoslavia.... The Russians had a mission
> with the Partisans, but its members, far from expressing any idea of introducing
> the Soviet system into Yugoslavia, had spoken against it.[7]

At that time, Tito was still one of Stalin's surrogates. How he came to
be his country's unchallenged wartime leader is another example of the
amazing efficacy of Stalin's international apparatus. A group of British
Communists in wartime Cairo, led by James Klugmann, a Comintern
agent, had systematically destroyed or delayed messages about the operations of Tito's rival in the guerrilla war against the Nazi invaders, Drazha
Mihailovic, leader of the 'Chetniks'. In this and in other ways, Churchill
and his War Cabinet were persuaded that the Chetnik leader was a Nazi
collaborator who had to be dropped in favour of Tito. The whole operation was part of the wider picture of Stalin's secret preparations for
his post-war offensive against the non-Communist world. In that sense,
Klugmann the professional, and others like him, supplemented the work
of Hopkins, who was an amateur in the sense that he was untrained,

although paid. (Later, when Tito split with Stalin, Klugmann the unconditional loyalist would denounce Tito in a book he wrote on Moscow's
orders.)[8]

With such deceptions and subversions, Stalin was well placed in 1945
to go ahead with his plan to take over Eastern Europe. Indeed, he made
his wider intentions clear in February 1946, by announcing that the doctrine of world revolution was still valid. Thus, at one stroke, he destroyed
the convenient myth that the main point at issue between him and Trotsky
had been the latter's insistence on carrying out Lenin's policy of spreading
Communism worldwide; whereas he, Stalin, had wisely opted for 'revolution in one country'.

In pursuance of this particular deception, Stalin had officially 'dissolved'
the Comintern in 1943, to reassure his wartime allies about his post-war
intentions. With the help of Harry Hopkins, Churchill and Roosevelt had
been duly reassured.

It was not until the 1970s that Western intelligence services learned
the truth: the Comintern had been rebuilt immediately after the war in
a more sophisticated form as the International Department of the CPSU's
central committee. Simultaneously, Stalin's Communist surrogates in
Western Europe created the vast network of international front organisations designed to disinform the public about Soviet intentions. The best-
known of these are the World Federation of Trades Unions (WFTU) and
the World Peace Council (WPC), created in 1945 and 1948 respectively.

WHETHER STALIN HOPED to gain post-war political advantages
from his close wartime relations with Roosevelt and Churchill we do not
know. Probably not. One look at FDR's gaunt face and emaciated frame
at Yalta would have told him that the President had not much life left in
him. As for Churchill, Stalin would have guessed that the Prime Minister's
confidence would not long survive the post-war betrayal of his trust.

As it happened, Stalin himself was the only political survivor of the
wartime Big Three. Two new leaders appeared unexpectedly: Harry
Truman in the United States, and Clement Attlee in Britain. Hopkins had
completed his 'job' by going to Moscow for one last visit in April 1945,
just after Roosevelt's death on the 12th. There, he helped to arrange the
Potsdam conference. Churchill made an initial appearance, then
was replaced by Attlee after Labour's victory in the general election of
16 July.

Neither Attlee nor Truman had had much experience of international affairs. Each, in Shakespeare's famous phrase, had had 'greatness thrust upon him'. Each, in his way, rose to the challenge. As a result, in each case, Stalin's secret offensive met with a suitable counter-force. The secret war was on.

In the US and Britain, a counter-force was created, but only two or three years later. In America, it was the Central Intelligence Agency (CIA), which grew out of the wartime Office of Strategic Services (OSS); in Britain, the Information Research Department (IRD) of the Foreign Office. There are important differences between the two, which need to be understood.

The British response was singular. Britain already had a long-established security and intelligence network, the best-known elements of which were MI-5 (the Security Service) and MI-6 (the Secret Intelligence Service). The new problem, in the immediate post-war years, however, was to counter the sudden and enormous flood of hostile propaganda directed from Moscow. For this, neither MI-5 nor MI-6 was equipped. The Foreign Office, at that time, had diagnosed the Soviet challenge, accurately and perceptively, in a wide-ranging paper, 'The Strategic Aspects of British Foreign Policy', prepared by the FO for the Chiefs of Staff and sent to them by the Permanent Under-Secretary, Sir Orme Sargent.

This important document, dated October 1946, assumed that the US would continue its policy of 'active intervention in all international questions', but expressed reservations. One was the mercurial character of the American people, 'unduly swayed by sentiment and prejudice rather than by reason or even by ... their own long-term interests'. Another reservation was the 'archaic' American Constitution, which handicapped governments, 'sometimes to the point of impotence'.[9]

The diagnosis was impeccable. The solution to Stalin's propaganda challenge was provided by a young member of Attlee's team, a junior minister named Christopher Mayhew. Aged thirty-two at the time, Mayhew was Parliamentary Under-Secretary of State for Foreign Affairs, with Hector McNeil as Minister of State and Ernest Bevin as Secretary of State. In his engagingly modest autobiography, *Time to Explain* (1987), Mayhew gives his diagnosis and his solution:

> At this time, Stalin's worldwide campaign of subversion and propaganda was at its most effective. Orchestrated from Moscow, or indirectly through the Cominform, scores of communist or communist-front organisations

maintained a relentless war against Western governments and institutions. The Soviet Union was presented as the exact antithesis of the West, that is, as the true enemy of Fascism, the champion of colonial peoples against imperialism, the ally of all peace-loving peoples against imperialism and the shining example of a workers' state in which capitalism had been abolished and where the workers prospered and were free.

To this flood of propaganda, the Western countries made no organised response at all (p. 106).

Cogitating on this situation, in December 1947, Mayhew proposed an ideological offensive against Stalinism. Bevin approved, and so did Attlee. The Prime Minister himself launched the offensive in a BBC statement broadcast by the World Service. The IRD was set up, as a new department of the Foreign Office, producing an ever-increasing flow of analytical papers, rigorously accurate but unattributable.

With his usual modesty, Mayhew goes on to record 'an extraordinary mistake'. At the suggestion of his immediate chief, Hector McNeil, Mayhew took on a man who demonstrated a dazzling insight into Soviet Communist methods. Not surprisingly, for the man's name was Guy Burgess. Not long after, Mayhew dismissed Burgess as 'dirty, drunken and idle'. It was not until 1951, when he fled to Moscow with Donald Maclean, that his true role as a Soviet spy became known. There is no suggestion that McNeil was aware of his KGB link: he had merely been impressed by Burgess's knowledge.

Over lunch at the Café Royal in London in 1990, I congratulated Mayhew on his stroke of inspiration in launching IRD. He smiled ruefully. 'Looking back, I think it was the best thing I ever did,' he said.[10]

When World War II broke out in 1939, the US was the only major power without a foreign intelligence service. This anomaly has to be attributed to the residual puritanism of American society, a point encapsulated by Roosevelt's War Secretary, Henry Stimson, when he remarked that gentlemen don't read other people's mail. True, the FBI under its long-time head, J. Edgar Hoover, did read plenty of other people's mail in a most ungentlemanly way, but he lacked the machinery for the systematic collection and analysis of international intelligence.

The attack on Pearl Harbor in December 1941 changed all that. In the ensuing panic, Roosevelt set up the Office for Strategic Services (OSS), initially run under the tutelage of the more experienced British. In the first wave of post-crisis impatience – an American national failing – Truman not only brought the boys home after victory in 1945, but also scrapped the OSS.

He realised his mistake when Stalin started taking over Eastern Europe. In July 1947, Congress passed the National Security Act, and the CIA was born. So, too, was the National Security Council, a kind of White House strategic advisory body, which held its first meeting in December that year. Now the US, too, started hitting back.

HARDLY ANYTHING of the above was publicly known at the time. Although the IRD was listed in the official *Diplomatic List*, its true purpose was not specified, and the secret was kept until it was dissolved in 1977. The truth about Harry Hopkins, and vital further details about James Klugmann, came out only after I had started writing this book.

For myself, I was already disillusioned with Stalin and the Soviet system when the first news of the takeover in Eastern Europe started coming in, in 1946–7. I remember clashing with my Communist friends (of whom I had a number) when the Stalinist purges began in Hungary, Bulgaria and the rest. By then, I was a sub-editor on the foreign desk of the (now defunct) *News Chronicle*, flagship of the Cadbury family's publishing ventures, known to journalists as 'the Cocoa Press'. Members of the Communist Party were numerous, and vocal, on the *NC*, as indeed they had been at Reuters, where I had served my apprenticeship in the handling of international news.

During this traumatic time, I read two books that changed my life. The one taught me how to *think* about politics; the other drew the veil off the hideous reality of Stalin's regime. The first, chronologically, was *The Machiavellians: Defenders of Freedom* by the American philosopher James Burnham. Sudden fame had come to Burnham with his instant bestseller *The Managerial Revolution*, published in the USA in 1941, which argued that Marx's economic determinism was mistaken and that Stalinism was not, as some critics were arguing, a temporary aberration, but inherent in Marxism. As he saw it, capitalism itself would evolve into dominance by a new, managerial class.

The interest in the book arose largely because it marked Burnham's break with Trotsky and with the Fourth International, of which he had been an active member. Although it remains one of the most famous of Burnham's books, it is the weakest for, when he wrote it, he had not yet thrown off the intellectual shackles of Marxism.

The Machiavellians, which was published in England in 1943, was a leap into full maturity, although it was little noticed at the time. I think I read it in 1946, in a library copy: the only books I could afford to buy in those days were Penguins and Pelicans. At that time, I was an assiduous reader of *Tribune*, and especially of its Literary Editor, George Orwell. To me, there was nothing incompatible between Orwell and Burnham: both men had been bitten by Marxism, then seen through its fallacies. Having joined Victor Gollancz's Left Book Club in 1937, in indignation against Franco's war against the Spanish Republic, I was still not quite cured of the Marxist infection a decade later.

The Machiavellians came as a revelation. A brilliant historical and philosophical analysis, it taught readers the vital distinction between real and formal meaning in politics: a fundamental point. Burnham's method was startlingly original. He compared Dante's *De Monarchia* with Machiavelli's *The Prince*. Writing in the thirteenth century, Dante presented politics in Utopian terms acceptable to the Church of Rome. Writing two centuries later, Machiavelli looked at facts and realities, with no attempt to idealise men's motives or intentions. That is why Machiavelli and his successors are 'defenders of freedom': they tell the truth as it is, not how politicians would like the facts to be gilded or otherwise distorted. Applied, for instance, to the final communiqué of the Yalta summit, or to the United Nations Declaration, the Burnham method throws a lurid light on the contradiction between Stalin's formal promises and his actual behaviour. Equally, however, it applies to the gap between electoral promises and actual intentions in a democracy.

The other book that influenced me deeply, but in a different way, was Victor Kravchenko's *I Chose Freedom*, one of the first and, I believe, the most important of the stream of books by defectors from Soviet Communism. I read it in 1947, the year of its appearance in Britain. Re-reading it in 1990, for the first time in forty-three years, I was struck afresh by the epic sweep of its narrative: a masterpiece in the tradition of the great Russian novelists, on a level with, say, Dostoevsky or Tolstoy. A whole tragic and brutal epoch comes to life.

Until I read *I Chose Freedom*, I still nursed residual doubts and misgivings about the Soviet system. To what extent, for instance, were its evident excesses attributable solely to the monstrous dictator in the Kremlin? Without him, would it not be possible, even now, to correct the errors of the past and move on to a classless society more in line with the vision (as I saw it) of Marx and Lenin?

After reading Kravchenko, I stopped asking myself such questions. I grasped the fact that this vast prison state, this society of spies and informers, was the inevitable, built-in outcome of the Leninist ideology and of millenarian Marxism. I saw Communism for what it was and is, as an irredeemable obscenity of history, condemning humanity to inescapable enslavement.

Kravchenko, a Ukrainian, was a pure product of the Revolution. He had joined the Communist Party not only because it was the road to advancement, but because he saw it as his duty to further the aims of the Party. Gradually, he comes to realise that everything he does and thinks is under the permanent scrutiny of the NKVD. The facts are what the Party and the secret police say they are. To state, or even to think, realities becomes treason.

Two brief quotations will illustrate a problem that remained unresolved well into the Gorbachev era, despite his *perestroika* and *glasnost*:

The first dividends of collectivisation were death.

Although not a word about the tragedy appeared in the newspapers, the famine that raged [in the 1930s] throughout southern Russia and Central Asia was a matter of common knowledge. We denounced as 'anti-Soviet rumours' what we knew as towering fact.

Kravchenko, *I Chose Freedom*, p. 111.

... collectivisation was a great historic act, the most important social change since 1917. Yes, it proceeded painfully, not without serious excesses and blunders. ...

Gorbachev, *Perestroika* (1987), p. 40.

The 'serious excesses', which Gorbachev conceded negatively, referred to the deaths, by massacre or starvation, of some fourteen million peasants (a figure now admitted by Soviet historians). This was the death crisis Kravchenko and so many others lived through. His distinctive act of courage was to have broken away from the system and revealed its horrors.

A trained engineer, Kravchenko was a member of a Soviet purchasing mission to the United States in August 1943. There, on 3 April 1944, he 'chose freedom'. Immediately, the great Soviet propaganda network went into high gear to vilify the defector. From the American *Daily Worker* to France's *L'Humanité*, and in all other capitals, Communist newspapers denounced him.

Soon came the threats. 'Comrade Starobin', in the *Daily Worker*, put it this way: *'The vigilant and avenging hand of forward-looking humanity catches up with [traitors] and finally erases them'*. (p. 477: italicised in original).

'Reading these words,' Kravchenko went on, 'I recalled that in Trotsky's case the avenging hand had gripped a pickaxe, with which it pierced his skull in Mexico City.'

IT WAS SIGNIFICANT that the word 'freedom' occurred in the titles of both the Burnham and the Kravchenko books. It was from this time, in 1946–7, that freedom became my life's motive. Because Communism was now the greatest threat to freedom, anti-Communism was an axiomatic requirement. The military threat of Nazism and Italian Fascism had been eliminated; and their ideological attraction to non-Germans and non-Italians was limited, except to society's marginalised drop-outs.

The Communist threat was more subtle, more insidious, more long-term. It invaded daily life, affected social mores, poisoned minds and institutions. Moreover, unlike Fascism, it appealed strongly to Western intellectuals, ever prone to self-delusion and to the lure of a social paradise somewhere else. I had felt this lure myself when only a few years younger. I now recognised its utter falsity.

IN 1945, still uncured of early illusions, I had voted for Labour. By 1948, life in Clement Attlee's Britain had ceased to hold the slightest attraction. Socialism reigned. The shops were empty; or, more accurately, they contained tempting items labelled 'Export Only'. I was saving half my salary for want of things to spend it on.

In October that year, we packed up (my wife, Lila, and our first three children, Katnryn-Anne, Isobel and Michael) and steamed to my native Australia, where I joined the *Sydney Morning Herald*.

NOTES

1 There are many versions of these early years. Perhaps the most useful is that of the British historian Christopher Andrew and the Soviet defector Oleg Gordievsky in *KGB: The Inside Story* (Hodder & Stoughton, London 1990). Henceforth, *Gordievsky*.

2 *Gordievsky*, p. 233.

3 Ibid.

4 My informant was Herbert Romerstein, one of the leading American official specialists on the Soviet intelligence system, whom I have known for many years. Romerstein's suspicions had rested on wartime cable intercepts with precise details of instructions to an NKVD agent referred to simply as 'H'. Although the US intelligence view was that the reference was to Hopkins, some officials inclined towards (Averell) Harriman (see Ch. IV). There is no evidence, however, that Harriman was working for the Soviets, although they had grounds to be thankful to him. When I mentioned this hardening of the Hopkins story to Gordievsky, over lunch, shortly after the publication of his book, he was delighted. Not long after, Romerstein gave further details in an article in the Washington weekly *Human Events* (Vol. LI, No. 7, 16 Feb. 1991).

5 One such was Phillip Knightley. Writing in the *Spectator* on 3 November 1990, Knightley's comment was: '... a smear which can only be described as shameful'. He went on: 'How can anyone be an unconscious *agent?*', thereby displaying an unexpected ignorance of intelligence jargon in one who has written so extensively on the subject.

6 Winston Churchill, *The Second World War* (1955), Vol. 12, Ch. 4: 'Yalta Finale'.

7 Ibid., Vol. 11, Ch. 6: 'Italy and the Riviera Landing'.

8 See M. R. D. Foot, *SOE* (BBC, London 1984), p. 47. The Klugmann operation from Cairo was first exposed by David Martin, a Canadian-born American, in his book *Patriot or Traitor: The Case of General Mihailovich* (Hoover Institution, 1978). His definitive study, *The Web of Subversion: Churchill's Yugoslav Blunder* (Harcourt Brace Jovanovich, New York 1990), established beyond doubt that Klugmann was a Soviet spy. Martin's findings were broadly confirmed by an independent television documentary, 'Tito: Churchill's Man?' (BBC TV, *Timewatch*, with Arts and Entertainments Network and Lionheart Television International, Inc.; produced by Peter Batty, 1992).

9 See Brian Crozier, 'What's Wrong with British Foreign Policy?', *Encounter*, July/August 1984.

10 Disillusioned with the Labour Party, Mayhew resigned his membership in 1974 and joined the Liberals. He was given a Life Peerage in 1981.

Containment in action (1947–58)

BY 1947, COMMUNISM was clearly on the move, not only in Eastern Europe, but in China, Vietnam, Greece and Turkey. Stalin had presented the Chinese leader Mao Tse-tung (later spelt Mao Dzedung) with huge quantities of Japanese weapons captured by the Soviets in their last-minute intervention in the Pacific War. As a result, Mao was now going on to the offensive against the Nationalist leader, Chiang Kai-shek, who in contrast had been deserted by his American allies. Although Mao would break with Moscow in the 1960s, he accepted satellite status under a thirty-year Friendship and Alliance Treaty with Stalin in February 1950.

In Vietnam, the Moscow-trained leader Ho Chi Minh had launched his insurrection against the French at the end of 1946. In Greece, in 1946 and early 1947, Communist terrorists and guerrillas had launched a threatening attempt to seize power. Turkey was at the receiving end of threats and diplomatic pressure from Moscow.

The immediate burden of countering Stalin's policies in Greece and Turkey had fallen on an exhausted and impoverished Britain. The Attlee government decided in February 1947 that it could carry that burden no longer. In a note to the US government on 21 February, the Foreign Secretary, Ernest Bevin, spelt it out.

On 12 March, President Truman asked Congress for $400 million to cover economic and military aid to Greece and Turkey. The 'Truman Doctrine' of help to nations struggling against Communist takeovers was born. Already, the US had launched its European Recovery Program, better known as the Marshall Plan. And let us not forget that, initially, the offer of American assistance was open to the Soviet Union and its satellites, but was turned down by Stalin. The last thing he wanted was US officials administering the plan poking about in the Soviet Union!

In July 1947 the American quarterly *Foreign Affairs*, a pillar of the East Coast liberal establishment, published an article that made history. Signed 'X', and entitled 'The Sources of Soviet Conduct', it prescribed what became known as the doctrine of 'Containment': that is, containment of encroaching Communist power. The author's name, it emerged later, was George Kennan, at that time head of the Planning Staff of the State Department and as such constrained to anonymity. It is hardly by chance that publication of the article, clearly authorised by the Administration, coincided with the passing of the National Security Act and the creation of the CIA.

Many people at the time, myself among them, were elated by the Truman Doctrine and by the containment policy. At last, we felt, the United States had a positive policy to deal with Communism. As events showed, however, the policy of containment was deeply flawed.

The flaws were exposed by James Burnham in a devastating book, *Containment or Liberation?* (1952). Four years earlier, in *The Struggle for the World* (1948), he had analysed the Soviet threat in terms that have stood the test of time. Now he exposed the limitations of the new policy in his succinct way: 'The policy of containment, stripped bare, is simply the bureaucratic verbalisation of drift.' Hard, but true. The need was not simply to resist further Communist encroachments, essential though this was, but to liberate countries that had fallen to the Soviet empire.[1]

In February 1948, Czechoslovakia's Communists seized power in Prague. It took the West another year to organise its collective defence in Europe, but on 4 April 1949 the North Atlantic Treaty was signed. The aim was purely defensive and the threat was conceived only in military terms. Although NATO was and remained essential for the defence of Western Europe in the face of the Soviet Union's gigantic military machine, it too was flawed, and in two principal ways: it made no provision for non-military forms of Soviet expansionism, such as subversion and terrorism; and it imposed inappropriate geographical limitations against a Soviet threat that was literally global.

By the time NATO was set up, this caveat had been dramatically strengthened by the launching of Moscow-directed insurgences throughout South-East Asia. In February 1948 – the same month as the Prague coup – the Communist-sponsored World Youth Conference in Calcutta drew up plans for these insurgences, which broke out in Burma in March, in the Philippines in April, in Malaya in June, and in Indonesia in September. NATO had no mandate to counter these offensives (for that is what they were), which had to be dealt with piecemeal, either by the newly independent governments (as in Burma, the Philippines and Indonesia) or by the colonial authority (as in Malaya, while the French bore the brunt in Indochina).[2]

A CRUCIAL DATE now stands out in the history of the secret war because of two events that took place many thousands of miles apart. On the night of 24/25 June 1950, the Korean War started when the North Korean army, created and trained by the Soviets, crossed the 38th Parallel into South Korea. That same night in West Berlin was born the Congress for Cultural Freedom (CCF).

The Korean War was, of course, an open event, massively covered by the press and radio (television was in its infancy). But some aspects of it remained secret and speculative until very recently. For example, the timing of the North Korean invasion showed that the Soviet Union, too, was capable of blundering.

At that time, the Soviet Union was boycotting the United Nations Security Council. This unexpected lapse enabled the United States to put a resolution for collective action before the UN without fear of a Soviet veto. The US thereupon led an international expeditionary force which fought the invading Korean Communists and their Chinese allies, not to victory, but to a standstill, preserving South Korea's independence but leaving the Communist regime in power in North Korea. A perfect example of containment in action.

Thanks to *glasnost* we now know that the Korean War was not (as Moscow had alleged and leftist apologists had accepted) a civil war started by South Korea, but an act of aggression from the North sanctioned by Stalin. For decades, the Soviet press and spokesmen had denied any such connection, but in 1990, at the height of *glasnost*, the truth was allowed to come out. The long-lasting North Korean dictator, Kim Il Sung, had gone to Moscow in 1949 on his own initiative, taking with him his plans for an attack on South Korea. Stalin gave him the 'go ahead'.[3]

On that same crucial date – 24/25 June 1950 – an assembly of Western intellectuals, many of them writers, was meeting in West Berlin to set up the Congress for Cultural Freedom. Because the origins of the initiative were not revealed at the time, no more than two or three of those involved realised the significance of what was happening. As always with the secret war, there were two aspects: the overt side, reportable and reported, and the covert side, known to few.

A number of those present later became friends and allies of mine. Among them were Julian (later Lord) Amery, and Melvin J. Lasky, best known later as the long-serving joint editor of *Encounter* magazine (which lived on until mid-1990). The historian Hugh Trevor-Roper (Lord Dacre) was there too, and so was my mentor, James Burnham. The most significant participants, however, were a number of prominent ex-Communists, among them Arthur Koestler, Ignazio Silone and Richard Löwenthal. All those present had one fundamental point in common: the realisation that Soviet Communism had stifled free debate and cultural freedom. For the ex-Communists, the realisation was embittering, but their future contribution to the anti-Communist cause was the more valuable because of that: they had seen the future and knew that it did *not* work.

The CCF went on to spawn an amazing number of high-quality literary magazines, including not only *Encounter* but *Survey* in London, *Cuadernos* in Buenos Aires, *Cadernos Brasileiros* in Rio de Janeiro and, in Australia, *Quadrant*. Intellectuals being by definition disputatious, there were many subsequent rifts and crises, but the Congress played a major role in combating the spread of the repressive ideology that had seduced so many Western 'intellectuals'.[4]

The key fact, unknown to the public at that time, was that the CCF had been an American initiative, planned and financed by the CIA. This, of course, made it an early counter-move in the secret war – as the West, at last, fought back. This fact, unsettling to many Congress stalwarts, was disclosed in *Ramparts*, a magazine of the extreme Left published in California, in March 1967. This exposure, I can now reveal, was handled by the Czechoslovak State Secret Service, the Statni tajna Bezpecnost (StB) on behalf of the KGB.

IN THE SECRET war between the Soviet Union and the West, the advantage was inevitably with the Soviet side: a hermetic society versus wide open ones. Secondary though spying is to the theme of this book, it is inevitably part of the background if only because the KGB was a major participant in both facets of the secret war: espionage and influence.

Until Mikhail Gorbachev introduced his *glasnost* policy of considerable, though limited, openness, the West was at a serious disadvantage, in that the Soviet side had an almost unlimited range of methods to influence public opinion and policy in the West. In contrast, it was almost impossible for the Western intelligence services to recruit agents of influence in the Soviet Union, if only because such agents would too easily betray themselves. The recruitment of spies, on the whole, was somewhat easier. For these reasons, the West was, in effect, limited to its broadcasting systems: the BBC Russian service; Deutsche Welle in West Germany; the Voice of America; and, most important of all, the US-financed Radio Liberty and Radio Free Europe from Munich. Except at times of relative détente, all these broadcasts were systematically jammed on the Soviet and East European side: a tribute to their importance.

Propaganda, whether overt or covert, is concerned with *perceptions*: the way people, including officials and politicians, interpret facts and realities.

No period better illustrates this aspect of the secret war than the great spy scare of the 1950s in the United States. That there was indeed a vast network of Soviet spies in America is a fact; where the Soviets scored was in their ability to blur the picture, so that the unmasking of spies was widely perceived to be hysterical or 'McCarthyite'.

The Republican Senator Joseph R. McCarthy, of Wisconsin, was a demagogue who seized on the spy issue to launch a sustained Red-baiting campaign which damaged the lives and careers of a number of innocent citizens. That is the public perception of McCarthy, and indeed it is true, though not the whole truth. The terms McCarthyism and McCarthyite are still used to discredit any charge of Communist links or persuasion by anybody against anybody else.

The facts, however, are not so black and white (or red and blue) as the McCarthyite myth makes out. Senator McCarthy, then hardly known, launched his campaign with a little-reported speech at Wheeling, West Virginia on 9 February 1950. His theme was that the conviction of Alger Hiss, a former senior officer of the State Department, on a charge of perjury, showed the (Democratic) Administration of President Truman to be 'soft' on Communism.

The Hiss case is one of the *causes célèbres* of this century. A disillusioned ex-Communist journalist, Whittaker Chambers, had denounced him as a fellow-Communist and a Soviet spy. Hiss, claiming that he had never met Chambers, sued him for libel. Chambers held his ground, and won his case, with Richard Nixon as his counsel. At that time, Nixon was a young Republican Congressman and a member of the House

Un-American Activities Committee (HUAC). Hiss was thereupon pros-
ecuted for perjury and jailed for five years after a second trial, the first
having ended with a hung jury.

Whittaker Chambers, a former senior editor of *Time* magazine, went
on to write his autobiography, *Witness*, one of the key books of our time
and a literary masterpiece.

James Burnham, in his succinct way, gathered the evidence in his book
The Web of Subversion (1954), proving conclusively that several dozen
agencies of the US government had been penetrated by the Soviet spy
network. These included the White House staff and the Departments of
State, Defense and Justice, and the Treasury. As he put it in a column
some years later: 'Just wrap a synthetic McCarthy-image in the properly
charged magical symbols, and you can count on the drugged Liberals to
carry through the demoralisation of a security system.'[5]

Sincere doubters may not be swayed by a declared anti-Communist.
For these, a better source would be the American historian Allen
Weinstein, who began his investigation of the Hiss–Chambers case
believing that Hiss had been unjustly convicted. He concluded his monumental study with the words: '. . . the body of available evidence proves
that he [Hiss] did in fact perjure himself when describing his secret dealings with Chambers, so that the jurors in the second trial made no mistake
in finding Alger Hiss guilty as charged.'[6]

A new twist to this complicated tale came many years later, on 29
October 1992, when Alger Hiss, in his eighty-eighth year, called a press
conference in New York to announce that his name had been cleared by
a senior official historian in Moscow. However, the press reports that
followed did not settle the matter. In London, for example, the *Guardian*
of 30 October 1992 reported that the man who had 'cleared' Hiss, General
Dmitri Volkogonov, was Chairman of Russia's military intelligence
archives; whereas, in fact, he was Chairman of the parliamentary archives
commission, with no access to intelligence archives, whether GRU (military) or KGB (civil).

It transpired that Hiss had written to Volkogonov in August asking him
to review the files. Thereupon, Volkogonov had asked Yevgeny Primakov,
head of Russia's Foreign Intelligence Service (successor to the KGB's
First Directorate), to send him the available files. On receiving them,
Volkogonov had found no incriminating references and had written an
exculpatory letter to Alger Hiss.

Volkogonov's non-intelligence archival job was pointed out by Allen

Weinstein, and further elucidation was provided by other leading authorities.

One of these was Herbert Romerstein, who talked to Volkogonov in November when the latter was in Washington to testify before the US Senate Committee on prisoners-of-war and persons missing in action. Volkogonov confirmed that he had not been given access to KGB or GRU files, but had merely examined the selection provided by Primakov. Back in Russia, Volkogonov, in a letter to the pro-democracy Moscow newspaper *Nezavisimaya Gazeta* on 24 November 1992, revealed that Primakov 'reasonably said that they give out no information about who is or is not a spy' before giving him the file that did not contain Hiss's name. He went on: 'Hiss wrote that he was 88 and would like to die peacefully, that he wanted to prove that he was never a paid, contracted spy.'

An exhaustive analysis of the case, and of the attempt to exonerate Hiss, appeared as a cover story in the New York magazine *National Review*, which pointed out that the evidence against Hiss available in the US was more than sufficient to prove Hiss's guilt, regardless of evidence produced or withheld in Moscow.[7]

IT WAS DURING this same early post-war period that the scandal of Britain's Foreign Office spies broke. The story of Maclean and Burgess, and later of Philby, Blunt and Cairncross, is well known. But the defections were not all on one side. In the early months of 1954, no fewer than four Soviet secret servicemen changed sides. In January, Yuri Rastvorov, who had been working in the Tokyo residency, defected to the CIA. The following month, Peter Deriabin, based in Vienna, did likewise.

April 1954 brought a more sensational defection when Nikolai Khokhlov, a professional assassin of the notorious SMERSH (the 'Death to Spies' outfit popularised in Ian Fleming's James Bond thrillers) called a press conference in Frankfurt, during which he displayed his murder weapon: an electrically operated gun firing cyanide-tipped bullets. He had been sent to kill a leader of the anti-Soviet émigré organisation, the Labour Alliance of Solidarists or NTS, but had decided he could not carry out the deed. That same month, the KGB's network being worldwide, a senior NKVD spy, Vladimir Petrov, defected in Canberra, Australia, with his wife Evdokia.[8]

IN ITS EARLY years, the CIA was both very busy and very successful in secret operations to counter Soviet moves in the secret war. Two of these secret operations reversed apparently accomplished facts in Iran, and in Guatemala in Central America; a third, however, was to change the course of history in Egypt and create a rift between Britain and the US over Suez.

Between 1951 and 1953, the Prime Minister of Iran was a curious personage called Mussadiq, who was a fervent nationalist, but in a specifically anti-Western way. Mussadiq was closely linked to the Communist Tudeh ('Masses') Party, which in turn was closely controlled by the Soviet International Department. He nationalised the Anglo-Iranian Oil Company in April 1951, and seized the giant Abadan refinery on the Persian Gulf, bringing unemployment and financial chaos. In August 1953, the Shah dismissed Mussadiq and appointed General Zahedi in his place. Mussadiq stood his ground, and brought the mob into the streets through the Tudeh. The Shah lost his nerve and fled to Rome.

At this point the CIA and Britain's SIS moved into action. In a brilliant operation, an alternative mob was brought into the streets. Not the poor, with nothing to lose but their chains, but a disciplined contingent of muscular athletes, recruited by Zahedi from all the capital's gymnasiums and athletic clubs. In no time the Tudeh mob had fled and the Shah and his consort, Queen Soraya, flew back from Rome on 22 August. Their exile had lasted only six days.

This counter-coup is usually attributed to Kermit ('Kim') Roosevelt, a distant cousin to the late President. A soft-spoken Agency man, Kim gave me his version of the counter-coup on one of my visits to America many years later. It was a joint Anglo-American operation; but the British, with the kind of modesty that goes with a truly secret service, have never claimed their share of it, and by not mentioning their role, Kim was merely respecting their wishes.[9]

A counter-coup of quite a different kind was successfully mounted in Guatemala in 1954, to oust a Communist-backed president, Jacobo Arbenz, who had come to power three years earlier. In a well-planned operation, a rival Guatemalan army officer, Colonel Carlos Castillo-Armas, at that time in exile in neighbouring Honduras, crossed the border with an unofficial air force provided by the CIA.[10]

MY THREE-YEAR CONTRACT on the *Sydney Morning Herald* expired in September 1951. I had started as number two on the foreign desk, was then in charge of it for the newly launched *Sunday Herald*, where I also had an art column and reviewed books for both the daily and the Sunday. I rejoined Reuters through its Antipodean partner, the Australian Associated Press (AAP), first in Melbourne, then in South-East Asia, early in 1952. My first stopping-place was Jakarta, my second Singapore, and my third Saigon. In all three areas, insurgencies were raging: minor ones in Indonesia, a major one in Malaya, and a full-scale war in Indochina. This was my first chance to study the phenomena of terrorism, guerrillas and revolutionary war.

In Saigon, the then capital of Vietnam, and in Phnom Penh, capital of neighbouring Cambodia, I had my first contacts with British and French intelligence. Ronald Lincoln (not his real name), my friendly contact at the British embassy in Saigon, was a cultured, self-effacing man with a distinguished war service record in 'little ships'. Before long, I found myself exchanging snippets of information with him: a two-way traffic of mutual benefit.

In Phnom Penh, a young French official told me that some controversial leaflets scattered on the streets had been drafted and printed by the French secret service. To be accurate, he did not actually 'tell' me: he presented me with facts that could not be interpreted otherwise. When I asked: 'So the leaflets were produced by the French High Commission?' his smile was complicitous. 'I wasn't the one who said it,' he remarked, jesuitically. This made another snippet for Ronald Lincoln.

In Singapore, the huge intelligence complex at Phoenix Park, staffed by career personnel from MI-5 and MI-6, became one of my prime sources of news. Acquaintances I made there blossomed into friendships in later years.

We left Singapore in October 1953, shortly after the birth of our third daughter, Caroline, and returned to London by easy stages. Money had run out, but luck soon returned.

I had renewed acquaintance with Ronald Lincoln, who had also come home. In September 1954, his confidential briefings brought me the job I had applied for as editor of *The Economist*'s 'Confidential' weekly bulletin *Foreign Report*. For *The Economist* itself, I wrote leaders, mainly on the Far East, and travelled to many countries as a foreign correspondent. Simultaneously, I delivered international commentaries for the BBC's overseas services, mainly in French and later in Spanish.

I also met a remarkable man, whom I shall call Ronald Franks, a brilliant eccentric, whom I assumed to be an intelligence analyst on the basis of a phenomenal capacity for correlating obscure names, dates and circumstances to draw inferences which invariably made sense. Acting on this hunch, I tracked him down to his desk at MI-6 headquarters by the simple expedient of asking for him by name on the number Ronald Lincoln had given me for himself.

I felt I had penetrated Britain's Secret Intelligence Service. At that time, however, my interest was not in spying but in acquiring new sources of information for *Foreign Report*.

Before leaving Singapore, I had brought myself up to date on the extraordinary case of Victor Kravchenko, whose *I Chose Freedom* had so impressed me some years earlier. His second book, *I Chose Justice* (1951), although less fundamental than the first, was illuminating in that nowhere else at the time could one find so detailed an account of the way the world Communist network responded to orders from Moscow.

On 13 November 1947, *Les Lettres Françaises*, a Communist literary weekly published in Paris, carried an article entitled: 'How Kravchenko Was Manufactured'. The article was signed 'Sim Thomas' – described as an American journalist who had received his information from a friend who worked in the wartime OSS.

According to this source, described as 'unimpeachable', Kravchenko had spent his time in Washington at night clubs, gambling and drinking, often arriving at his office next day still completely drunk. Weighed down by debt and about to be shipped back to the USSR to answer for his bad behaviour, he was described as an ideal tool for the OSS to use against the Soviet Union. According to 'Sim Thomas', the OSS had paid Kravchenko's debts, then spirited him away from Washington. It was at that point that 'his' Americans had decided he should write an anti-Soviet book.

By that time, Kravchenko was living in New York under an assumed name. He took the brave decision to sue *Les Lettres Françaises* for defamation of character. Fourteen months elapsed before the case came to trial in Paris. Kravchenko gives a vivid description of the harassment he suffered at the hands of the NKVD. He had thought himself secure. One morning, he noticed on a table in his New York apartment an object that had not been there the previous day: a bullet. Shortly afterwards, his publishers sent him a letter mailed in France and unsigned. The writer said he was an NKVD agent, and proved it with a wealth of details about Kravchenko's movements in the United States. He warned Kravchenko not to come to Paris, which, he added, would prove fatal. Night after night, Kravchenko was awakened at intervals by voiceless telephone calls and audible breathing.

The Kravchenko trial became a *cause célèbre* in Paris and internationally. French Communist Party members acted throughout as Stalin's agents, and the witnesses produced by the Soviet side had been carefully drilled in systematic falsehoods. They included Kravchenko's first wife. Kravchenko, however, had prepared his case meticulously, and produced many witnesses, including some who had spent years in Stalin's gulags. He won his case and was awarded damages, initially of $150, later reduced on appeal to 3 francs – about 1 cent – on the ground that the publicity around the trial had compensated him by increasing sales of his book. *Les Lettres Françaises* was saddled with the far heavier costs, however.

The French Communist Party was the second largest in the Western world (after Italy's), and at that time attracted about thirty per cent of French voters. The Kravchenko trial proved beyond all doubt that the Parti Communiste Français (PCF) was a mass weapon at Stalin's disposal.

On 25 February 1966, Victor Kravchenko's body was found in the flat he occupied in Manhattan in the name of Peter Martin. A bullet had been fired through his right temple and a .38-calibre revolver was next to his body. A 'suicide note', apparently in his handwriting, was also found, and the police listed the death as 'apparent suicide'. These words summarise the reports that appeared in the *New York Times*, the *New York Herald Tribune* and the *Washington Post* of 26 February.

The following day, however, the *New York Journal American* recalled recent secret testimony released by the Senate Internal Security Subcommittee, which gave details of the Soviet assassination network and techniques. It recalled various cases, of which the most important was the killing of General Walter Krivitsky, found dead in his Washington hotel room in almost identical circumstances in 1941, complete with bullet in the right temple and a nearby .38-calibre gun. Kravchenko had had several death threats and, in 1949 alone, had survived four attempts on his life.

ON 29 APRIL 1954, shortly before I joined *The Economist*, an international conference had opened in Geneva, with the stated aim of bringing peace to Indochina and Korea. The Korean side of the talks merely confirmed the military stalemate. The Indochina side handed victory to the Vietnamese Communists, led by Ho Chi Minh. As the only journalist then in London with personal experience of covering the Indochina war, I was much in demand as a broadcaster and lecturer.

In March, Ho's Commander-in-Chief, a military genius named Vo Nguyen Giap, had begun to attack the French-held fortress of Dien Bien

Phu, near the Laotian border. The new French C-in-C, General Henri Navarre, had in effect invited the attack, by choosing to fortify this remote village, isolated from the main French forces, in the belief that General Giap would be bound to attack and would then be decisively defeated.

Navarre's intelligence, however, was disastrously wrong. He knew that the Vietminh (as the Communists were known) had no heavy guns and believed that they had no way of bringing any to the scene. At best, his intelligence reports told him, they could not hope to bring in more than two divisions, with 20,000 coolies to supply them. In the event, 80,000 coolies, wheeling bicycles laden with arms and food through the jungle, kept four Vietminh divisions supplied. And the heavy guns were already there: Soviet weapons sent across the vast and still friendly expanse of Communist China.

The outcome was total victory for Giap, whose forces overran Dien Bien Phu on 6 May and captured the survivors of the garrison. The French could have fought on, but had lost heart. In Paris, the Socialist leader Pierre Mendès-France came to power in June with a pledge to end the war within a month or resign. In the Palais des Nations in Geneva, the clocks had been stopped at midnight on 20 July, to enable Mendès-France to claim, tongue in cheek, that he had met his pledge. That 'midnight' lasted several hours. Early on 21 July, the terms of peace were agreed. Vietnam was partitioned into two roughly equal halves, along the 17th Parallel.

The dividing line had been the subject of long and acrimonious dispute. The Vietminh, with their Soviet and Chinese big brothers, had pressed for the 13th Parallel, which would have given them about two-thirds of the divided country. Some time after the event, it became known that a tacit and secret bargain had been struck between Mendès-France and the Soviet Foreign Minister, Vyacheslav Molotov.

The Soviet aim was to stop the project for a European Defence Community (EDC), which was due to be debated in the French National Assembly in August. The French Foreign Minister in the previous government, Georges Bidault, who had headed the French delegation at Geneva before Mendès-France's arrival, had flatly refused to discuss the matter with Molotov. Mendès-France was more amenable for reasons that in no way indicated a sympathy for Communism. As a Jew, and so soon after the Second World War and Hitler's massacre of the Jews, he simply could not stomach the idea of French and German troops serving side by side (as provided by the EDC Treaty).

In the debate on the EDC in the French Assembly on 30 August, Mendès-France let it be known that he would ignore the Communist votes. He simply allowed the Treaty to be rejected on a point of procedure; for which his political opponents never forgave him. Six months later, he lost the premiership.[11]

SOME OF THE public events of 1956 are relevant to the secret war. In February, at the Twentieth Congress of the ruling Communist Party (CPSU) in Moscow, its leader, Nikita Khrushchev, startled the comrades with a speech, intended to be a secret, in which he denounced, selectively but in detail, some of Stalin's crimes. A copy of the speech reached the CIA, which distributed it to the press.

The Italian Communist leader, Palmiro Togliatti, who had spent Italy's Fascist years in Moscow dutifully supporting Stalin, thereupon announced a new doctrine of 'polycentrism' (meaning that individual parties would henceforth go their own way). Although the doctrine was not accepted by the Soviet leadership, it undoubtedly weakened the Kremlin's hold on foreign Communist parties.

October and November of 1956 brought the almost simultaneous crises of Hungary and Suez. On 3 November, Yuri Andropov, at that time the Soviet ambassador in Budapest, lured the Hungarian Defence Minister, Pal Maleter, to a banquet with a promise of negotiations. While the banquet was in progress, the KGB chief, Ivan Serov, stormed the hall with armed men and arrested all the Hungarians.[12] Next day, the capital was heavily bombed by Soviet warplanes. Within a few days, the Hungarian revolt was crushed.

A point of special interest today is that it was Andropov who, many years later, as Chairman of the KGB, talent-spotted the promising young party activist, Mikhail Gorbachev, and became his mentor and protector. It was 'bad form', however, during the West's 'Gorbymania' years, to mention Gorbachev's KGB background.

The Anglo-French expedition to the Suez Canal culminated in paratroop landings in the Canal Zone on 5 November 1956. It then ended in fiasco when operations were halted within forty-eight hours. Although the Soviet leaders, Bulganin and Khrushchev, brandished their rockets and claimed the credit for the British Prime Minister Eden's decision to withdraw, the decisive pressure came from President Eisenhower and his Secretary of State, John Foster Dulles. To the public, and to many observers at the time, this Anglo-American rift was puzzling. There was, however, an explanatory factor, kept secret then and for many years.

The secret factor was that the CIA had played a decisive role in the coup of 23 July 1952, which ultimately brought Colonel Gamal Abdel Nasser to power in Egypt (although the 'front man' at the time was General Mohammed Neguib). The inside story was given (for the first time in public, to my knowledge) by one of the operators involved, the late Miles Copeland, a well-known ex-CIA man.[13]

As with the Iran coup two years later, the principal operator was his CIA senior colleague Kim Roosevelt. Towards the end of 1951, when Churchill returned to power after six years of Labour rule, the British decided to teach the Egyptians a lesson for abrogating the treaties under which the British forces garrisoned the Suez Canal Zone. The British destroyed a village from which Egyptian saboteurs had been operating, then attacked Egyptian posts near Ismailia with heavy loss of Egyptian lives. The outcome was 'Black Saturday', 26 January 1952, when mobs in Cairo went on the rampage, destroying all the British-owned properties they could find, including Shepheard's Hotel, and throwing British babies out of windows in the British hospital.

The Americans were anxious that this anti-British feeling should not spread to them. At first, Kim Roosevelt's idea was to make a deal with King Farouk, the royal voluptuary known in the US diplomatic world as the 'Fat Fucker'. The King, however, was more interested in orgies than in making international deals, and Roosevelt toyed with the idea of backing some religious leader who would (it was argued) be friendly to the US in return for American generosity.

His moves in that doomed direction failed, but he was able to meet Colonel Nasser, leader of the Free Officers, who were plotting to overthrow the King. There were several meetings, and (says Copeland):

> The American CIA ... broke off official contact with the British SIS and Kim's project ... was on the way. It was approved by Allen Dulles[14] over tea in his Georgetown house on the Sunday afternoon following Black Saturday.

This secret American operation helps to explain the Anglo-American rift over the Suez crisis of 1956, since the real (though unstated) aim of the British and French in their joint expedition was to bring down America's protégé, Colonel Nasser.

The disaster was thus manifold. It split the 'special relationship' at a time when Anglo-American unity was most needed in the face of Soviet brutality in Hungary; and it estranged the French, who wanted to fight on against Egypt, from the British, who did not.

Moreover, the United States got nothing out of helping Nasser in his early days. At first, the Nasser card had looked promising, and the US had, in effect, bought Nasser's goodwill by offering to help finance Nasser's ambitious project to build a high dam at Aswan. However, Nasser (like Nehru in India, Sukarno in Indonesia, and Tito in Yugoslavia) had decided on neutralism in the Cold War. In July 1955, immediately after the first Eisenhower–Khrushchev summit in Geneva, the Soviet leader had sent his son-in-law, Dmitri Shepilov, to Cairo where he negotiated a massive arms deal with Nasser.

A year later, on 19 July 1956, the US withdrew its offer of help over the high dam, and Nasser, the following week, nationalised the Suez Canal Company, precipitating the great Suez crisis. This deepened Nasser's dependence on Soviet support. Huge shipments of arms from Moscow's Czechoslovak satellite were made; Soviet 'advisers' arrived in Egypt in their thousands, and in the end, the high dam was built under Soviet supervision. An ironical finale to a secret American operation aimed at forging lasting links with Nasser.

NOTES

1 For a fuller version of the argument, see Brian Crozier, *Strategy of Survival* (Temple Smith, London; Arlington House, New Rochelle, NY, 1978), pp. 106–11. See also David Rees, *The Age of Containment* (Macmillan, London; St Martin's Press, New York, 1967).

2 For the Calcutta meeting, see J. H. Brimmell, *Communism in Asia* (Oxford University Press, 1959, pp. 256–63). See also Brian Crozier, *South-East Asia in Turmoil* (Penguin, 3rd ed., 1968).

3 Moscow's role in the Korean War was first revealed by the Soviet historian Mikhail Smirnov in an interview on Radio Moscow on 20 April 1990. The following day, the BBC's World Service broadcast the Smirnov interview in Korean, quoting Smirnov as follows: 'The Pyongyang side prepared this war. Over this issue, the study of history in the Soviet Union has had the following view, that is, approximately ten divisions of the South Korean armed forces launched a surprise attack across the 38th Parallel against the North Korean territory early in the morning of 25 June 1950. I think that all of this is contrary to fact....' This version of events was confirmed by Stalin's successor, Nikita Khrushchev, in his massive archive of audio tapes, made available to *Time* magazine by his son Sergei. The first version of the tapes, made available in 1973–4, and later published under the title *Khrushchev Remembers:*

The Last Testament, omitted the relevant passages (and many others). This was an act of self-censorship, by Sergei, because of the possible consequences at that time. Khrushchev's spoken description of Kim Il Sung's visit to Stalin appears in *Khrushchev Remembers: The Glasnost Tapes* (foreword by Strobe Talbott, translated and edited by Jerrold L. Schecter with Vyacheslav V. Luchkov, Little, Brown, 1990, pp. 144–7).

4 For a well-researched but occasionally flawed history of the Congress for Cultural Freedom, see Peter Coleman, *The Liberal Conspiracy* (Free Press, Macmillan, 1989). See also Brian Crozier, 'A Noble Mess' in the *Salisbury Review* (London), December 1990.

5 *National Review*, New York, 8 February 1958. From *The War We Are In* (collected columns, Arlington House, 1967).

6 *PERJURY: the Hiss–Chambers Case* (Knopf, New York, 1978), p. 565. The KGB defector Oleg Gordievsky, in the book co-authored with Christopher Andrew (see Ch. I, note 1), reveals that in a KGB lecture in the Lubyanka, (Iskhad Abdulovich) Akhmerov had mentioned Hiss briefly (p. 233). In a later passage (p. 273), he names Hiss as 'the KGB's main source within the State Department'.

7 The first account of Volkogonov's exonerating statement appeared in the *New York Times* of

29 October 1992. See also: Allen
Weinstein, 'Reopening a Cold War
Mystery' (*Washington Post*,
3 November 1992); Herbert
Romerstein, 'The Alger Hiss
Whitewash Hoax' and 'The Alger
Hiss Whitewash Hoax Collapses'
(*Human Events*, Washington, DC,
28 November 1992 and 2 January
1993 respectively); Jacob Cohen,
'Innocent After All?' and Amos
Perlmutter, 'Soviet Historiography,
Western Journalism' (both in
National Review, 18 January 1993).
In London, the *Guardian* returned
to the charge on 9 January 1993,
with a special supplement
misleadingly entitled 'Alger Hiss:
the spy who never was', which took
Volkogonov's original statement as
proof of Hiss's innocence,
dismissing his retractive further
statement.

8 *Gordievsky*, p. 353; Vladimir and
Evdokia Petrov, *Empire of Fear*
(André Deutsch, London;
Frederick Praeger, New York,
1956), p. 351; also Michael
Bialoguski, *The Petrov Story*
(Heinemann, 1955). The best

account of the Khokhlov case is in
John Barron, *KGB: the Secret Work
of Soviet Secret Agents* (Reader's
Digest Press, 1974), pp. 311–13.

9 In an otherwise detailed and
accurate account, the American
writers David Wise and Thomas B.
Ross do not mention the SIS
participation: see *The Invisible
Government* (Jonathan Cape,
1965), pp. 110–11. Henceforth,
Wise and Ross. See also Brian
Crozier, *The Masters of Power*
(Eyre & Spottiswoode, 1969),
pp. 305–6. Henceforth, *Masters*.

10 *Wise and Ross*, pp. 165–83; and
Masters, pp. 307–8.

11 See Donald Lancaster, *The
Emancipation of French Indochina*
(Oxford, 1961), pp. 336–7.

12 See John Barron: *KGB* (op. cit.),
p. 72.

13 In *The Game Player* (Aurum Press,
1989), Ch. 15, 'The "Moslem Billy
Graham"'.

14 Allen Dulles was Director of the
Central Intelligence Agency. He was
the younger brother of John Foster
Dulles, Secretary of State under
President Eisenhower.

III

From 'passive' to 'active' (1958–61)

THE MAN SEATED next to me on the Air France flight from Algiers to Paris in February 1958 was reading something that caught my eye at an oblique angle: a letter from General Raoul Salan thanking him in unusually warm terms for the series of talks on psychological war he had been giving to the French Army in Algeria.

In French military argot, the man next to me had been doing a *tournée des popotes*: a tour of the officers' messes. This seemed a promising encounter. So I asked my travelling companion what he thought of the situation in Algeria. This was one of the times when I was thankful I had spent seven of my childhood years in the 1920s in France. Assuming I was French, the man launched into a hair-raising torrent of revelations.

His main theme was the prevailing state of mind within the French armed forces. It was a question not so much of damaged morale as of revolutionary aspirations – not Communist aspirations, but nationalism of the extreme Right. Stunned by their unforeseen defeat in Indochina, the French had begun, late in the day, to translate the works of Mao Tse-tung on revolutionary war. They were not prepared to contemplate a second defeat. France had to fight its way back to 'greatness'.

Apart from an occasional supplementary question, I just listened. After more than an hour of it, I thought I should let my interlocutor know that I was British, not French. He looked surprised, but soon recovered his composure. On learning that I was the editor of *The Economist*'s *Foreign Report*, he told me that he had long been a regular reader and admirer of 'my' bulletin.

He introduced himself as Colonel Antoine Bonnemaison of the French Ministry of National Defence. He was a lively personality, with large brown eyes and a deep voice. Bonnemaison changed my life.

Before we parted company at Orly airport, he advised me to get hold of the last few issues of the official 'house magazine' of the French armed forces, the *Bulletin Militaire d'Information*, and to pay special attention to the articles of one Colonel Lacheroy.

I had never heard of the *Bulletin Militaire d'Information*, but the British Museum Library had a complete file of it. I soon saw what Bonnemaison meant. Although the articles were couched in severe intellectual and analytical terms, they were explosive in the context of the Algerian War and of political tensions in Paris.

On 20 February 1958, *Foreign Report* carried my account of the state of mind within the French services, under the title 'Towards Militarism in France'. I remember adding a question mark to the title, then deleting it.

A storm of another kind then broke around my head. The deputy head of the Foreign Office News Department summoned me peremptorily for a carpeting. The British ambassador in Paris, Sir Gladwyn Jebb (later Lord Gladwyn) had telephoned in a fury to complain that the article was inaccurate, unfounded and damaging to Anglo-French relations. I found it hard to understand why an analytical piece in a confidential newsletter which did not even hit the daily headlines could have been found so important, but such was the mystique of *The Economist* and its 'bluesheet'.

I stood my ground. 'I believe my information to be accurate,' I said firmly.

Came 13 May, and the 'second coming' of Charles de Gaulle. To the lasting credit of the Foreign Office, the same official called me in again, this time to apologise. 'You were right, and we were wrong,' he said magnanimously. 'We knew nothing about all this.' In retrospect, this was perhaps the biggest scoop in *Foreign Report* during my time.

I called on Antoine Bonnemaison, when I was next in Paris, to tell him about my victorious confrontation with the Foreign Office. His office was in a basement on a back street off the rue des Capucines, in the 9th *arrondissement*. It was a modest establishment, cluttered with files, and occupied only by Bonnemaison himself and a quiet, efficient secretary. He ran a mysterious outfit called the *Centre de Recherche du Bien Politique*. There was an Aristotelian ring to this untranslatable name: a

Research Centre for the Political Good – 'good' in its sense as the antithesis of 'evil'.

One day in 1959, Bonnemaison invited me to join one of the international *colloques* he had been running since 1955. The venue chosen was Frankfurt, and Antoine explained that, for reasons to be clarified later, he would introduce me as 'a member of the *French* delegation'.

Bonnemaison had been speaking in riddles. 'A few of us meet, twice a year, to see what we can do ...'

'In what context?' I asked. 'Can you be more specific?'

'To try to find ways ... To talk about problems,' was all he would say.

I mentioned this to Ronald Franks, my SIS friend, the 'mad genius', who expressed great interest. Already, in return for the occasional scoops he had given me, I had been tipping him off whenever something of special interest came my way on my travels.

The propriety of such exchanges, between a journalist and an intelligence service, is hotly contested. I know a number of reputable journalists of various nationalities who have done as I did. In part, the motivation is professional: new sources, exchanges of information. In some cases, too, patriotism plays a part: it is obviously good for one's country that its foreign policy should be based on information known to be sound. Among left-wing journalists, however, the prevailing pressure is to denounce such collaboration. This of course puts a premium on the recruitment of left-wing journalists as spies, since their public criticism of intelligence services may shield them from suspicion. The protests of the 'holier than thou' can be hypocritical.

The Frankfurt meeting took place in the German equivalent of a stately home. The atmosphere was mysterious and intriguing. There were about thirty-five participants. The French delegation numbered ten, plus myself. On this, as on later occasions, I was the only journalist present. Bonnemaison had explained that the proceedings would be strictly confidential. Specifically, the fact that these meetings were taking place was not to be mentioned publicly. However, there was nothing to prevent me from using any information imparted during the meeting. There were only two other delegations: from the German Federal Republic and the Netherlands.

Although Bonnemaison remained reticent, the truth about the *colloques* emerged in the private exchanges I had with other participants. Assuming that, as a member of the French delegation, I must have been briefed before my arrival, the Dutch and Germans treated me as an insider. The *colloques* had been launched by Antoine Bonnemaison as an exercise in Franco-German rapprochement. Under the normal cover of his military rank in the cavalry, Bonnemaison was in fact a senior officer of the French equivalent of MI-6: the *Service de Documentation Extérieure et de Contre-Espionnage* (SDECE).

Bonnemaison was the organising secretary, but the French delegation was led by General Jean Olié, de Gaulle's Chief of the General Staff, with whom I struck up a cordial relationship. The blend of 'delegates' was basically the same in all three groups: intelligence, both civil and military; leading academics; non-academic political or economic specialists; one or two trusted politicians; leaders of industry; trade union leaders; and clerics of various denominations.

The German delegation was led by General Foertsch, an impressive man who had served as a senior deputy to the better-known General Reinhard Gehlen, creator of the post-war West German Federal Intelligence Service, the BND (*Bundesnachrichtendienst*). Two regulars were Professors Lades and Kernig, both specialists on Communism in general and East Germany in particular. There was a German equivalent of Bonnemaison's Centre: the *Deutsche Vereinigung für Ost–West Beziehungen* (the German Alliance for East—West Relations). The Vereinigung was based in Munich, appropriately close to the headquarters of the BND at Pullach.

The Dutch delegation was led by a massive and delightful man named Einthoven, lately retired as head of the Dutch security service. With him was a younger man, C. C. ('Kees') van den Heuvel, tall and athletic, who had played a heroic role in the Dutch Resistance during the Nazi occupation.

I was captivated by these meetings, which were very productive in terms of facts, background, analysis and intelligent discussion. The *colloques* took place alternately in France and Germany. Between the first and second of those I attended, Bonnemaison had revealed my true nationality, discreetly, to the other delegations.

These meetings often yielded exclusive material for *Foreign Report*, and I occasionally saved the most secret details for Ronald Franks. To my mind, this was one modest way to help fill one of the gaps created by Britain's self-exclusion from Europe. In June 1955, the Foreign Ministers of the original member states of the European Economic Community had met in the Sicilian capital, Messina, to consider the next steps after the Treaty of Rome which they had signed. They had invited Britain to join them, but Britain's Prime Minister, Sir Anthony Eden, had turned down the invitation.

The predictable consequence was that the British had no say in drafting the rules of the EEC. France's clever *hauts fonctionnaires* had a clear run. The Common Agricultural Policy was one of the undesirable outcomes. A sizeable 'bus' had been missed.[1] And an intelligence gap had been created.

In his own time, Bonnemaison explained to me that his main function was to coordinate the work of the French psychological war organisations, known collectively as the *Cinquième Bureaux*. His specific target was Leninism. 'What about Marxism?' I asked. He looked grave. 'Marxism is a philosophy. It has a right to existence. Leninism is activism and a threat to the State.' I owed much to Bonnemaison. With his warm personality he had an intellect of exceptional power. After his military career, he had emerged into civilian life to take a string of higher degrees. In some ways, he would have been happiest as a university professor. But professionally, he was an activist.

He was a close, indeed a penetrating student of the French political scene, and especially of the social realities behind it. He opened up new horizons for me by teaching me the basic principles of indirect action behind the scenes. He transformed me from passivist to activist.

BY THE TIME I started attending Bonnemaison's meetings, I had at last overcome a lingering reluctance to meet Germans. The anti-German sentiments inculcated at the Lycée of Montpellier in the 1920s were still strong in me in the 1950s, deepened by moral revulsion against Nazism. So strongly did I feel this that I had turned down several chances to visit Germany at *The Economist*'s expense. Germany, however, was now becoming increasingly important, and I decided that I needed first-hand experience to do my work intelligently.

In Montpellier, aged twelve, I had carried off a prize for German. In 1958, aged forty, I spent some months trying to turn childish memories into an adult command. I had been cultivating contacts at the German embassy in London, and I was invited to tour the Federal Republic. Unusually, this was a personal invitation, not as part of a group.

In West Berlin (before the Wall), I visited one of the debriefing centres for the many thousands of refugees pouring across the border: nearly 30,000 a month at that time. I was struck by the depth of indoctrination on the Communist side, so that those I spoke to expressed their detestation of Communism in formal Marxist language.

'I am fleeing to capitalism,' said one earnest young man, a student, 'because our socialist rulers are violating the teachings of Marx and Engels, and exploiting our working class.'

An American colleague, Seymour Topping, then of AP and later Executive Editor of the *New York Times*, drove me into East Berlin, where I saw for myself the deserted streets, the thin traffic, the wedding-cake Stalinist architecture. He introduced me to John Peet, a former Reuters correspondent, who now ran a propaganda bulletin for the Socialist Unity (Communist) Party, which I already knew.

Two things Peet said stuck in my mind. One was that he had long given up attending Party lectures, out of sheer boredom. The other struck a defensive note: 'I've always been left-wing,' he said, almost as though admitting to an embarrassing social disease. . . .

I had been granted an appointment to see the Federal Chancellor, Dr Konrad Adenauer, but a cancelled flight from Berlin wrecked the arrangement. Instead, I met an imposing but lesser figure, the President of the Federal Republic, Professor Theodor Heuss. With me was *The Economist's* Bonn correspondent, Karl Robson, an old friend and colleague from *News Chronicle* days. To me, the most arresting thing the Professor said was in response to a question: whether he feared that the Federal Republic's involvement in the European Common Market and NATO would make the reunification of the two halves of Germany even more difficult than it already was.

'On the contrary,' said President Heuss in his deep, rumbling voice, 'membership of the Common Market and the Atlantic Alliance will make it easier to reunite the three parts of Germany: West Germany, Central Germany and Eastern Germany.'

This was an educative moment. Back in London I asked to be put on the mailing list of the information bulletin of the West German embassy. Its cover carried a map of Germany in its pre-war frontiers. What we called 'East Germany' our German allies called 'Central Germany'. 'East Germany' meant the territories, now under Polish rule, east of the Oder–Neisse line, from which the Germans had been expelled after the war to compensate the Poles for the land further east seized by Stalin when Hitler invaded Poland in 1939.

At that time, it would have been impossible for anybody to imagine the deal which Chancellor Kohl would make with President Gorbachev thirty-one years later, still less united Germany's renunciation of the evacuated territories.

                    *   *   *

FOR EIGHT MONTHS in 1959, most of my spare time was spent on researching and writing what became my first published book, *The Rebels*, which delved into the origins of insurgences in Palestine, Cyprus, Malaya, Indochina, Algeria and elsewhere since World War II. The publisher was Chatto & Windus, through Peter Calvocoressi, whose distinguished career had included the mammoth task of writing the Chatham House *Survey of International Affairs* for five consecutive years. I had been brooding over the subject since my time in South-East Asia, and my absorption with it had grown with my visits to North Africa and a brief stay in Cyprus at the height of the Greek terrorism.

The Rebels was an instant critical success. By far the most pleasing of many reviews were two lengthy ones, in *Encounter* and *The Times Literary Supplement*. Both were by C. M. Wodehouse, recently retired as Director-General of Chatham House, but only the *Encounter* one was signed.

I had met Wodehouse a few times at Chatham House, in the company of others, but at the time knew nothing of his background. 'From the Foreign Office' was an unspecific description. I learned only later of his prowess as the British colonel who had headed the liaison group with the Greek guerrillas during the war. His *Encounter* review (September 1960) included the following prophetic passage about 'stasiology': the study of the breakdown or paralysis of the State.

A theory of rebellion can perhaps be elaborated: 'Stasiology' would be no more bizarre than some other social sciences that have recently burgeoned and Mr Crozier has made a pioneering contribution to it.

The first foreign translation of *The Rebels* was in German. Some months later, an American edition came out (Beacon Press, Boston), and the US government obtained permission to translate key passages into Greek, Turkish and Arabic, and to distribute these passages to all member governments of NATO. There were pirated editions in Arabic (Lebanon) and Chinese (Taiwan). In distant Colombia, the Army paid a modest sum for the privilege of publishing a Spanish-language edition for the benefit of its hard-pressed security forces.

Soon *The Rebels* was used as a textbook in a course on counter-insurgency in the US Foreign Service Institute. The same arrangement was made in national defence colleges in Israel and other countries, but it was not until 1972 that the full impact of my essay in stasiology became clear. I was on a tour of US defence institutions, culminating in a lecture

at the US Army Institute for Military Assistance at Fort Bragg, North Caro-
lina. After my talk, the senior officer took me to the library and showed
me a copy of the first counter-insurgency course at the Institute. It was
based entirely on my book, at that time the only relevant text available.

Stimulated by the Vietnam War and by revolutionary violence in many
countries, stasiology became a minor industry. Hundreds, perhaps thousands, of books on the subject were published.

In deference to my connection with *The Economist*, I had written
impartially. On the colonial issue, in particular, a number of readers
would tell me that they were not at all sure, on reading the book, which
side I was on. In future books I would give priority to objectivity (respect
for the facts) over impartiality (equality of praise and blame).

This change of approach led to a breach with Calvocoressi, whose
knowledge, intellect and lucid style I much admired but whose standpoint, to my mind, was soft liberalism incarnate.

DURING THE FOUR-YEAR period of 1959–62, the Soviet Union
scored several important successes in the secret war; and suffered at least
one serious reverse. Such is the nature of the secret war that the facts in
each case remained unknown for some years.

By far their most important success was in Cuba. On the last day of
1958, the Cuban dictator, President Fulgencio Batista, fled to the United
States. Two days later, Fidel Castro and his band of guerrillas entered
Havana in triumph. Initially, Castro posed as a romantic Cuban patriot,
deceiving his own followers as well as the outside world. Fourteen years
later, a detailed Allied secret document came into my hands which
revealed the concealed reality of a Soviet takeover. Posing as a TASS
agency correspondent, a senior KGB official, Aleksandr Alekseyev, arrived
in Havana shortly after Castro's victory. His mission was to guide Castro
in the creation of a secret intelligence agency that would, in time, serve
the needs of the Soviet Union.

After his initial reconnaissance, a group of five Soviet KGB advisers
turned up in Havana. The report gave detailed physical descriptions of
them.

It took Alekseyev and his colleagues about two years to set up a Cuban
equivalent of the KGB: the DGI (*Dirección General de Inteligencia*). The
original Director-General of the DGI (from 1961 to 1969) was Manuel
Piñeiro Losada, known as *Barbaroja* ('Red Beard'). On a smaller scale,
the departments of the DGI closely paralleled those of the KGB.[2]

Castro's ego being what it was, the DGI in its initial years was by no means as docile as the Soviets would have liked. In time, however, it was brought under total Soviet control. The real significance of this extraordinary operation was that for the first time Soviet imperialism had found a way of breaching the barrier of distance, thus apparently confirming the faith of the Leninists that Communism could indeed be extended to all countries of the world.

Until the Cuban operation and its success, the prevailing orthodoxy among students of Communism had been what was sometimes called 'the theory of contiguity'. Indeed, all the victories of Communism, whether in Eastern Europe or in Asia, had been achieved under the proximate threat of military power. Now, for the first time, a new technique had proved itself: the extension of power through the creation of an ultimately docile secret service.

TWO OTHER SOVIET successes in this period were of totally different kinds. The secret details of both were revealed by General Jan Sejna, of the Czechoslovak secret service, the StB, when he defected to the West in 1968 during the 'Prague Spring'.

In February 1962, the German Federal Republic and the Western Alliance itself were shaken by the '*Spiegel* affair'. A highly classified NATO document, giving full details of a forthcoming military exercise, had been leaked to this mass-circulation weekly news magazine.

Enraged, the Defence Minister, the Bavarian leader Franz Josef Strauss, ordered the arrest of the publisher, Rudolf Augstein, the editor, Konrad Ahlers, and a couple of colleagues. The Liberals (FDP) in Chancellor Adenauer's coalition accused the Minister of acting unconstitutionally, and threatened to resign unless Strauss stepped down. This he was forced to do. It broke his hitherto spectacular career, at least for some years, and wrecked his chances of succeeding Adenauer as Federal Chancellor.

One of my papers of that period throws an interesting light upon the *Spiegel* affair. It was a memorandum to the editor of *The Economist*, recording a talk I had some months earlier at the Foreign Office with Sir Frank Roberts, at that time British ambassador in Moscow. The relevant paragraph reads:

Sir Frank had Mikoyan to dinner recently. Mikoyan argued that the West Germans were getting stronger, that the present government was all right, but that Adenauer was getting older, and who knew what would come after him?

It would be dreadful if Strauss came to power. In that event, there really would
be a revanchist attitude in West Germany and an attempt to unify Germany
by force.

At that time, Mikoyan, the Armenian Bolshevik and great survivor of
the Stalin purges, was First Deputy Prime Minister and a senior Politburo
member. Clearly, he was telling Sir Frank what the Politburo wanted the
British ambassador to hear.

General Sejna revealed in 1968 that secret papers which had crossed
his desk in Prague gave details of a Politburo decision to launch a KGB
operation to stop Strauss. According to Sejna, it was decided that the
actual operation should be entrusted to the Czech equivalent of the KGB,
his own StB. One of the key ploys was to obtain classified defence documents and plant them on *Spiegel*.[3]

Having defected to the US, Sejna was of course debriefed by the CIA,
and later by the Pentagon's DIA (Defense Intelligence Agency). The American debriefers, however, seemed only mildly interested in the Strauss
affair, and did not want to know Sejna's sensational revelations about the
Soviet 'Drugs-for-War' offensive.

With other Warsaw Pact officials, Sejna had been present at a secret
meeting called by Khrushchev in Moscow in the autumn of 1962. Khrushchev sketched out a strategic programme to disseminate drugs in the
United States, with the object of demoralising the American armed forces,
and other sectors of society, including schools. In the initial phase of the
plan, Czech secret service officials were instructed to work with the
Cubans to infiltrate the United States and Latin American countries to
produce and distribute drugs in the United States.[4]

DURING THIS PERIOD, the Soviets also suffered serious reverses
in Africa. In June 1960, Belgium decided, with excessive haste, to confer
independence upon the Belgian Congo. It had made no long-term preparations for this decision, and at that time there were only seventeen
graduates among the black Congolese. The new Prime Minister, Patrice
Lumumba, had many Communist friends and must have been regarded
in Moscow as a malleable tool. Indeed, the Belgian Communist Party had
provided the new government with 'technical advisers'. Moreover, the
Belgian-trained Force Publique (a kind of militia) mutinied. The classic
preconditions for a Communist revolution appeared to exist.

The Soviet Union started a massive airlift to the Congo, introducing arms and Communist agents. The United Nations decided to intervene, and the Russians represented their airlift as a contribution to UN operations, while publicly casting discredit on the UN intervention. On 5 September 1960, *The Times* reported that the Soviet and Czech embassies in Léopoldville between them had at least 200 diplomats and 'technicians' in the country without counting medical teams. The experienced Soviet ambassador, Mikhail Yakovlev, was on good terms with Lumumba.

A few days later the projected coup ended in fiasco. The new President, Kasavubu, dismissed Lumumba, and on 14 September Colonel Mobutu, Commander-in-Chief of the so-called Army, announced a takeover, and gave the Communist embassies forty-eight hours to leave the country. During the next day and night, the Soviet and Czech embassies made large bonfires of incriminating documents. On 17 September, the entire staffs of both embassies left Léopoldville by air.

Mobutu explained that a Soviet radio transmitter had been operating in Léopoldville, where the Russians had set up a spy ring.[5]

Some weeks after Mobutu's coup, I arrived in Léopoldville on the last lap of a tour of mainly Francophone West Africa. I was travelling in a dual capacity, as correspondent of *The Economist* and commentator for the BBC French Language Service. The atmosphere was tense. Lumumba was under house arrest. On the evening of my arrival, as a guest of the suave and unflappable Sture Linner, a Swede in charge of the civilian side of the UN mission, we heard a prolonged crackle of gunfire.

It was the fledgling Congolese Army, clashing with UN troops who (without any justification in international law that I could discover) were protecting the home of the unaccredited Ghanaian, Nathaniel Welbeck, who claimed to be his country's chargé d'affaires. Mobutu had given him twenty-four hours to clear out, and sent troops to make sure he did.

The UN force, wearing the usual blue helmets and arm-bands, were known as 'ONUC' or 'UNOC' (*Opération Nations Unies Congo*, or United Nations Operation Congo). The locals thought the ONUC or UNOC were a tribe. The confusion is illustrated by a cruel story.

One day Congolese and UNOC troops clashed. The UNOC troops were Tunisians of fair complexion and the Congolese had not heard of Tunisia. A Congolese sergeant shouted: 'Filthy UNOC imperialists.' Bewildered, a Tunisian remonstrated. He told the Congolese about the French colonialists and added: 'You see, we ourselves only got our independence four years ago.' 'Only four years,' replied the astonished Congolese, 'and already you're white!'

The local BBC man, Neil Fraser, lent me his ancient Pontiac, which only worked in second gear. The Congolese driver was very nervous. We headed for the residence of the British ambassador, Ian Scott, but the driver lost his way, and we found ourselves outside the villa in which Lumumba was under house arrest. Fierce-looking helmeted Congolese troops surrounded us with drawn bayonets. The trembling driver whispered to me: 'Don't put your head out. They are without pity!' Ignoring him, I put my head out of the window and asked politely if the soldiers could direct me to the British ambassador's residence. The nearest one grunted and waved us on with his bayonet.

In the trigger-happy atmosphere, Ian Scott maintained an unflapped British presence. His view was that the Congolese were frightened, but that a friendly overture made them relax. At the height of the troubles, Scott had set an example of calm by bringing his wife out to join him.

On my way to the Congo, I had interviewed three African presidents. The first was Léopold Senghor of Senegal, the erudite grammarian of the Constitution of the French Fourth Republic, and philosopher of *Négritude*. The next was Modibo Keita of neighbouring Bali, an elongated Nilotic man nearly two metres tall, whom General de Gaulle was said to enjoy meeting because he was the only leader of a former French colony who could look him in the eye. Sékou Touré of Guinea, however, was the only one worthy of Soviet attention because, alone of the Francophone African leaders, he had contemptuously spurned de Gaulle's offer of a place in the French Community. The Guinean people, he declared, 'prefer poverty in freedom to riches in slavery'.

De Gaulle retaliated by cutting Guinea off without a franc. A wheat ship on its way to Conakry was diverted. The departing French officials even ripped out the telephones on their desks. With his heavy dose of anti-colonial bitterness, Sékou Touré had a metallic voice laced with acid. Although he denounced Communism and hoped the West would strike a balance between the two world blocs, he was himself the arch-exponent of a kind of African peasant Communism, remarkably similar (minus the culture and 4000 years of history) to the peasant Communism of Mao Tse-tung. He said to me:

We have the most advanced democracy in the world. I challenge you to name a more advanced one. Whereas in countries like the United States *and the Soviet Union* [my emphasis] the ruling party is only a small fraction of the population, here in Guinea it is everywhere.

Guinea was indeed the ultimate example of 'participatory democracy' – a negation of democracy as we understand it in the West. Once Sékou Touré had taken de Gaulle at his word, he had little option but to turn to the Soviet bloc. The East Germans, for instance, had printed Guinea's worthless banknotes. Guinea was also the receiver of a bizarre example of the perils of central economic planning: the Soviet aid programme deliveries included a snow plough. In fairness to Sékou Touré, I have to add that when the Soviet ambassador in Conakry started the usual Soviet job of inciting unrest, which led to widespread riots, Sékou Touré expelled him without ceremony in December 1961.

On my way home, I stopped briefly in Ghana, then in Nigeria for the independence celebrations. In Lagos, in the splendid Federal Palace Hotel, I bumped into my unlikely friend Kingsley Martin of the *New Statesman*. He was in good form and told me a story against himself. He had once had a conversation with Seretse Khama, later Prime Minister of Bechuanaland, and later still the first President of independent Botswana, on a visit to London. 'The trouble with you, Seretse,' said the socialist sage of Great Turnstile, 'is that you're the nigger in the woodpile.'

NOTES

1 For a lively account of the Messina affair, see Michael Charlton, *The Price of Victory* (BBC, London, 1983), Ch. 6, ' "Messina! Messina!" or the Parting of the Ways'.

2 *Conflict Studies No. 35*, 'Soviet Pressures in the Caribbean: the satellisation of Cuba' (Institute for the Study of Conflict [ISC], London, May 1973).

3 In the early 1980s, Sir James Goldsmith was sued by *Spiegel* magazine after he had said in a speech that the affair had been 'orchestrated by the KGB'. (See Ch. XVIII.)

4 See Joseph Douglass, *Red Cocaine* (Clarion, Atlanta, 1990); Brian Crozier, *The Gorbachev Phenomenon; 'Peace' and the Secret War* (Claridge, London, 1990). Henceforth, *Phenomenon*.

5 For a fuller account of these Soviet reverses, see Brian Crozier, *The Struggle for the Third World* (Bodley Head, London, 1966), pp. 66–73.

IV

France: the first breach (1961–4)

THE LAOS CONFERENCE opened in May 1961 and dragged on for fourteen months, bringing me repeatedly to Geneva. It was the perfect example of the Communist view of diplomacy as the continuation of war by other means. Under earlier agreements, the Vietminh surrogates, Pathet Lao, had been formally 'integrated' with the Royal Army, but full integration never happened. A hard core of Communist guerrillas stayed in the jungles to fight on. Unfortunately for this enchanting backwater, the Western powers were not prepared, when the crisis came, to protect the kingdom from its predatory neighbours.

That 'grand old man' of American diplomacy, the multi-millionaire Averell Harriman (1891–1986), made the point clear in the run-up to the Conference. He had been President Roosevelt's ambassador to Moscow during World War II (1943–6). Like Harry Hopkins (see Ch. I), he fell under Stalin's influence in later years; unlike Hopkins, he was never a recruited agent, but he was nevertheless a constant appeaser of the Soviet Union.[1]

At a press conference in Vientiane on 25 March 1961, Harriman said that in the American view Prince Souvanna Phouma was not dominated by the Communists and would do everything to create a truly neutral government. He added that the Soviet Union was working in good faith to bring about a peaceful solution.

The Soviet leader, Nikita Khrushchev, had coined the 'troika' formula, conjuring up images of frozen steppes and a sleigh drawn by three horses. It came to mean a 'neutral' government consisting of neutralists, Communists and anti-Communists.

In effect, the Laos Conference was a continuation of the 1954 conference which had ended France's war in Indochina. The British and Soviet Foreign Ministers – Lord Home and Andrei Gromyko – alternated in the chair.

My friend from Singapore days, the affable and equable Malcolm Mac-Donald, took over the co-chairmanship from Lord Home, and invited me for a drink. MacDonald, an ex-Labour minister turned roving envoy, was always forthright. In one of his public interventions, he exclaimed:

> We all know that there are military advisers, military technicians from the Democratic Republic of Vietnam in Laos ... and therefore we are entitled to get a straight answer from the representatives of the Democratic Republic of Vietnam.

The British estimated that there were 8000 North Vietnamese troops in Laos; the Americans put it at 10,000. The Americans themselves had 800 advisers there. On 21 July, the conference reached agreement on Laotian neutrality and the withdrawal of foreign troops. By early October, all the Americans had left. As for the Vietnamese, they did withdraw a token number of their men, as a reluctant admission that a few might, inadvertently, have strayed across the Laotian border. The bulk of them stayed behind.

The conference had got the Western powers off the hook, but the 'peace' it brought Laos was short-lived. In due course, Laos was simply incorporated into the new empire of Greater Vietnam. Khrushchev's 'troika' had worked.

BEFORE LEAVING LONDON in 1961 for a six-week lecture tour of the US as a guest of the English-Speaking Union, I briefed my colleague Andrew Boyd, who was to run *Foreign Report* in my absence. Among the notes I left him was this one:

> *H. A. R. Philby.* Lazier as time goes by. Ought to be stirred up now that Kurds and Syrians are erupting.

At that time I did not know that 'Kim' Philby was a Soviet spy. I was in the Far East when he had been investigated by the British Security Service (MI-5). After a period of loneliness and penury, Philby, sponsored by the Foreign Office, had been taken on by the *Observer* and *The Economist* as their joint correspondent in the Near East, based on Beirut. An indifferent foreign correspondent, he could have worked harder than he did to make his cover convincing.

My SIS friend, Ronald Franks, also had an entry in my memo to Andrew Boyd. It read: 'His piece on the state of China caused a first-class row within the FO, and he is chary of adding fuel to the fire.' It was not only within the FO that Franks had stirred up controversy. He was also at the British end of a major clash of opinion between MI-6 and the CIA over the Sino-Soviet split. Franks himself had told me about the row within the Foreign Office, but he had not mentioned the much bigger row between MI-6 and the CIA, about which I learned much later.

At issue was the correct interpretation of events in China. Was the split real or was it a deception to confuse the Western intelligence services? A Soviet defector from the KGB, Anatoly Golitsyn, had been advising the Head of Counter-Intelligence in the CIA, James Jesus Angleton, not to fall for the flood of evidence that there had been a great split between the Communist parties of the USSR and China. He gave apparently convincing reasons for interpreting it as a vast deception exercise by the KGB. Angleton, by nature and training disinclined to take anything at face value, listened to Golitsyn.[2] The truth, as presented by Ronald Franks and his colleagues, was therefore suspect.

I was involved in the dispute, at the margin, because Franks had contributed his analysis to *Foreign Report*. He had also published a detailed article, under the name of David A. Charles, in the CIA-sponsored *China Quarterly*. The row in the Foreign Office was over the propriety of an SIS man thus making his views known, even under a pen-name. Both Franks and Angleton were credited with genius-level intelligence by their respective colleagues.

The case of the British traitor George Blake came to light during that period, and Philby was under investigation. Moreover, the memory of Burgess and Maclean was still recent. During the years in which Angleton and some of his colleagues persisted in denying the fact of the Sino-Soviet rift, Ronald Franks was thus regarded with deep suspicion at Langley. As Ronald Franks had explained, at the heart of the Sino-Soviet rift was China's former Defence Minister, Marshal Peng Teh-huai. Peng was a moderniser, who doubted the value of Mao's theories of peasant guerrilla warfare and wanted a professional army. Above all, he wanted nuclear status for China, and since Moscow was China's only supplier of modern weapons, he wanted to keep in with the Soviets. Rashly, he had criticised Mao's policies in a letter to the Soviet Communist Party, without even consulting the Chinese Politburo. Khrushchev had encouraged him and had refused to apologise for intervening in Chinese affairs. It was this that had brought the latent dispute into the open.

There is a sad footnote to this story. Some years later Ronald Franks enrolled at the Massachusetts Institute of Technology, at the other Cambridge near Boston, to write what should have been the ultimate treatise on the origins of the Sino-Soviet dispute. Having finished it, but neglected to make a carbon copy, he left it in a taxi on a short ride in Boston and lost it. This catastrophe sent his mind over the edge, and he sank into deep melancholia. This, at least, was his account. Some time later, his SIS chief, Maurice Oldfield, told me he doubted whether Franks had ever actually written the book, and assumed that he had lost his notes for a work he never committed to paper.

Whatever the reason, he never fully recovered. He died in an accident.

BONNEMAISON AND I had discussed problems of presentation in our fight against Communism. We had agreed that in the prevailing climate, a phase of 'anti-anti-Communism' would be desirable. There had been a surfeit of anti-Communist articles, books or speeches, which gave ammunition for the mindless but effective smear of 'McCarthyism'.

In this mood, I left on my American tour. The American scene offered tempting targets for anti-anti-Communism. Extremist groups proliferated. In their sweeping condemnation of anything marginally right of centre, they were counter-productive.

I had discussed this theme with Melvin Lasky of *Encounter*, who commissioned from me a reportage on the extreme Right in the US. One of my targets was the fanatical John Birch Society, whose wild and virulent accusations far exceeded the worst excesses of the late Senator McCarthy.

In one of its publications, Birchites were told that 'Dwight Eisenhower is a dedicated, conscious agent of the Communist conspiracy'; and that 'the chances are very strong that Milton Eisenhower is actually Dwight Eisenhower's superior and boss within the Communist Party'. Others listed were the Dulles brothers: Allen, head of the CIA, and John Foster, Secretary of State. One might, just as plausibly, have labelled Khrushchev as a closet Republican. . . .

On my way back to London, I dropped in on the left-wing weekly the

Nation in New York. Delighted to meet an apparently dedicated British leftist, the editor commissioned three articles from me.

My *Encounter* article of March 1962, 'Down Among the Rightists', caused a dual stir, from Left and Right.

The theme of anti-anti-Communism was aired at length at Bonnemaison's next *colloque*, in the picturesque setting of Mont Saint-Michel, in the late spring of 1962. Two newcomers were there. One was an Australian who had served in both the ASIO (Australian Security Intelligence Organisation) and SIS. His name was C. H. ('Dick') Ellis. Aged seventy and long retired, he was multilingual, and had served in Washington during the war as special assistant to the legendary Canadian 'Bill' Stephenson ('Intrepid').

The other newcomer was Professor Maurice Allais of the Sorbonne, who at that time was swimming hard against the French academic and intellectual left-wing tide. Allais was an uncompromising advocate of free-market economics and of strong but limited government. His clear presentation rid me of my last shreds of socialist illusion.[3]

I DEVOTED much of 1962 to the Algerian War. Among some unique sources was the Swiss writer Charles-Henri Favrod, author of the first book on the war (*La Révolution Algérienne*, 1959). Favrod was also acting for the French SDECE as go-between with the Provisional Government of Algeria: a role he later authorised me to reveal.

BUT DOMINATING that year was the Cuban missiles crisis of October 1962. President Kennedy's determination to outface Khrushchev was made possible by the high-level intelligence brought to the Western secret services by Colonel Oleg Penkovsky, who had been recruited by Britain's SIS. In 1959, the CIA had reported a substantial 'missile gap' in the Soviet Union's favour. The mass of photocopies brought over by Penkovsky on his fleeting official visits to London and Washington made it clear that it was America, not the USSR, which had the nuclear advantage.

Before and during the crisis, Ronald Franks had kept me informed, although he did not mention Penkovsky initially. In April, nearly six months before the crisis, Franks corrected the 'missile gap' fallacy by giving me Penkovsky's evidence. Penkovsky's exploits did not become public knowledge until the Soviet authorities brought him to trial in May 1963. Ronald Franks, one of the senior men who had debriefed Penkovsky, brought me the full story. Surprisingly, a number of Western commentators remained sceptical.

A later Soviet defector, the first from the GRU (military intelligence), Viktor Suvorov, described how Penkovsky was executed: burned alive in an open coffin.[4] If true, this should dispose of lingering suspicions that Penkovsky was an *agent provocateur* or a double agent.

When Khrushchev backed down and removed the Soviet missiles from Cuba, Kennedy was hailed in the West as the victor. He was indeed, but he paid a heavy price for his victory, for in return for the dismantling of the missiles the Americans withdrew their own missiles from Turkey and dropped plans to deploy missiles in Italy (while leaving the Soviet Union's intermediate-range missiles in European Russia intact). Moreover, Kennedy gave Khrushchev a solemn undertaking to refrain from any further attempt to remove the Castro regime in Cuba. Thus, on balance, the Soviets were better placed after they had backed down over Cuba than before they installed their missiles on the island.

The attitude of *The Economist* shocked me. It took the same line as the leftish *Guardian*, advising scepticism over the US evidence and caution in response. This was not the paper I had joined in the days of Geoffrey Crowther, who, I learned later, had been equally shocked and had let it be known that he would ask the board to replace Donald Tyerman as editor. It grieves me to say this, as Tyerman – a brave man who had overcome the handicap of legs crippled by polio – had been invariably kind to me, despite our political divergencies. In fact, Tyerman stayed on until 1965, when Alastair Burnet took over.

THERE WAS an ambiguous symbolism in the venue of the next *colloque* at the end of March 1963: Bad Godesberg, outside Bonn, was where Neville Chamberlain had had his second meeting with Hitler in 1938. On that occasion, he rejected Hitler's demands; but Munich loomed ahead. When Bonnemaison greeted me, I could see he was agitated. I asked him if anything was the matter, but he merely shrugged.

Three days later, when the meeting ended, he was in tears in the presence of three of his intimates. This was his last *colloque*, he revealed. General de Gaulle had decided to close down all the *Cinquième Bureaux*, and with them Antoine's Centre. Having said this, he corrected himself. To be accurate, he had been told by his superiors at the Ministère de la Défense Nationale that he could continue to run the Centre, but only on condition that it drop its anti-Leninist activities and devote itself to

research and information in favour of de Gaulle's *force de frappe* –
France's independent nuclear deterrent.

Bonnemaison had told his chiefs that this condition was unacceptable,
and resigned. Because of his exemplary record, his pension was upgraded
to the level it would have reached at the retiring age of sixty-five. At the
time he was fifty-seven. France's abandonment of its counter-subversion
arm was the first breach in the Allied united front against Soviet Active
Measures.

The background was illuminating, and discouraging. Nobody but
de Gaulle could have steered Algeria to peace and independence as he
did, under the Evian agreements of March 1962, without provoking a civil
war in France itself. He had returned to power with the backing of the
partisans of *Algérie Française*. With subtle patience he moved in succession to 'the Algerian personality', to 'Algerian Algeria', and finally to
'independent Algeria'.

His concealment of his true motives was masterly. He had never been
interested in retaining Algeria as a fictitious extension of France. To him,
the Algerian question was an unwelcome obstacle in the way of his real
ambition, which was to turn France into a nuclear power and legitimate
partner of America and Britain: a formula he had tried to launch in
letters to Prime Minister Macmillan and President Kennedy, proposing
an 'Atlantic Directorate' of the three powers. He did give France its *force
de frappe*, but failed to get his Atlantic Directorate, a failure that
embittered him.

There were two other elements in his decision to close down the
Cinquième Bureaux. One was that they had been taken over by the more
extreme military partisans of French Algeria, and thus constituted a threat
to the Gaullist State. The other was that Charles de Gaulle, in common
with another erudite politician, Enoch Powell, saw history in terms of
nation-States and empires, and failed to understand the ideological
dimension that was the basis of the Soviet threat.

During his twelve years in the wilderness (1946–58), he had formed his
Rally of the French People as a national movement transcending political
parties. In many speeches he had condemned the Communists as *les
séparatistes*. Now, back in power, and having been snubbed by the 'Anglo-
Saxons', he wanted a free hand to seek a rapprochement with Russia.
About Communism, as such, he had developed a kind of complex of
inevitability. General Olié, in conversation with me, quoted a remark
which de Gaulle had made in his hearing towards the end of 1961: 'I

myself shall bring Communism to France, to avoid Soviet Communism and its totalitarianism.' Some academic critics have dismissed this remark as a *boutade*, but Olié took it seriously, and so did I.[5]

Shortly after his traumatic forced retirement, Antoine Bonnemaison revived his organisation under another name: the *Centre d'Observation du Mouvement des Idées*. No longer State-supported, he raised the necessary funds from leading French industrial enterprises, including Péchiney and Air Liquide. His fight against Leninism continued, but the international dimension had been greatly reduced. Henceforth, the *colloque* participants were almost exclusively French. I was usually the only foreign participant, although on occasion I brought other Britons in as guests.

Although France had officially dropped out of the Western State-run anti-subversive network, Britain's IRD was at the height of its performance. The Germans, Dutch and Americans were still in. Shortly after the Bad Godesberg *colloque*, van den Heuvel set up the International Documentary Centre in The Hague, with which I was involved from the start. Better known as INTERDOC, it depended largely on West German subsidies. The British end was run by Dick Ellis, with the help of an ex-MI-5 man. As a gesture of courtesy, General Olié attended the first INTERDOC meeting, with a small French delegation. Neither he nor his compatriots, however, joined in the discussions, although in private they were friendly and communicative.

NOTES

1 See Joseph Finder, *Red Carpet* (Holt, Rinehart and Winston, New York, 1983), which examines 'the connection between the Kremlin and America's most powerful businessmen'. Ch. 8 is devoted to Harriman.

2 The most thorough examination of the Golitsyn case is in Tom Mangold, *Cold Warrior: James Jesus Angleton – the CIA's Master Spy Hunter* (Simon & Schuster, London, 1991). The Golitsyn case is complex, however, and his own book, *New Lies for Old* (Wheatsheaf Books, London, 1984) repays careful study.

3 In 1988, Maurice Allais was awarded the Nobel Prize for Economics.

4 In his book *Aquarium* (1985), Suvorov does not identify the victim, but he told me that he understood the man was Penkovsky. In a later and otherwise exhaustive account, *The Spy Who Saved the World* (Scribners, 1992), the co-authors, Jerrold L. Schecter and Peter S. Deriabin, merely record Penkovsky's execution (p. 373).

5 Crozier, *De Gaulle* (Eyre-Methuen, 1973), Vol. II, 'The Statesman', p. 613. At that time, I was not able to reveal Olié as my source.

V

Into the secret world
(1964–5)

WITHIN DAYS of leaving *The Economist* at the end of February 1964, I was approached by two secret services, and within weeks by a third. I already had three BBC contracts, with the French, Spanish and Latin American services, and a one-year contract with the *Sunday Times*.

The first 'secret' approach was from a long-time IRD friend, H. H. ('Tommy') Tucker. I had already turned down a full-time job proposal from him, but he now made me an offer which I accepted immediately: a part-time consultancy for IRD. Tommy, six and a half feet tall, and thin to match, had started as a journalist, then married into the Foreign Office. He was now, at thirty-eight, the youngest Counsellor in the foreign service. He was also shrewd and highly skilled.

Before leaving *The Economist*, I had already, on contract, transformed a thick folder of IRD documents into a short book called *Neo-Colonialism*, published some months later by the Bodley Head as one of a series of 'Background Books' edited by Stephen Watts. Predictably, howls of rage from the Left had followed. The point of the book was to demolish the Communist claim that 'imperialist' companies continued to exploit colonies after independence had been granted. Furious exchanges of letters in the press helped sales.

One reviewer who took me to task was R. Palme Dutt, resident guru of the Communist Party of Great Britain (CPGB), who disputed my assertion that the term 'neo-colonialism' had originated in the Kremlin. It was he who had launched the concept, he claimed, in a book written in 1956 and published in 1957, when he described the 'new tactics of imperialism' as the 'new colonialism'. The term had been translated into French as *'le néo-colonialisme'* and into German as *'das Neokolonialismus'*.

In fact, if we are talking about a concept rather than translations of a term, the originator was none other than Khrushchev who, in his report to the 20th Congress of the CPSU, in February 1956, had declared: '. . . the colonial powers, in addition to suppression by force of arms, are resorting to new forms of colonial enslavement under the guise of aid to underdeveloped countries, which brings them colossal profits.'

One point the controversy had confirmed was that 'neo-colonialism' was indeed a Communist label, whether manufactured in Moscow or in London.

As a consultant to IRD, I would be required to spend one morning a week at IRD's crumbling quarters in Carlton House Gardens, advising various departments. I would also write occasional research papers.

The next approach was from Ronald Franks of MI-6, who wanted me to know that he hoped I would continue to provide occasional material that I might pick up in the course of my work *and* my travels. He even hinted that his 'firm' might on occasion contribute travelling expenses. On this front however nothing concrete happened. Indeed for some months Ronald became somewhat elusive and even evasive on the few occasions when we did meet. Obviously 'something' was happening, which he did not feel at liberty to reveal.

Some weeks after leaving *The Economist*, I was approached by Tony (Anthony C.) Hartley on behalf of the Congress for Cultural Freedom. He asked me if I would be prepared to take over the features services of the CCF and commercialise them. There were three such services: Forum Information Service in English, *Preuves-Informations* in French, and *El Mundo en Español* in Spanish. The English one was distributed in London, and the French and Spanish ones in Paris, from the headquarters of the Congress on the Boulevard Haussmann. All three were 'giveaway' services, but doubts had been raised about the value of this formula.

I thanked him for the offer but turned it down. Apart from my reluctance to take on a regular job, I was too busy with existing commitments to contemplate the offer. In addition to the contracts, I was writing for newspapers in a dozen countries, lecturing a lot, and trying to finish a book on South-East Asia commissioned by Penguin.

A few weeks later, Tony Hartley came back with a specific but more limited proposal. Would I be prepared to spend some weeks travelling around Latin America? The prime purpose would be to meet the local representatives of the *Congreso por la Libertad de la Cultura* and newspaper editors in the capitals, and produce a professional report on the usage of the CCF's Spanish-language service. I would also be expected to write two articles for *Encounter*, and could combine all this with coverage for the *Sunday Times* and the BBC.

At the time, I knew nothing about the CCF beyond the fact that it had been established at a conference of leading writers and intellectuals in Berlin in June 1950, and had spawned *Encounter* and a wide range of similar publications in many countries. Nor had I ever investigated the Congress, but a conversation some years earlier with Peter Calvocoressi stuck in my mind. I had asked him what he thought of the Congress. 'It's a rum organisation,' he muttered. 'Very rum.' He had declined to elaborate. I accepted Hartley's offer.

I finished the Penguin book before leaving and arranged for the proofs to be sent to me in care of the British embassy in Caracas, Venezuela. I spent August and September in Latin America. The other cities I visited were Santiago, Chile; Buenos Aires, Argentina; Rio de Janeiro and Brasilia, Brazil; Lima, Peru; and Mexico City. I have described my trip in detail elsewhere[1], and confine myself here to events of later relevance.

On hearing of my forthcoming journey, Ronald Franks had expressed interest. He introduced me to a colleague specialising in Latin American affairs who asked me to report if I came across material I felt I could spare from my existing commitments. I started at the deep end, in Chile, where I teamed up with a CCF man from Paris called Luis Mercier Vega, who told me he was half-Chilean with a French mother. His accent in each language was consistent with this claim.[2]

We had both gone to Chile to observe and report the presidential elections of 1964. The worrying factor, locally as well as internationally, was the candidacy of the Socialist *bon viveur* and demagogue, Salvador Allende. Accepting the highly disciplined, Moscow-line Chilean Communist Party – the largest in Latin America – as a partner in his Popular Unity coalition (UP), Allende offered a programme of sweeping revolutionary change. A medical doctor, round, vigorous, jowled and slightly shifty, Allende was in fact going to have to wait another six years for his chance to run Chile.

In the one quiet room of his coalition's ragged, gesticulating *Casa del Pueblo*, Allende received me after the vote but before the final result was known. I asked him whether he really thought he could keep the Communists under control if elected President of the Republic.

He said, sweepingly: 'There is no problem. I am the President of Chile and have the President's prerogatives. The Communists have made no requests and I have made no promises.'

In the event, victory went to the Christian Democratic candidate, Eduardo Frei, an ex-lawyer and journalist, pale, hawk-beaked and intense. On paper, and as he explained it to me after his victory had been confirmed, Frei's programme was remarkably similar to Allende's. The difference was that Allende was a fanatic and meant it; Frei, a well-meaning muddler, did not.

In Buenos Aires, I found the Argentinos anxious for a rest from Peronismo, which had ruined what should have been one of the richest countries of the world by a huge expansion of the State sector and by buying off the trade unions. They were getting it under the gentle guidance of a quiet, honest doctor from Cordoba, President Arturo Illia. In the huge presidential room in the pink neo-rococo *Palacio Rosado*, Illia greeted me informally, patting me on the shoulder and inquiring colloquially: *'Cómo le va?'* ('How goes it?')

With his ascetic, wrinkled face, white hair and opaque brown eyes, the doctor thought I needed a lesson on the Islas Malvinas, which we called the Falkland Islands Dependencies. He pointed to a wall map. This, he said, was the continental shelf; the Malvinas were part of it, and the Argentine Antarctic was a natural prolongation of it.

Writing today, more than twenty-five years later, and with the memory of the Falklands War still vivid, I am inclined to believe the Foreign Office must have read what I wrote on my return about these islands with 600,000 sheep and 2000 humans:

> The humans are not, as the Argentinos say, a transient population of temporary migrants: 80 per cent were born there and have no wish to come under Argentine rule. Nor are they an oppressed colony: the 'colonialism' issue is absurd; there is no national liberation movement in the Falklands. On the other hand, do we really still want the Falklands, Gibraltar and other scattered bits of real estate that once seemed so essential? Is there not a basis here for long-term bargaining: a delayed transfer of sovereignty in return for solid economic concessions, for instance special rights for British fishing?

WHILE I WAS in Mexico City, my last stopping place, in October, events of world importance were taking place in Britain and in Moscow.

Sir Alec Douglas-Home's short-lived Tory government had been beaten in a general election, and Harold Wilson and Labour were now in power. In Moscow, the ebullient Nikita Khrushchev had been ousted in a palace coup in favour of a duller but more orthodox Party functionary, Leonid Brezhnev.

Back in London, I wrote a formal report to the Congress for Cultural Freedom, recommending that the Spanish press service from Paris should be professionalised, along with the others, and sold instead of given away to interested newspapers. I also strongly recommended that the services should cease to carry articles about Congress activities of no special interest to Latin American readers. Having delivered my report, through Tony Harley, I put the Congress out of my mind.

I WAS SCARCELY back when Ronald Franks telephoned me to suggest an urgent lunch at his club, the Athenaeum. He told me he had been authorised to take me to SIS headquarters and introduce me to some of his colleagues. 'You'll find we're still a gentlemanly outfit,' he said.

After lunch, we took a taxi to Century House, the 1960s high-rise building south of the Thames which now housed SIS. At the security checkpoint at the entrance, I was issued with a temporary pass, and Franks escorted me to an upper floor, where he introduced me to the head of his department, which dealt with Sino-Soviet questions. This was my first shock. I had met the man, Noel Cunningham (not his real name), several times. That day and on future days, I met a number of people whom I had talked to, in the Travellers or elsewhere, in the belief that they were 'Foreign Office'. One of them I had known as a colleague when he had worked for *The Economist* Intelligence Unit.

Later on, at Century House, I met a number of non-officials whom I had known for years, whose 'contact' with MI-6 was similar to mine. They included academic friends of mine specialising in matters of interest to me, including Vietnam and the Soviet Union.

Ronald Franks was right in his choice of 'gentlemanly'. Friendly though enigmatic smiles were on every face. Speech was soft, and in public tended to come out of the side of the mouth: tell-tale professional quirks of the intelligence world.

From Noel Cunningham, I learned the reason for the reticence I had noted over some months in my relations with Ronald Franks. From its headquarters in Langley, Virginia, the American Central Intelligence Agency, I was told, had raised objections to further SIS contacts with me on the ground that on several occasions *Foreign Report* had carried stories that presented the CIA in a bad light. So *that* was it! I laughed, remembering the stories. They had come from a woman journalist based in India, and I had not regarded them as hostile. The real objection, it seemed, was to the fact that I had carried the stories, because they were accurate. In the end, Langley had accepted British assurances that I was in no way against the CIA, but the process of persuasion had taken the best part of a year. We were now in November 1964.

Cunningham wanted to know if I would be prepared, on occasion, to write analytical reports on themes in which I had specialised, such as international Communism and insurgencies. I readily agreed. This would involve occasional access to material not publicly available.

He told me about GCHQ (Government Communications Headquarters) at Cheltenham, the highly secret signals intelligence interception organisation. 'It's a veritable *industry*,' said Noel, adding with relish: 'That's the stuff that really gives you an intellectual erection.' It did not follow, however, that I would have access to this erectile stuff.

The fundamental rule of access to material not publicly available is 'need to know', and the rule was rigorously observed. To write this first analysis, I 'needed to know' a great deal because of the ground to be covered. I was asked to write a full report on Sino-Soviet subversion in the Third World. This was indeed the acid test of the contested genuineness of the great split. I had already dealt with this theme in an article entitled 'The Struggle for the Third World', published in the Chatham House quarterly *International Affairs* in July that year. In it, I had argued that the subversive operations of the Soviet Union and the Chinese People's Republic were in conflict everywhere in the Third World, in East Asia as in Africa and Latin America. Having identified the phenomenon, I had called it 'competitive subversion'.

The question now was to submit the thesis to the test of the material not available to the general public. Having studied the evidence, it confirmed my view, and Ronald Franks's, that the split was indeed genuine.

The ground covered was immense and the time I could spare from other commitments was limited. At last, several months into 1965, the report was finished.

At this point, I was introduced to the bureaucratic obstacle. Every specialist in every area covered had to see the draft and comment on it. The draft also had to go to the IRD specialists. In the end, Noel assembled two or three dozen of the commentators at a boardroom table, with himself in the chair, and me next to him, answering questions or dealing with queries or contestations. It was only after that gauntlet had been run that the revised report could be issued and distributed.

After the document had been 'sanitised' by the excision of secret material, I was allowed to take the scissored typescript home. The report formed the core of a further 'Background Book' with the same title as the Chatham House article, *The Struggle for the Third World* (1966). This one was yet another sequel in the series started with *The Rebels*.

Sometimes, a piece of information may not be secret, but remains classified because of its source. *The Struggle for the Third World* contained an interesting example. One day, at Century House, one of my new semi-colleagues, a large man called William, invited me to his office and showed me a Top Secret CIA report on the then current crisis in the Dominican Republic.

At the end of April 1965, President Lyndon B. Johnson, acting on his own executive authority (that is, without consulting Congress), ordered the US Marines to land in the Republic to protect American lives in the civil war that had broken out there. This was his stated pretext, but the true reason for his decision was implicit in the report William showed me, the contents of which he encouraged me to note.

For months, Dominican Communists trained in various countries, including Cuba and Czechoslovakia, had been smuggled back into their half of the island of Hispaniola (the other half of which was the wretchedly poor Haiti). The training the Communists had been given covered sabotage, terrorism and guerrilla warfare. A military revolt by followers of an ex-President was their signal. The Communists used their own military contacts to gain access to the arsenals, and within hours distributed arms to hundreds of well-prepared citizens.

If Johnson had not intervened, it is safe to say that the Dominican Republic would have joined Cuba as an outpost of the Soviet empire (as indeed happened many years later with Nicaragua and the island of Grenada). The intervention, however, caused an outcry from the Left, from American liberals and from well-meaning others who were unaware of the true circumstances. There was much talk of blows to America's peace-loving image and to Dominica's budding democracy, and of a return to Theodore Roosevelt's 'Big Stick' behaviour.

Had President Johnson stated the true reason for the intervention, he would have at least disarmed some of the critics, although he would not have appeased the leftists. He weathered this little storm better than the much deeper one in Vietnam, and a presidential election in Dominica on 1 June appeared to vindicate his action and enabled him to pull the Marines out.

The CIA had actually compiled a list of fifty-five Communist ringleaders of the projected takeover, though without giving the necessary background. The correspondents who flocked to the island to cover the crisis were surprised and indignant not to trace any of them. I was astonished at their naivety. Did they really suppose the Communists would stay on to be exposed?

At that time, I had become a regular contributor to the *Spectator* which, as a stop-gap, was being edited by the Tory MP Iain Macleod, who had declined to serve in the Douglas-Home Cabinet. I wrote the story (minus the attribution) which duly appeared; and duly attracted indignation from my critics.

RONALD FRANKS shared an office with a tall, reserved colleague, whom I shall call Derek Parsons. More controlled than Franks, better organised, he was on the same high level intellectually. He had served in Moscow and was, in the view of some leading experts, the best Sovietician in the country, although the least known by the nature of his career. I shared that view.

In general, I found the level of intellectual attainment and rigour of analysis higher in SIS than in any other institution with which I had dealings. In those days, MI-6 was required not only to obtain secret intelligence by whatever means was judged necessary, but also to produce analyses for the benefit of the Joint Intelligence Committee, and of course of that committee's Foreign Office component. In later years, I understand, the analytical requirement was considerably reduced; mistakenly, in my opinion.

To recognise the intellectual level of the SIS analysts is not to disparage the attainments of the Foreign Office personnel, in comparison. The factor that gave the edge to SIS was corporate. Foreign ministries are constrained by the nature of diplomacy to seek accommodations or agreements, often with hostile powers or groups. This imperative, which I call 'pactitis', inevitably involves compromise, whether territorial or thematic. In the end, more often than not, *any* agreement is held to be better than none. This constraint is a powerful disincentive to objectivity in analysis. In contrast, intelligence analysts have a constraint of another kind. Their requirement is the objective truth, even if it is hurtful or obstructs the negotiating of a possible pact.

WITHIN DAYS of Khrushchev's overthrow in October 1964, his successor, Leonid Brezhnev, had invited the National Front for the Liberation of South Vietnam (NFLSV, the political front for the Vietcong guerrillas in the Vietnam War) to open an office in Moscow. This amounted to a formal commitment to its cause. Shortly after, the Vietnam War acquired a British political overtone with the 'Warbey affair', in which I played a part that made me, more than ever, a target for the extreme Left.

William Warbey, at that time a Labour MP, was one of his party's most steadfast fellow-travellers, as those who collaborated with the Communists without joining them were known. In the Christmas break at the end of 1964, he had visited North Vietnam and came back with a Communist propaganda film. In speech and in writing he had been expressing anti-American and pro-Communist opinions about the war. From Ronald Franks, I learned that Warbey's travelling expenses and hotel bill had been paid by the Communist-controlled Vietnam Fatherland Front. In a live BBC Television discussion with Warbey and others, I challenged him on this point towards the end of the discussion, and he lost his composure when I pointed out that the Fatherland Front was no different from the proscribed organisations listed annually at that time by the Labour Party. Warbey started shouting and gesticulating, and the programme was brought to an abrupt end.

The incident made front-page headlines. The BBC Overseas Service cancelled a radio discussion featuring Warbey, the well-known Vietnam specialist Patrick ('Paddy') Honey and myself. The producer, David Wedgwood Benn, was the younger brother of Tony Benn, at that time Labour's Postmaster-General.

In his 'Spectator's Notebook', signed 'Quoodle', Iain Macleod accused the BBC of censorship, as did the *Daily Telegraph*. Warbey lost a formal complaint to the House Committee on Privileges, by 159 votes to 114.

In a letter to the *Spectator*, Warbey defended the Fatherland Front and claimed that the NFLSV was an autonomous Southern body, not controlled by Hanoi.

In my *South-East Asia in Turmoil*, which was published by Penguin in January 1965, I assembled a lot of evidence, which seemed to show that in fact Hanoi's control was absolute. When the North Vietnamese Army overran South Vietnam's defences in April 1975, the NFLSV vanished without trace.

Some months after my clash with Warbey, he resigned as an MP.

In this and other controversies, Macleod invariably supported me when the shafts started flying. My aim, in all such cases, was not to shock people but to face them with what I believed to be realities. Illusions are perhaps more comforting to live with, and I was making many enemies.

South-East Asia in Turmoil went into three editions and twenty-two languages. The English original sold 100,000 copies – four times the original estimate – and became required reading for all personnel of the South-East Asia Treaty Organisation (SEATO).

Qualified praise came from an unexpected source. In the *New Statesman* (19 March 1965), Graham Greene wrote:

> To write in less than 180 pages a clear account, unclogged by detail, of the revolutions and counter-revolutions since 1941 in Malaya, Siam, Burma, Korea, Indochina and Indonesia would have been an extraordinary achievement, even if the result had been a dull textbook. Mr Crozier is never dull.

The author of that sourly anti-American novel, *The Quiet American*, added however: 'I would have liked to ask this intelligent observer whether he sees any favourable future, save Communism, for South-East Asia.' The deferred answer has come in the prosperity of Singapore and Thailand and the misery of Communist Vietnam, with the desperate exit of the 'boat people'. It is fair to add that neither Singapore nor Thailand was devastated by decades of war.

The controversies continued. One of them marked my definitive break with the liberal Establishment, though not with the Establishment as a whole. I publicly criticised some of the staff appointments made by Kenneth Younger, Director of Chatham House and a former Labour Minister of State. I had in mind three committed leftists he had taken on. He wrote me two furious letters. The first led to a reconciliation lunch; in the second, he called me 'contemptible', leaving me no option but to resign from the Royal Institute of International Affairs, after eleven active years.

NOTES

1 'Latin American Journey',
  Encounter, December 1964/
  January 1965.
2 Mercier also claimed to be a
  Spanish Anarchist and to have
  fought with the Anarchists during
the Spanish Civil War. He
committed suicide some years later.
See Peter Coleman, *The Liberal
Conspiracy* (Free Press, Macmillan,
1989), pp. 207–8.

VI

The CIA's Congress (1965–8)

I HAD FORGOTTEN about the Congress for Cultural Freedom, but the Congress had not forgotten me. Tony Hartley surfaced again. He wanted me to meet the American Executive Secretary of the CCF, John Hunt. The meeting took place at the Stafford Hotel, St James's, on the morning of 3 May 1965. Hunt, a novelist, was a calm, civilised man.

The Congress, he said, had accepted my recommendations. However, 'professionalising' the services, as I had proposed, implied financial backing, and a very substantial backer had been found: John Hay Whitney, proprietor of the *New York Herald Tribune*, had been the US ambassador in London in the late 1950s during my *Economist* years, and I had been among the privileged few journalists invited to his small lunches at the Connaught Hotel, and to the more formal receptions at his residence in Regent's Park. In these new conditions, Hunt wanted to know, would I be prepared to take over the whole operation and supervise it?

At first I demurred, as before, on the ground that I was not looking for a job. Hunt was persuasive, as well as persistent. It would not be a full-time job, he argued. With office back-up and an efficient secretary, two days a week would probably be enough.

He won me over, and I accepted in principle, but I laid down rigorous conditions. The CCF would have to withdraw entirely. I had nothing against the Congress, I explained, but it was a ramshackle organisation in no way qualified to run press feature services. I would have to be given full editorial control. Moreover, I insisted that the French- and

Spanish-language services should be transferred to London. All these points were accepted, at least orally.

I asked Hunt about office accommodation, and he said that was already taken care of: a suite of offices had been leased at Kern House, which ran between Kingsway and Lincoln's Inn Fields.

In anticipation of my assent, Hunt had already appointed an editorial team of three to run the proposed service under my guidance. One of them was the editor of the existing giveaway Forum Information Service, Murray Mindlin, whom I had already met. The other two were Gene Gately and Tarzie Vittachi. Mindlin was a Jewish intellectual from New York, who had spent many years in Europe and spoke excellent French and German. Gately was another American who, Hunt had told me, had had an earlier career in Madison Avenue, which was to American advertising what Fleet Street was to London journalism. Vittachi, a Ceylonese, was a journalist who had run the International Press Institute's Asia Programme. To break the ice and discuss plans for the future service, I invited all three for drinks at my home in Temple Fortune, on the evening of 7 May. Gately, a quiet and very polite young man of middle height, made a favourable impression, though I remember thinking that he lacked the brashness I had, perhaps mistakenly, associated with the advertising world. Vittachi, a very dark-hued man in his late forties, wore a sombre expression. Mindlin was clearly ill at ease.

There was in fact some ill-defined tension in the air: the 'ice' to be broken. Gins and whiskies loosened tongues. After much discussion, all three accepted my proposal that the press service should be styled 'Forum World Features' (FWF), with 'Kern House Enterprises' as the holding company, after the Kingsway offices that had been leased.[1]

The deal was sealed over lunch, appropriately at the Connaught, much patronised by American diplomats, on 17 May. Those present, apart from Hunt and myself, were Jock Whitney; Samuel C. Park, his financial adviser, a tall, slim, courteous man in his fifties; Melvin Lasky of *Encounter*; Gene Gately; and Murray Mindlin. Whitney – tall, vigorous but shy – was reputed to be worth about $200 million. His main business interest was encapsulated in the name of his holding company: Communications, Inc. He had little to say, but listened carefully to the rest of us.

On my next visit to Century House, I mentioned the tentative arrangements to Ronald Franks, who said pensively: 'The Congress is CIA, you know.'

I remembered Peter Calvocoressi's remark some years earlier about the 'rum' character of the Congress for Cultural Freedom, on which he had declined to elaborate.

The British had suggested to the CIA that it would be a good idea to provide a broader intellectual haven for Western writers, especially after the Communist takeover of Czechoslovakia in 1948. The Americans had responded with characteristic generosity, and the CCF was born in 1950; much as, three years earlier, President Truman had taken over Britain's burdens in the Middle East, with the policy of 'containment'.

I listened, fascinated, but felt more probing was needed. I told Franks I had been given to understand that the funding was mainly from the Ford Foundation. 'Oh,' said Franks, 'they're just notional donors.' It was the first time I had heard that expression, which henceforth became part of my vocabulary. It seemed obvious that Whitney himself was probably another 'notional donor', and I decided to find out. Having enjoyed the effect of his revelations, Ronald Franks added: 'I'm glad you've taken this on. It should be interesting.'

More than three weeks of silence followed. I was beginning to wonder whether the deal was off when a long letter from John Hunt in Paris reached me. It was dated 10 June 1965, and I read it in mounting disbelief. Almost everything in it was at variance with the terms we had agreed.

Not only was the CCF not pulling out, but Hunt declared that Mr Whitney had asked him to be 'the Board member directly responsible for liaison between the stockholders and the company'.

He mentioned Gene Gately, who would handle the administration, and Charles Johnson (as I shall call him), who would do the auditing, and whom I had not yet met. There would be small-scale Spanish and French services run from London, and a competent translator would be found. As for myself: 'There will be no need for you to get involved in administration and finance since the time which you can give the company will be limited and therefore precious and your role is connected with policy and substance rather than with administrative detail.'

I would be the President of the new company, with Gately as Vice-President and Treasurer, and Tarzie Vittachi as Vice-President for African and Asian affairs; and Murray Mindlin as Secretary. Mr Whitney was planning to put $100,000 a year into Forum, but this year's budget would depend on the size of the terminal grant from the Congress. Hunt added that one of the most important sources of material for the service would be good articles from the European press, to be made available to me through Leo Labedz, a multilingual officer of the Congress and at that time associate editor of the quarterly review *Soviet Survey*.

The clear message was that things would go on much as before, with the Congress running the show through John Hunt and my own role largely ornamental.

From Century House, where I had gone on the day Hunt's letter arrived, I rang him in Paris. In ill humour, I asked him what was the point in reaching an oral agreement if all the main details were to be changed? He was very emollient, and put the blame on Mr Whitney, who had thought that the Congress connection and experience should be made available to the new service.

Next day, a further letter from Hunt informed me that there would be no money to continue Preuves-Informations even in reduced form: a further departure from the oral agreement.

Logically, I should have opted out at this point, but by then my interest was aroused. For one thing, I now had a connection, though not yet a formalised one, with the CIA. I was intrigued by the possibilities this link might open up. Clearly, however, the continuing presence of the Congress raised problems. On thinking it over, I decided that to drop out at this point would be the weaker of the two alternatives I faced. It would be more interesting to stay on, give the job a try, and resist any unwelcome pressures that might come from Hunt and his boss, Michael Josselson, President of the Congress, who operated from Geneva and whom I had met only briefly in London the day after the Whitney lunch, which he had been unable to attend.

I wrote to John Hunt, to stress my displeasure at Mr Whitney's decision to change the terms that had been agreed orally. I added that I would nevertheless give the arrangement a try, while reserving the right to resign if there was too much, or unwarranted, interference by the CCF.

HAVING MADE my decision, I phased out my BBC contracts and moved into my new office at Kern House on the agreed date, 1 July 1965. That day, I met Charles Johnson, who was in overall charge of financial arrangements, and his assistant, Chewn Jotikasthira. Of Thai origin, Chewn had served in the British Army and spoke English with a Cockney accent, although he had taken US citizenship and become a patriotic American who displayed the Stars and Stripes from the rooftop of his home. The arrangement was that Chewn would be Forum's accountant, while John-son would handle and allocate the cash flow from Mr Whitney and the 'terminal grant' from the Congress. He had his own office, a few doors away.

Johnson, prematurely grey, was about my age. At our first meeting on that first day, he told me that arrangements were in hand for the registration of Mr Whitney's new company, for tax reasons, in the State of Delaware. My suggestion had been accepted, and it was to be called 'Kern House Enterprises, Inc.' There would be a British equivalent, which he would run. The set-up was that Sam Park, whom I had met at the Connaught lunch, would handle the funds at the US end. He added that he was a businessman who handled other accounts besides this one.

In this long first talk, Johnson explained that Jock Whitney was a philanthropist and a patriotic American who was not in this for the money, although he would doubtless wish to break even after a while. His main objective was to provide a first-rate service for newspapers in the Third World.

I commented that, while I agreed that this was an important goal, it did not seem the best way of breaking even. Surely we would need to break into the European and American markets. Johnson replied that while Europe was not ruled out, Mr Whitney saw little point in selling the service in America, both because the competition was excessive and because the American public already had a superfluity of news and feature services.

The significance of this curious little speech escaped me at the time. Professionally speaking, it was discouraging. I was being asked to commercialise a feature service while being denied access to the main commercial outlets.

Ronald Franks, who lived in his own world of intellectual cogitation, evidently did not immediately report his conversation with me to his chief, Noel Cunningham. When he did, in his own time, Cunningham was furious and summoned me to his office in Century House. What had made him angry was to have learned in this indirect way that the CIA, as he put it, had recruited 'one of our contacts' without informing SIS, in breach of the secret arrangement between the United Kingdom and the United States: the core of the famous 'special relationship'. He did not explain how the CIA would have known that I was in touch with SIS.

In retrospect, I believe this was a comedy of errors. The CIA, as such, had not 'recruited' me; the Congress had. At some point, there must have been a failure of communication between the CCF and the CIA. The way the whole thing had been handled made it evident that the Congress had intended to recruit me as an 'unconscious' agent, not as somebody already in contact with SIS.

Noel Cunningham now revealed to me that the President of the CCF, Michael Josselson, was in fact a senior official of the Agency. He suggested that I should see Josselson as soon as possible, to 'level' with him. Meanwhile, he would be making a strong protest to the CIA's London station.

A few days later, on 12 July, I flew to Geneva, where Josselson lived and worked. Josselson, a naturalised US citizen of Lithuanian Jewish origin, had served in the US Army after escaping from Hitler's invading forces. He was a small man, about sixty, with intense dark eyes, highly intelligent and an excellent organiser.

He told me he had been startled to learn that I was in contact with MI-6. I repeated some of the points I had made to John Hunt, about interference from the Congress. If the intention was indeed to 'professionalise' Forum, any contributions or suggestions from Congress would have to be judged strictly on their news merits. He looked doubtful, but said I would obviously have discretion in such matters. We parted on friendly but inconclusive terms.

Having reported back to Noel Cunningham on my meeting with Josselson, he introduced me to a senior CIA man in London. I was anxious for a precise explanation of the apparent reluctance to sell the proposed service to Western newspapers, and to the American press in particular. The CIA man, whom I shall call James Craig, was ready with an answer which I found cryptic: 'We can't sell Forum in the US,' he said, 'because we are not allowed to propagandise the American people.'

As I learned later, there was indeed a long-standing revulsion against such 'propagandising', born initially of the manipulation of the American public during World War I, by the British as well as the American government. The revulsion was deepened by the example of Hitler's master propagandist Joseph Goebbels during World War II. The CIA had made matters worse during its early years, by its use of American student groups and foundations for the funding of special activities. In line with this revulsion, the United States Information Agency (USIA) is still not allowed to circulate its material in the United States, and the texts of Voice of America broadcasts are not available in the US.[2]

In line with the 'propagandising' ban, the main target for FWF was indeed the Third World, which was being inundated with Soviet propaganda. It was not a question of disseminating counter-propaganda from the Western side, but of providing first-class background coverage to pre-empt space that might otherwise go to Communist disinformation. There was no ban on selling the service in Western countries, apart from America, but this was not the main point of the exercise.

I asked the obvious question: 'What happens if an American newspaper picks up an article that has appeared elsewhere?'

The answer was immediate: 'We have no problem with that. This is what we call "fall-out".'

It was clear from my talk with the Agency man at Century House that Charles Johnson had to be a colleague. I had drawn the same conclusion from the fact that he handled the money. It was also clear that despite my meeting with Josselson, and the representations made by Noel Cunningham, the CIA was still not being frank with me.

The following evening at Kern House, when the staff had left, I brought Charles Johnson over for a drink. I mentioned my talk with Josselson and said: 'I have to assume you and he are colleagues.'

He looked alert suddenly. 'Are we levelling?'

I agreed that this was a fair way of putting it, and he admitted that he was indeed an Agency man. In one respect, at least, life was going to be simpler.

The next few weeks were far from easy, however. I had instructed Gene Gately and Vittachi, in particular, to research market possibilities for the proposed press service in the Third World, and to sound out potential contributors in various countries.

My main problem was the editor I had 'inherited': Murray Mindlin, who was totally uncooperative. I could not decide, initially, whether his reluctance to work with me was due to natural indolence, of which he had a large share, or to other factors, in particular his satisfaction with the previous state of affairs, after years of running a giveaway service of two articles a week, most of which reached him ready-made from Paris.

He never turned up at the office before noon, and when he did, seemed permanently engaged in other things, such as dictating letters or reading. I had begun to commission articles, at £25 a piece, from various journalists, as a kind of trial run for Forum World Features. We had commissioned a striking logo-type, based on the initials FWF. The main remaining problem, apart from the stream of suggestions or material from Paris or Geneva, was the non-cooperating editor. I had given Mindlin an article in French to adapt and edit in English. It took him three days. When another French article came in from Paris, I demonstrated how to do the same job in forty minutes by direct dictation to a typist.

In this twilight period, my own authority to hire and fire was in doubt. Technically, Mindlin was still employed by the CCF: Kern House Enterprises was not yet functional. I decided to have a showdown. The date was 3 September 1965, and on the 4th I reported on it in a 'private and confidential' letter to John Hunt, with a copy to Josselson. The gist of it was simply that Mindlin was not doing the job for which he was being paid.

I went on to complain, not for the first time, that the job *I* was doing was not the job that was originally offered to me. I had been shocked at the decision to delay, perhaps for a year (the latest proposal from Paris), the transfer of the Latin American service to London. I added: 'I should like to make it clear that I would not have been tempted to terminate my BBC contract and embark on major readjustments of my working schedule by an offer of the job as it now stands.' I said, however, that I would of course see the Forum expansion programme through but might thereafter have to reconsider my commitment in the light of any further decision about the Servicio de Prensa.

On Mindlin, Hunt's response was immediate. He came over within a few days and sacked Mindlin as editor of Forum Information Service, retaining him for the other duties to which he was devoted. It was agreed, however, that he would stay at Kern House until mid-December.

By mid-September, we had put together a presentation package of well-written articles on a variety of themes: in effect a salesman's sample bag. We offered two services: Service A, consisting of high-quality signed articles, and Service B, consisting of shorter, unsigned research pieces on countries or subjects in the news.

I sent Gately and Vittachi on a major sales expedition to East Asia and Australia, from which they returned with some forty contracts worth, on paper, about $30,000 a year. One of the subscribers was my old employer, the *Sydney Morning Herald*.

During the whole of this preparatory period, I had been bombarded with offerings from Paris, most of which I spiked as unsuitable for a professional features service. Furious telephone exchanges usually followed. This was exactly the situation I had feared. It had become a war of attrition.

On the return of our travelling salesmen, I learned (from Gene Gately) of a new problem. Tarzie Vittachi, it appeared, also worked for a religious sect called Subbud, with the title of 'international courier'. The problem was keeping Subbud's expenses distinct from ours. This one was satisfactorily resolved.

While Gately and Vittachi were on their travels, I had appointed a successor to Mindlin: John Tusa, an energetic young producer for the BBC's World Service at Bush House. For the past few years, Tusa had produced many of my own talks and discussion programmes, and I thought highly of him.

With Tusa at Kern House, and Kern House Enterprises functional at last, we launched Forum World Features on 1 January 1966. Our forty subscribers were scattered in some twenty countries.

By now, however, a personal problem had intervened. My two main contracts for a proposed historical biography of Franco (with Eyre & Spottiswoode in London and Little, Brown in Boston) had come into force, with further contracts in Paris and Munich under negotiation. I would soon be running out of research material in London and would need to move to Madrid to do the job properly. I seemed to be losing my war of attrition with the Congress, and decided to ease myself out of Kern House by stages.

My first ploy took the CCF by surprise. On 4 December 1965, in a long letter to John Hunt, I spelled out the situation at that stage. On the new service, FWF, soon to be launched, I pointed out that the contracts sold by Gene and Tarzie, though a good beginning, were no more than that. There was a long way to go, and unless the European and American markets were tackled, commercial viability was unlikely to be achieved. 'Clearly,' I wrote, 'the more commercialised we are, the more our output will be dictated by the demands of the market we have created. There will be no room in such a service for cultural articles of restricted appeal or for the kind of publicity for Congress activities that might call in question our claim to be a commercial service, detached from the Congress.'

As for my own role, I repeated, yet again, my objections to the job I had been doing, as distinct from the one I had been offered. As our salesmen had been offering the new service under my name as 'Director-General', I proposed to leave my name on the FWF masthead, but to reduce my involvement to one day a week, at a fee reduced by £750 a year (35 per cent).

Under this arrangement, I would no longer need a secretary, and since Mindlin would be taking his own secretary with him, a further sum could be saved. I offered to provide professional guidance, if required, or, alternatively, to pull out altogether.

Evidently puzzled by so unusual a suggestion, Hunt accepted my proposal for a pay cut, but expressed the hope that I would continue to head the service as it was indeed being offered in my name.

Sad to say, the launching of the new service and of the commercial company brought no improvement in relations with the Congress. If anything, the interference from Paris and Geneva got worse. By mid-March, I had had enough. On the 19th, about eleven weeks after my voluntary pay cut, I wrote to Josselson to let him know that I would be giving notice at the end of the month, with effect from the end of June. My main reasons, as I spelled them out, were 'the method of indirect control through John Hunt' and 'the differences between the offer originally made to me and the job as it has actually turned out'.

As I saw it at that point, I had lost my battle with the Congress for Cultural Freedom. However, an unexpected development turned defeat into victory. On 4 May, four senior members of my staff wrote me a joint letter, pleading with me to stay on. The signatories were Gene Gately, John Tusa, Tarzie Vittachi, and our executive secretary, Patricia Stonebridge. I was touched by the letter, which said, in part:

It is quite clear that the loss of your name would by itself be a blow to FWF ... would it not be possible for you merely to take leave of absence for a year? After all, real crises could be referred in an emergency. Failing that, could you not remain as honorary Chairman?

I decided that I could not ignore this appeal and wrote to John Hunt, enclosing a copy of the letter and offering to act as 'chairman in absentia' during my working year in Madrid. Shortly after, the Agency transferred Gene Gately to other duties. His cover story was that his Texan wife's father had offered him a better job in an oil company.

The crisis of my making produced the result I had been fighting for from the start. Mike Josselson came to London to tell me that henceforth all links between the Congress for Cultural Freedom and Forum World Features would be severed. From now on, with the full agreement of SIS, I would deal directly with CIA personnel. He introduced me to my contact man, a bustling, energetic middle-ranking Agency officer whom I shall name Ray Walters.

*   *   *

LITTLE, BROWN, of Boston, had made my contract for the proposed biography of Franco conditional upon my interviewing him and obtaining assurances of access to Spanish archives.

In November 1965, on the last day of an exploratory week in Madrid, I was received by the Caudillo. A taciturn man, he replied to my questions in monosyllables until, after a quarter of an hour, I asked him when he became aware of the threat of Communism. At this point, he became voluble. He had seen the threat as early as 1917, he said, and had begun to study Communism seriously in 1928.[3]

I made it clear both to Franco and to his officials that I was nominally a Protestant, a man of liberal views, and that I had supported the Republican side during the Civil War; but that I had been anti-Communist for nearly twenty years. It must have been this last factor that tipped the balance. I was promised access to archives.

The promise was honoured, and my 'access' extended to high officials, including the Director-General of Information, Carlos Robles Piquer, a fervent Catholic, and his political boss, the Information and Tourism Minister, the ebullient, impatient Manuel Fraga Iribarne.

The degree of my access was naturally of interest to Century House. As a parting shot after lunch one day at the Athenaeum, Maurice Oldfield asked me if I would be prepared to place a 'bug' under the desk of a high official I was seeing regularly at the Foreign Ministry. I declined without hesitation, partly because I thought I would be extremely vulnerable to detection, but also because I did not think the potential gains were of sufficient interest to justify the risk. The only matter of interest to Century House seemed to be the Spanish attitude to Gibraltar, on which my own views were neither pro-British nor pro-Spanish.

I have often wondered whether Oldfield was being serious. On balance, I think not. It had been a good lunch.

The SIS man in Madrid was a self-effacing but intelligent man who had the professional eccentricities of his trade to a high degree. I was impressed by his ability to glide across a room with guests to see me in my study without manifesting his appearance, and for telling me things, just audibly, out of the corner of a static mouth.

Hardly any worthwhile intelligence came my way during the busy first eight or nine months of my stay. Towards the end, however, with the book completed apart from the indexing, I did provide SIS with some useful material, notably a detailed account of a one-on-one talk I had with Admiral Carrero Blanco, at that time Franco's successor-designate, but later assassinated by the Basque terrorist gang, ETA.

MY NEW ARRANGEMENT with the CIA and FWF worked satisfactorily, but before I left England another crisis had to be dealt with. I had become increasingly critical of what seemed to me to be a pro-Soviet and anti-American bias. There were also, it is true, articles reflecting the American and Allied viewpoint, but it was clear that John Tusa and I were out of harmony on the definition of 'balance'. My view was that in a weekly press feature service, as distinct from a radio discussion, balance could only be achieved within each weekly batch of articles. His own was that an anti-Western piece could be balanced in a later batch of articles. Tusa was of course unaware of the CIA connection.

I wrote a forceful letter to him, after inconclusive arguments, and he resigned. He went on to rejoin the BBC and, many years later, was appointed Managing Director of its World Service. I discussed this new crisis with Ray Walters, who had already thought about it and told me he had a replacement in mind. Indeed, he was bringing the man over from South Africa.

His name was Cecil Eprile. On paper, he certainly had the right qualifications. A Scottish Jew, he had emigrated to South Africa as a young man, and made a career in journalism, latterly as editor-in-chief of the controversial *Drum* publications, which provided a voice for the Republic's black population.

He was a thin, wiry man with black eyes and a small moustache, not unlike Franco's. He was afflicted by a monumental stammer. Professionally, he seemed right for the job. He had brought cuttings with him which showed real talent, with an attractive light touch. But I wondered whether the stammer would damage his authority. He told me there was one thing he could guarantee: if appointed, he would be absolutely loyal to me in my absence and at all times. I offered him the job and he gave me no cause to regret it.

Four times during my short year in Madrid I flew to London for consultations with my FWF staff, and twice I brought Cecil Eprile to Madrid where we conferred with Ray Walters. The service was doing very well and reaching more and more countries. With Eprile in charge, Forum World Features was running itself, and I could get on with the biography in peace of mind.

Visitors came from various countries. One, who dropped in unannounced, made a great impact on my life. I interrupted my morning typing
to answer the doorbell. I saw a man of medium height and silver-grey hair,
plump and bland in appearance. 'You don't know me, but I've heard a
lot about you,' he announced. 'I am Frank Barnett, and I run the National
Strategy Information Center in New York.'

Not liking to be disturbed without notice, I must have been less than
cordial. I soon yielded to his charm, however, and we were deep in
conversation about the Soviet problem and what to do about it. The NSIC,
he told me, was a non-profit organisation which coordinated the efforts
of scattered scholars in the field of strategy. We had a number of mutual
friends. Right now, I was entirely absorbed by Franco. This he understood,
but he hoped I would come over to the United States, and he would give
me some useful introductions. I did, and he did, but not until 1968.

Franco: a Biographical History came out in London in 1967 and in
Boston, Paris and Munich, then, finally, in Madrid. It brought me at least
temporary fame, and long-term hostility. I knew there would be hostile
reactions. Franco was, and remains, a hate-figure, not only on the Left
but among well-thinking (*bien-pensants*) liberals, who need hate-figures
to divert hostility from themselves.

The Spanish translation was by my friend Esteban Perruca, who was in
charge of the newsreels section of the Information Ministry. It was admirable, with tiny exceptions for political motives. One of these did seriously
tamper with my meaning, however. Where I had said, of Franco's reprisals
after the Civil War, that he had 'chosen vengeance', Perruca had written:
'Franco opted for punishment' (*'Franco optó por el castigo'*).

The Spanish edition (Magisterio Español, Madrid) carried footnotes by
the translator, where the authorities disagreed with my interpretation of
events. The first edition in particular carried many hostile footnotes. That
first edition, in 1969, was declared *'tolerado'*, which meant that no book-
shop could display more than one copy at a time. On noting the interest
aroused abroad, however, the authorities changed their minds, and
reclassified the book *'aprobado'*, deleting some of the footnotes. Thereupon, it went into several impressions, became a bestseller, and, as the
critics put it, *'la más citada de las biografías del Caudillo'*.

In retrospect, I often wonder whether my *Franco* did me more harm
than good. There were many 'rave' reviews, and almost as many hostile
ones, especially in Paris. Many years later, I learned that some of my
natural allies, notably within the Congress for Cultural Freedom, had

decided to boycott me for the mere fact of having written a book on Franco that was not a denunciation. Only around 1990 did I understand, at last, why for long years my contributions had become unwelcome to *Encounter*, flagship of the Congress.

IN 1968, the KGB made a first attempt to wreck Forum. An American voice on the telephone told me he was a journalist representing *Ramparts*, a magazine in California, and would like to interview me. The manner was unfriendly, but I had no reason not to see him. His name was Daniel Schechter.

In my office, Schechter was positive and aggressive. His magazine, he said, had firm evidence that FWF had been launched and was funded by the CIA. I told him the story of the approaches I had had from the Congress for Cultural Freedom, of my initial unawareness of its CIA connection, of my efforts to get the CCF out of my hair, of my success in so doing, and of my current excellent relations with Jock Whitney. I showed him the elaborate, glossy publicity folder we had prepared for selling purposes, with the mastheads of newspapers in many countries which now subscribed to our service. My visitor was determinedly sceptical, and I sent him to Kern House to see for himself that our sales were genuine and that we were running a straight, 'normal' press service.

At the time of Schechter's visit, I knew nothing about *Ramparts*. The standard epithet used by its enemies, I soon learned, was 'muck-raking'. In its issue of March 1967, it ran a long article packed with revelations about secret CIA funding of labour unions and a variety of other organisations, of students and intellectuals among them. I learned years later from an MI-6 source that the *Ramparts* scoop had been provided by the Czechoslovak StB, under the control of the KGB. I know of no evidence, however, that *Ramparts* was aware of the role played by these agencies.

The harm was initially limited to US organisations, the funding of which by the Agency had been banned by the Katzenbach Committee. But in May 1967, it was compounded from an unlikely source: Thomas Braden, the CIA man who had set up the International Organizations Division of the Agency. That month's issue of the *Saturday Evening Post* carried a gloating article by Braden, entitled 'I'm glad the CIA is immoral'. In it, Braden mentioned the creation of the Congress for Cultural Freedom to counter Communist propaganda.

The author's intention was doubtless to defend the Agency's record in counter-attacking the KGB in the Cold War (and incidentally to claim the credit for it) but the roll-on effects on the Congress and its international network of publications were disastrous. Doubtless *Ramparts'* interest in Forum was a natural, though unplanned, consequence. FWF had not been specifically named, however, and we weathered the storm better than the Congress, confirming my view that Forum had to be kept independent of Josselson and his ramshackle empire.

NOTES

1 Some years later, press reports suggested that the company had been named after a former CIA man named Kern, whom I had neither met nor heard of.

2 The 'propagandising' ban later became known as 'the Katzenbach amendment', which was CIA shorthand for the recommendations of a committee appointed by President Johnson in February 1967 and chaired by his newly appointed Under-Secretary of State, Nicholas deB Katzenbach, who had previously served as his Attorney General. In correspondence with me in 1992, Mr Katzenbach confirmed these circumstances. (See also Peter Coleman, op. cit., p. 226.)

3 For a fuller account, see Brian Crozier, *Franco: a Biographical History* (Eyre & Spottiswoode, London; Little, Brown, Boston, 1967), Ch. 1.

VII

More own goals
(1965–70)

BEFORE BEING FORCED out of the French secret service, Antoine Bonnemaison had introduced me to a colleague of his who had resigned at the same time. I shall call him Gabriel Decazes. Tall and thin, he was fiercely anti-Communist.

By mid-1965, President de Gaulle's international behaviour had become increasingly eccentric. Since the rebuttal of his project for an Atlantic Directorate, his wartime anti-American attitude had deepened. To the extent that Britain, since the collapse of the Suez expedition, normally supported the United States, his attitude was also anti-British. More alarmingly, especially to the West Germans (and in the face of the Franco-German Treaty he had signed with Chancellor Adenauer), he became increasingly pro-Soviet, in the sense that he felt good relations with the Soviet Union would help to reduce the weight of the United States in Western Europe.[1]

From Bonnemaison and Decazes, I was kept well informed on these matters. Both men, and a small group of former participants in the *colloques*, felt (as I did) that de Gaulle's eccentric attitude constituted a growing threat to the unity of the Western Alliance. I remember one discussion in particular at which the two Frenchmen solemnly agreed that the General had become *l'ennemi*. We agreed that something had to be done about it, mainly by monitoring his intentions. Gabriel Decazes, in particular, was well qualified, for he had kept close and friendly links with his former colleagues in the SDECE and the Ministry of Defence. Indeed, he had well placed and talkative sources inside the Elysee Palace as well. Moreover, his motivation was impeccable: a deep commitment to NATO and to the anti-Communist cause. In effect, what our small group had decided on was the need for an informal spying operation against the General's government.

As the only 'Anglo-Saxon' member of the little group, I was asked whether I was prepared to report any major hostile plans on de Gaulle's part, to the British and American governments. At that time, I had not yet developed a well placed network of American contacts, but I felt sure that my existing contacts in Whitehall and Westminster would pass on anything we learned that was of direct concern to Washington. The plan of action was discussed and agreed in the spring of 1965.

IN THE EVENT, our first spy operation was a joint one. I had argued the case for a detailed understanding of General de Gaulle's machinery of power. Specifically, we need to know how the Elysee staff functioned, the orders it was getting from the General, who was doing what under his supreme command. With his Elysee contacts, Decazes was able to give partial answers, with special emphasis on defence, but an overall view was lacking.

I, too, had contacts, and I suggested to the group that the easiest way to find the answers we wanted would be for me to spend a morning at the Elysee Palace, ostensibly to gather material for an article. The stratagem worked. The published outcome appeared under my name in *Encounter* of October 1965, in the form of a Letter from Paris, headed 'The System at the Elysee'. I have to add that Melvin Lasky, to whom I had 'sold' the idea, was and remained quite unconscious of its ulterior purpose. Nor of course did he (or *Encounter's* readers) learn the substance of some of the more revealing talks I had that morning, which I reserved for our group.

The picture that emerged was, not unexpectedly, of a cultured man of gigantic ego; but more interestingly, of an ego increasingly frustrated, to the point of paranoia, by his inability to operate on the world stage in a manner commensurate with his own vision of France as a world power and of himself as the man of France's destiny. In his frustration, he was desperately searching for a *coup de théâtre* that would demonstrate

France's independence of the Anglo-Saxon superpower and its British smaller brother.

De Gaulle was, as one would expect from a man of his background, an exacting taskmaster, though not a tyrant. Although his decisions were solitary, before deciding he would always listen to counter-arguments from his carefully chosen and highly qualified team. So great was the workload, however, that too often, according to one of his counsellors, he merely read a report, marked it 'seen' and took no action, as though he had literally 'seen' a report but had not actually read it.

'It is as though,' a prominent Gaullist told me, 'you were on a ship sailing for the North Pole and an officer put a piece of paper before the captain, proposing a change of direction to the South Pole. The captains reads it, marks it 'seen', and the ship sails on, heading north.' (From the *Encounter* article).

BEFORE THE END OF THE YEAR, de Gaulle had settled on the theatrical symbolism he needed: France was going to pull out of NATO. Decazes gave me the news in December. It was indeed a major intelligence coup, and he urged me to pass it on to London and Washington immediately. I did what I could, which was to write a succinct memo, which I passed on to Ronald Franks, with the necessary background explanations.

Four months later, on 9 March 1966, de Gaulle announced his decision to withdraw France from the integrated command of the Atlantic Treaty Organisation (while remaining formally committed to the Alliance itself). A year later, on 1 April 1967, he went further and expelled the Allied forces from France.

It is sad to recall that, as in the more important case of Richard Sorge's tip-off to Stalin about the impending Nazi invasion of Russia in 1941, Decazes's intelligence about de Gaulle's intentions was received sceptically in MI-6, in the Foreign Office and in Washington, and was simply ignored. In other words, no action was taken to forestall de Gaulle's coup, to kill it by advance publicity, or try to mount pressure on him within his own team.

After the March 1966 announcement, Ronald Franks wrote me a note of warm congratulations, and of apologies for official scepticism. The Decazes group had been deeply dismayed by the lack of active response from the 'Anglo-Saxons' to the scoop he had handed them, through me. Although he had kept his detailed plans, if any, to himself, I had surmised that he had banked on swift and firm action from London and Washington, in the hope that in the ensuing crisis, his friends in the Armed Forces would find a way of ousting de Gaulle.

Shock and dismay greeted de Gaulle's announcement, not only among France's Allies but even in his immediate entourage. As Decazes told me, the General had not bothered to consult his Cabinet on this momentous decision. Soon, NATO headquarters was transferred from Paris to Brussels.

Some years later, Aleksei Myagkov, the first defector from the KGB's Third Chief Directorate – which operated within, and spied upon, the Soviet Armed Forces – revealed that France's March 1966 withdrawal from NATO was regularly cited in officer training courses as a major KGB success.[2]

The attribution of this decision to KGB influence supports the thesis that the KGB probably had an agent of influence inside the Elysee. Allegations to this effect by Thyraud de Vosjoli, the SDECE liaison man with the CIA in Washington, inspired the best-selling novel *Topaz* by the American writer Leon Uris.

Gabriel Decazes knew Thyraud de Vosjoli, and told me he was known among his colleagues as '*Joli roti de veau*' (a phonetic anagram). Decazes, too, was convinced that the KGB did indeed have an agent of influence in the Presidential Palace.

De Gaulle's decision to pull out of the NATO organisation was of course a major blow to the Western Alliance, both self-inflicted by a leading member, and a positive success for the enemy.

Despite his deep disappointment, Decazes continued his spying operation within the Elysees for nearly three years. Some of the information he kept to himself, but there was enough left over to keep me, and other members of the group, well informed about policies and political trends. Although there were no further dramatic scoops, his information was particularly useful to me during the great crisis of May-June 1968 in interpreting the Soviet-directed role of the French Communist Party. Paradoxically, by calling a general strike, the PCF broke the student challenge that had come within an ace of ousting de Gaulle. The Communists had no desire to be shown to be outflanked by the anarchic New Left; nor did they want de Gaulle to be brought down, for his anti-American policies had proved useful.

At this time, Decazes lost heart and decided to retreat into the privacy of his retirement. I never saw him again.

THE NEXT ALLIED 'own goal' I was involved in (though after the event) happened in Germany, with the advent of Willy Brandt as Federal Chancellor in October 1969. Brandt was undoubtedly a controversial figure, in that he was both widely revered and reviled. His declared admirers included British ex-Labour Cabinet minister and future Social Democrat Shirley Williams, the Labour Cabinet minister Denis Healey, and the future Conservative Prime Minister Edward Heath.

Personally, I am not among Brandt's admirers, although I recognise that he played a staunch role during his period as Mayor of Berlin, from 1957 to 1966. As Chancellor, it could be argued that he was a disaster for the Western Alliance, not only in the visible Cold War but also, less visibly, in the secret war.

The first sign I had that a major change was on the way came at a meeting of INTERDOC which ended on 21 September 1969, exactly a month before Brandt's election victory. The British contingent in particular noticed a new reticence on the part of the Germans. Anticipating an election defeat for the Christian Democrats, they made speeches advising caution towards the Soviet Union, and hinted at a probable change in foreign policy, with emphasis on a possible rapprochement between Bonn and Moscow.

Their advance information, and their political instinct, proved accurate. On 28 October, Chancellor Brandt made his much-anticipated foreign policy speech in the Bundestag, launching his *Ostpolitik* of friendly overtures to the Eastern bloc.

In fact the old hardline policy of Chancellor Adenauer and his immediate successors had not produced any tangible benefits to the Federal Republic. Brandt reckoned he could get more out of the Soviet Union by being more flexible, and many Germans vested their hopes in him. This was particularly true of divided families, members of which yearned to visit their relatives in the East.

While Mayor of Berlin, Brandt had fallen under the influence of Egon Bahr, his Press Office Director. On becoming Chancellor, Brandt appointed Bahr as State Secretary in his own office.

Egon Bahr advocated normal relations between West Germany and the countries of the Warsaw Pact; recognition of the German Democratic

Republic; negotiations between the two rival military alliances; and, finally, a collective security system in Central Europe.

Interestingly, Bahr revealed his thoughts on these questions in an interview with the American strategic expert Walter F. Hahn in January 1969, seven months before Willy Brandt's election victory.[3] The policies he advocated, then and over the ensuing years, were clearly in line with Soviet policies.

Brandt's Ostpolitik led to a string of treaties with the Soviet bloc countries and to recognition of the German Democratic Republic (GDR).

Many Germans on both sides applauded these arrangements. But there was a heavy price to pay in the secret war. The Soviets opened a consulate-general and a trade mission in West Berlin, while the GDR opened a large mission in Bonn. The Federal Republic was now wide open to East German spying on behalf of the KGB. The full extent of this espionage by the East German Stasi (State Security Service) was only revealed when the East German regime collapsed in 1989–90 and the two Germanies were reunited under the West German Chancellor, Helmut Kohl.

For this reason alone, Chancellor Brandt's Ostpolitik was open to criticism. But there was worse. Unknown to the public, one of Brandt's first decisions on coming to power was to make it mandatory for the sources of all West German intelligence to be disclosed not only to himself as Chancellor, but to every member of his Cabinet as well. As any professional intelligence officer would confirm, the human sources of secret intelligence must be protected, not only for their own safety and survival but because any secret agent whose identity is revealed will simply 'dry up'.

When the Chancellor's decision became known, a number of the most seasoned members of the West German Federal Intelligence Service, the BND, resigned in protest. Thus, not only were the Stasi and the KGB given a tremendous boost, but West German intelligence was virtually emasculated: a victory of some magnitude for the wrong side in the secret war. As it happens, I was a beneficiary of this unfortunate turn of events, but this story belongs to a later chapter.

There is an ironical justice in the fact that East German espionage, which Willy Brandt had unwittingly done so much to help, was his undoing when he was forced to resign in 1974 over the disclosure that his private secretary, Guenther Guillaume, was an East German spy.

IN THE LATE 1960s, I brooded over what seemed to me a gap in Western efforts to counter Soviet propaganda. FWF was doing useful work, but the products of a press agency are by their nature ephemeral. What was needed was a series of short books on current affairs, each to be written by an acknowledged expert. The Background Books series, to which I had contributed two titles, was still useful, but I envisaged something sharper and stronger, with greater impact.

I discussed the idea with my SIS and CIA friends, who readily agreed. As I saw it, the project was financially viable, and would therefore not need secret contributions, although the Agency was ready to meet expenses in the event of a special project acceptable to me and to the publishers (who would not be made aware of any CIA interest).

In 1969, I put my proposal to Maurice Temple Smith, the publisher who had commissioned my Franco biography but had moved since to Secker & Warburg. He accepted with enthusiasm and proposed the general title of 'World Realities'.

My guiding principle was expressed in a quotation from Niccolò Machiavelli's *The Prince* which would adorn each cover:

I have thought it proper to represent things as they are in real truth, rather than as they are imagined.

To emphasise this principle, I added the following paragraph:

This series presents political, economic and social issues as they really are, and not as sectarian, partisan or official interests would have us believe they are, thus conforming to the best tradition of Machiavellian analysis. Each book will be rigorously objective and as accurate as a partnership of editor, authors and researchers can make it. But they will not necessarily be impartial, since each author will express his views on the known facts.

I had some difficulty in making Temple Smith see the point. A tall, gaunt man with piercing blue eyes, Maurice was highly intelligent, but intellectually every idea to him was equal to every other idea. We discussed the possibility of a book on Marxism. His view was that such a book should be written by a Marxist. My view was that a Marxist would, by definition, be incapable of objectivity. Since Marx was the source of political totalism, I would no more ask a Marxist to write on Marxism than turn to a Nazi for a study of Hitlerism. Marxists had their own outlets, in abundance, as was their right. We were not going to provide yet another. This was one idea we did not pursue.

The first author I commissioned was Lord Gladwyn. Over lunch I reminded him, delicately, of the objections he had raised from his Paris embassy to my *Foreign Report* story on the political pressures within the French Army; diplomatically, but unconvincingly, he professed ignorance of the matter. His book, *De Gaulle's Europe or Why the General Says No*, was well received. So were the ensuing ones, which included Max Beloff on *The Future of British Foreign Policy*, and *The Future of Soviet Foreign Policy*, by Sir William Hayter, lately retired as Britain's ambassador in Moscow.

TOWARDS THE END of the 1960s, the Vietnam War was escalating ominously, dividing friend from friend in the academic world and in journalism. The case of one friend, in particular, makes the point and throws light on an aspect of the secret war.

I had known James Cameron, a big name in journalism, for many years. After a trip to North Vietnam, he sold a series of articles to the London *Evening Standard*, reprinted in 1966 in a short book entitled *Witness*, which I reviewed for the *Sunday Times*.

He later told me by telephone that he had been approached by a man he had known when both were on the now defunct *Picture Post*. The man, by now an East German, asked Cameron if he would be interested to go to North Vietnam. His fare and expenses would be advanced by a loan from an agency named Report Press Services and he could pick up his visa in Prague. When Cameron repaid the loan from the fees he earned, Report Press Services simply vanished.

I passed these curious facts on to SIS, which assessed them as a perfect example of a KGB Active Measure.

This was the last contact I had with James Cameron. He had committed himself to the Communist side, and I to the American side, albeit critically. Not long after, he started crossing the street if he saw me, and pretending he hadn't seen me if we happened to be in the same club room at the same time. Another 'friend' of earlier years, Richard Harris, the China-born Far Eastern specialist of *The Times*, did likewise. Neither man was a Communist. Harris in particular was a sentimental supporter of Mao and his achievements.[4]

THE YEAR OF international student violence, 1968, had rekindled my old interest in political rebellion. In this as in so many other ways, the Vietnam War was a catalyst.

Especially in the US, in France, Italy and Germany, the so-called New Left was in ferment. The heroes of the embattled students were: Ho Chi Minh of Vietnam; Fidel Castro of Cuba and his ex-guerrilla leader, 'Che' Guevara, who had lost his life in a failed uprising in Bolivia; the Brazilian advocate of 'urban guerrillas', Marighella; Guevara's French admirer, Régis Debray; the black French writer, Frantz Fanon; the American guru, Herbert Marcuse; and the young German Rudi Dutschke with his telling Maoist slogan 'the long march through the institutions'. In France in 1968, the Paris students almost brought down General de Gaulle. In the US, President Johnson opted not to run for a second term.

IN MY IRD CAPACITY, I wrote a paper about the New Left, which was circulated in Whitehall, entitled 'The New Apostles of Violence'. I also produced a condensed version of the paper for FWF, under the title 'The New Brotherhood of Violence'. It found its way into the *Washington Post* (which clearly had a soft spot for the New Left), and then into the London *Times*.

By 1969, when my IRD paper was circulated, subversion had become a major international problem. The evidence made available to me made it clear that the so-called New Left was asserting its ideological independence from Moscow. But this merely complicated still further an already complex situation. The Soviets seemed as puzzled by the phenomenon as were the Western agencies, and it was clear that the Kremlin's international apparatus was going to do all it could to bring the New Left groups under its control.

As for the Soviet Union's own subversive efforts, they were clearly on the increase. Either in the USSR itself or by arrangement with surrogate regimes, such as Cuba, East Germany or Czechoslovakia, training was available for terrorist groups, along with arms and money. The Soviet-controlled World Peace Council was active in many Western countries in support of the view that the Soviet Union (unlike the United States) was working for peace. Soviet money was also provided to Communist parties in many countries.

The relative lull of Khrushchev's last two years (after the Cuba missiles crisis of 1962) had ended with his overthrow in October 1964. His successor, Leonid Brezhnev, was too readily dismissed in the West as a dull party apparatchik, whereas his long reign of eighteen years would be marked by the biggest expansion of the Soviet Union's empire since

Stalin. In the West, the facts about Soviet involvement in subversion and terrorism were little noticed, whereas much attention was (rightly) given to Soviet naval expansion and the growth of the Soviet nuclear arsenal.

IRD, WHICH HAD MOVED from the rambling, decaying premises at Carlton House Terrace to Riverwalk House, a high-rise block on the corner of Vauxhall Bridge, had put an office at my disposal. There, on the basis of a vast supply of classified documents, I wrote my next book, under the uninspiring title suggested by my British publishers, Eyre & Spottiswoode: *The Future of Communist Power*. The American publisher, Coward McCann, brought it out under the more eye-catching title of *Since Stalin*. It incorporated, with slight amendments, the paper on political violence I had produced for IRD.

In this increasingly threatening situation, I saw a serious gap. Existing institutes or research centres (or 'think tanks' as the Americans called them), however worthy, were either too academic, or too neutral, or too heavily concentrated on hardware strategy, such as the study of naval and air forces. Such studies were of course useful and needed, but they failed to take account of the more dangerous Soviet strategy of takeovers by *non-military* means, such as subversion and terrorism. This criticism applied in particular to Britain's Institute for Strategic Studies (ISS).

In 1968, I had been invited by its then Director, Alastair Buchan, to deliver a paper on 'The Strategic Uses of Revolutionary War' at the tenth annual conference of the ISS at St Catherine's College, Oxford.[5] But Buchan died soon afterwards and his successor, François Duchêne, an able ex-colleague of mine from *The Economist*, took over and the ISS became the IISS (the first 'I' standing for 'International'). In its new guise, the orientation of the Institute became markedly more neutralist; that is, less willing than before to draw public attention to Soviet involvement in the matters that seemed to me to be of fundamental importance.

The need, as I saw it, was for a research centre which would produce studies on the ever-widening range of groups and forces bringing violence, chaos and disruption into our societies, but always in the context of Soviet strategy. My first thought was to make use of the existing facilities of Forum World Features, including the research library I had established there with the gift or loan of my private collection of books, other publications, and press cuttings. I gave the new venture a clumsy but explicit name: the Current Affairs Research Services Centre (CARSC). I knew nothing of fund-raising, and very little of the world of money. I wondered whether I could persuade Jock Whitney to back CARSC financially.

In conversation, I aroused only marginal interest in Whitney and Sam Park. I had also mentioned the idea to my CIA friends, whose show of enthusiasm was no greater. They thought of an ingenious way of killing it with minimum pain. At their suggestion, Whitney and Park commissioned an independent assessment. They sent a New York stockbroker, John Train, to London to look at the situation. By then, I had published the first of a monthly series of monographs under the general title of *Conflict Studies*.

Train was a man of culture as well as money. He had lived in Paris and seemed as interested in the arts as in stocks and shares. He spent a week in London and told me he was interested in our first product, but sceptical about the commercial viability of the project as a whole. Back in New York, he wrote a report (which I never saw) advising Jock Whitney not to invest in CARSC. John Train was in the full sense an unconscious agent. He had been briefed by Sam Park, who in turn had been briefed by the CIA.

I was disappointed but not surprised. In Train's place I should probably have given the same advice. His job was to protect his client's financial interests. A negative verdict could not harm those interests; a positive one, however, might have placed them at risk. His caution was in no way reprehensible.

It looked as though I would have to find the money independently.

I had been seeing a good deal of Professor Leonard Schapiro, the well-known Sovietologist, who held the Chair of 'Government with particular reference to Soviet Studies' at the London School of Economics and Political Science (LSE). Schapiro had a well-deserved reputation for wisdom. A man of few words, he had impenetrable, pale amber eyes, bushy eyebrows and a gigantic Semitic nose, which dominated his craggy face – a Biblical figure in appearance.

Born in Glasgow, but brought up in St Petersburg until the age of twelve, he was bilingual in Russian. After St Paul's and London University, he had been called to the bar through Gray's Inn. His favourite monosyllable, after a prolonged pause, was 'Yes', which signified no more than non-committal appraisal.

Over lunch at the LSE, he listened to me with no other than his usual

monosyllables. When I suggested the creation of a research centre, however, he objected. A research centre, he declared, had no identity of its
own. It had to be attached to some university or college. What we needed
was an *institute*, with its own status and autonomy. Moreover, an institute
could attract tax-exempt 'charitable' funds. He accepted my proposed
name; thus was born the Institute for the Study of Conflict (ISC).

Over the next few weeks, I proposed the names of a number of distinguished figures to join the Founding Council. Leonard Schapiro was to
be the Chairman. The others were:

Max Beloff: Gladstone Professor of Government and Public
    Administration, University of Oxford, and Fellow of All Souls College
Maj.-Gen. R. L. Clutterbuck: Senior Army Instructor, Royal College of
    Defence Studies
Geoffrey Fairbairn: Lecturer in History, Australian National University
S. E. Finer: Professor of Government, Manchester University
Hugh Seton-Watson: Professor of Russian History, School of Slavonic
    and East European Studies, University of London
Sir Robert Thompson: former Permanent Secretary for Defence
    Studies, Malaya; Head, British Advisory Mission to Vietnam
    (1961–5)
Brig. W. F. K. Thompson: military correspondent, *Daily Telegraph*
J. H. Adam Watson: British Ambassador, Havana (1963–6); now
    Diplomatic Adviser, British Leyland

The only member I had not met was Professor Finer, a personal friend
of Schapiro's.

The façade of the edifice was complete. I now needed 'boys' for the
back rooms. Above all, I needed a fund-raiser. I telephoned friends in
the higher reaches of the Foreign Office and of the Ministry of Defence.
The FO candidates were unsuitable. Defence sent me a large, amiable,
soft-spoken soldier, Lieutenant-General Fergus Ling, who had lately
helped to raise funds for quite different purposes. In the event, he never
did raise any money, although he did persuade the armed forces to buy
certain issues of *Conflict Studies* in bulk. The Agency had permitted me
to produce the first five *Conflict Studies* under CARSC as a commercial
imprint.

This, at least, was the situation as it appeared to the outside world. The
reality was more interesting. Despite John Train's adverse report, I had

asked not only the CIA, but IRD and SIS as well, to provide enough money, jointly, to launch the Institute, although not necessarily to sustain it thereafter. However, the new Permanent Under-Secretary at the Foreign Office, Sir Denis Greenhill, vetoed any British financial contribution to the Institute for the Study of Conflict. In the insider parlance of the Diplomatic Service at that time, Sir Denis Greenhill was a 'better notter', with the standard characteristics: a distaste for stretching the rules, and for unwanted publicity. Faced with two British defections, the CIA decided to drop out as well. No member of the ISC's Council, however, not even Schapiro, was aware of these machinations.

I was on my own, but rashly – with a tiny reserve and no further money in sight – decided to press on. The first five issues of *Conflict Studies* had carried the CARSC imprint and the Kingsway address of Forum World Features. The sixth, a study on the Irish situation by Iain Hamilton, a former editor of the *Spectator*, was the first published by the Institute for the Study of Conflict, and carried my office address at 199 Piccadilly. It aroused interest (manifested by a bulk order) in Army quarters. I then wrote No. 7 as a guide to future staff and contributors: 'The Study of Conflict'. In effect, No. 7 was a condensed sequel to *The Rebels*, summarising virtually all that was known at the time about terrorist groups around the world, their links and their methods. I submitted it for comment to all members of the Council so that I could present it as 'the consensus of views' of the Institute.

BY THEN, I was under contract to write a biography of General de Gaulle, while still supervising FWF, and now trying to find money for the Institute. In my Piccadilly office, I was clerk, accountant and manager, as well as director, editor and Director of Studies, writing to potential authors, commissioning print orders, licking stamps and entering the names and addresses of subscribers. Among the first of the latter was the Soviet embassy, which indeed had sent a representative to the offices of FWF/CARSC the day after the first of the *Conflict Studies* had appeared: a sure sign of their importance to the enemy, even if the British authorities concerned had cancelled their support.

When money started coming in, I brought over Michael Goodwin as Administrative Director. I had known Goodwin for eight or nine years from the time he had commissioned a long study from me on Communist China's steel industry. A publishing venture he was involved in had collapsed, and I had helped to find him a job with the Congress for Cultural Freedom; from which I now lured him. Although not intellectually impressive, he brought valuable administrative and publishing skills to the fledgling Institute.

Sir Robert Thompson was the first to produce funds: oil money from Shell and British Petroleum. Shell put up £5000 a year for three years, BP £4000 for two years. It was a good start, but the Agency now came up with something bigger, in the private sector. It arranged for me to meet the American businessman and philanthropist Richard Mellon Scaife, part-heir to the Mellon fortune and a major shareholder in Gulf Oil.

I flew to Pittsburgh to meet him. Already, through Frank Barnett, I had met the man who handled his charitable funds, R. Daniel McMichael. Deeply versed in Communist strategies, Dan McMichael picked the right outlets for the funds at his disposal. I formed an instant rapport with his chief, Dick Scaife, as he liked to be called – a tall, fair-haired man with film-star good looks. The initiative was successful. Dick Scaife not only took over the FWF burden from the ageing Jock Whitney, but sanctioned a grant of $100,000 a year to my Institute, from his Scaife Family Charitable Trusts. This was a *real* grant, not a 'notional' one.

From that moment, the ISC took off.

DURING THIS troubled time, my relations with the CIA grew closer. Three or four times a year, I flew to Washington, DC, then on to other places for my own purposes. Usually, I spent a whole day at Langley, where specialists on the major areas and problems of the day were brought in to brief me and discuss whatever problem was raised. As at Century House, I was impressed by the high calibre of the researchers and analysts, some of whom became long-term friends.

My main links were with the Covert Action department, headed by Cord Meyer, who hosted the stimulating lunches on the top floor. A Yale man, Cord had lost an eye to the Japanese during the invasion of Guam.

Contrary to the popular view of the CIA, as disseminated not only by the Left but by the liberal media, the prevailing ethos of the Agency was itself intellectually liberal, in the American sense. This was certainly true of Cord, a cultured, civilised man who had indeed attracted the unwelcome attention of the FBI, and had been suspended without pay for some weeks while the CIA investigated his past association with pro-Communist people and groups. He was cleared, of course, or I would never have met him at Langley, where he held the post of Deputy Director.[6] But unfortunately I did not meet Richard Helms, the highly professional Director of Central Intelligence, during the nine years of my association with the Agency, although I did meet him after his retirement.

Once rid of the CCF and its constant interference, FWF prospered. We launched a Spanish service, to run which I recruited a senior member of the Spanish service of the BBC; then an occasional French service, and finally a Chinese one, run by Eric Chou, a distinguished scholar and journalist who had been kept in solitary confinement in Peking for nearly four years and brainwashed before being sent back to Hong Kong (where he edited the pro-Communist *Ta Kung Pao* daily) to spy on the British. One day, he had gone to the airport with a small suitcase and flown to London, where he was granted asylum. He wrote of his experiences in a book whose title echoed Kravchenko's, *A Man Must Choose.*[7]

The Agency submitted his Chinese versions of the FWF articles to its own Chinese experts, who pronounced them first-rate.

IN ONE OTHER Far Eastern matter, however, CIA expertise proved faulty. Since the massacre of twenty-five bystanders at Lydda airport (Tel Aviv) in May 1972, the Japanese Red Army had been much in the news. The Agency's Japanese specialists in Covert Action had an idea that was bright but insecure. They had produced a hand-written diary, allegedly written by a member of the Red Army, which, if published, would have helped to discredit the terrorists, both in Japan and internationally.

It was arranged for one of my CIA contacts to drop it into my letter-box early one morning, and I was asked to find a way of getting it into the Japanese press. I had my doubts about this operation, not least because, not being a Japanese scholar, I could not judge the text for myself. I discussed it with one of my IRD friends, who shared my misgivings.

In the end, I took it to a Japanese journalist in London, with whom I was on good terms. I told him, truthfully, that this text had been dropped into my letter-box, and untruthfully that I had no idea where it came from and that I would be grateful if he could cast an expert eye over it and tell me what he thought of it. In fact the text had come with a few typed lines in English claiming that this was the diary of a Red Army terrorist which exposed the division within the organisation and gave details of the torture of recruits to enforce unconditional obedience.

Within two days, my Japanese friend telephoned me to say: 'This diary is a forgery.'

'I'm not surprised,' I replied, 'but please tell me how you know.'

'It can't be genuine, because of the characters that he has used. Some of them are very old-fashioned and wouldn't be used by this generation.'

It turned out that the Japanese man who had written the diary for the Agency was indeed a senior citizen who had lived in America for a long time. As far as I know, the operation was dropped.

As regards the content of FWF's services, gone were the clashes and frictions of Congress days. Relations were cordial and productive. The occasional suggestions from the Agency were nearly always justified by the criteria of news value which the CCF had failed, or declined, to grasp.

The only real clash I can recall was illuminating. I had received an unsolicited article by Tibor Szamuely, the Soviet defector, whom I had known for more than ten years. Tibor had received part of his schooling in England and was, as a result, bilingual. The article was powerfully written and well argued. The subject was Richard Nixon, and the problem was that it came out unequivocally on Nixon's side, notably in the matter of his defence of Whittaker Chambers against Alger Hiss (see Ch. II).

My CIA friends, however, declared the article unacceptable. At that time Nixon was already President of the United States, having won the race handsomely in 1968. He was now running for a second term, which of course was the topical 'peg' for the article. I was astonished by the CIA's attitude. 'You realise what you are saying?' I asked. 'As an official agency of the US, you want to ban an article defending your own President.'

'Well,' the answer came, 'he does have a rather unsavoury past.' Szamuely's article had pointed out that in his historic clash with Alger Hiss, Richard Nixon, the lawyer, had been proved right. The fact that the CIA did not want me to run the article was a perfect illustration of the liberal ethos within the Agency, mentioned earlier. To be fair, the Agency probably did not want to be found guilty of praising *any* American politician, even the President.

I felt strongly about this, and on 1 October 1970 I wrote a memorandum to Don, my main 'case officer' in London, pointing out that the article was a powerfully reasoned defence of a man who had been consistently denigrated by the media, but who, in a crucial matter, had been vindicated by the verdict of the courts. 'To suppress the article,' I went on, 'would be to lay ourselves open to two serious charges: that we believe Hiss to have been wrongfully convicted; and that we do not wish the American President to be defended against his present-day detractors.' I pointed out that in any case the article would not be distributed in the United States.

My concluding paragraph deliberately created a potentially difficult situation for the London station of the Agency to cope with:

> I hope ... that my arguments will be accepted locally. If, however, they are not ... then I request that the matter be referred to head office, together with this memorandum. In the event of a further negative, I propose that the President himself should be consulted.

Perhaps this was 'hitting below the belt'. At all events, I won and Szamuely's article went out in FWF's service. As far as I am aware, there were no unfavourable repercussions in the US.[8]

Twice during the FWF years I had to turn down a request from an influential friend of Frank Barnett's who later became a household name: William J. Casey. Bill was one of the first people Frank had introduced me to in 1968. He was a founder member of Frank's National Strategy Information Center (NSIC). He had worked for the American wartime OSS, from London, and had gone on to a lucrative New York law practice. In the early 1970s, he had been, among other things, Under-Secretary for Economic Affairs and President of the Export-Import Bank (under President Nixon).

A tall, lanky man, he was a lazy speaker, and was once introduced by Frank Barnett as 'the mumbling pimpernel'.

First in my Piccadilly office, then again some months later over breakfast in Paris, he had come to me with a proposal. So impressed was he with Forum World Features that he was putting together a syndicate of high-powered businessmen with a view to taking it over and marketing it in the US. Nothing would have given me greater pleasure, but I was up against the 'Katzenbach Amendment' and my lips could not have been more sealed.

On the first occasion, when he merely sounded me out on the proposal, I simply said that I did not think Mr Whitney would be interested. The second time, in Paris, he was full of self-confidence, and had actually put his syndicate together. This time, I told him firmly that I had discussed the matter with Mr Whitney who was determined to stick to his original idea of a press service mainly aimed at the Third World.

Many years later – in November 1980 – we were both guests at William F. Buckley's party at the Plaza Hotel in New York, to celebrate the twenty-fifth anniversary of his influential magazine *National Review*. Ronald Reagan had just won his landslide election victory and was President-elect of the US. He had appointed Bill Casey as his Director of Central Intelligence. Bill had been Reagan's highly effective campaign manager, and I had attended his press conference in London some weeks earlier.

On this occasion, I had telephoned him to make sure he would be attending the Plaza dinner, as I had something important to tell him. At the preliminary cocktail party, while Henry Kissinger was attracting the attention of other guests, I took him by the arm and we sat together on a couch. I reminded him of his attempts to take over FWF, and explained why his proposal was a non-starter. He mumbled: 'I guessed as much.' But I felt sure he had not.

NOTES

1 For a fuller account of de Gaulle's policy at the time, see Brian Crozier, *De Gaulle* (1973), Part VI.
2 Aleksei Myagkov, *Inside the KGB* (Foreign Affairs Publishing, London, 1976): 'In 1968, the Head of KGB School No. 311, in a lecture to future officers about the organisation's activities abroad, stated plainly that, in the opinion of the Politburo, events in France were a positive result of the efforts of the Soviet government and of the successes of the KGB' (p. 24).
3 The interview was not published until 1973, in the winter issue of ' *Orbis*, Vol. 16, No. 4; see also Geoffrey Stewart-Smith, ed., *Brandt and the Destruction of NATO* (Foreign Affairs Publishing, London, 1973).
4 See, for example, Richard Harris, 'Ready response to idea of an ordered and effective society' in a China supplement to *The Times*, 30 September 1975, which lists and comments on Chairman Mao's 'achievements' without a reference to the mass executions and other atrocities of his regime.
5 Reprinted in *Problems of Modern Strategy*, foreword by Alastair Buchan (Chatto & Windus, London, 1970).
6 Peter Coleman, op. cit., pp. 47–8.

7 Longman, 1963.
8 Four years after this incident, the Watergate affair burst around President Nixon, forcing his resignation in 'disgrace'. His numerous enemies, especially in the liberal media, had their revenge on the man who had dared to side with McCarthy and expose Alger Hiss. Although I did not discuss the matter with the CIA officers concerned, who had moved on to other assignments, I imagine they must have felt justified in the line they had taken in 1970.
My own view, as expressed in my book *Strategy of Survival* (p. 120–21), is that Nixon's main error in the Watergate affair was excessive loyalty to his staff. He should simply have fired the guilty ones and carried on. In his book *In the Arena* (Simon and Schuster, 1990, p. 41), Nixon expresses the same view.
I did not meet Richard Nixon until the mid-1980s, since when we have exchanged many letters. In my view, his books are by far the most compelling analyses of the US role in world affairs. In his own country, though still under attack from his former enemies, he is now widely revered as an elder statesman.

VIII

Into battle
(1970–4)

THE DECADE of the 1970s was dominated by the concept of 'détente', meaning a slackening of international tensions. The concept was misleading. Throughout my period as Director, the Institute for the Study of Conflict was involved in exposing the fallacies of 'détente' and warning the West of the dangers inherent in a policy of illusion.

'Détente' meant different things on each side of the Iron Curtain. In the West, advocates of 'détente' (some of whom believed in it) hoped it would lead to a general reduction in the burden of armaments, by reducing the fear of war. Many even hoped, against all the evidence, that in time 'détente' could persuade the Soviet leadership that the USSR should now abandon its ideological war against the West and indeed against all countries not already in the Soviet orbit. A period of peace was envisaged, during which trade would make the Soviet Union more prosperous and therefore more ready to stop its subversion of other countries.

On the Soviet side, the aspirations were strikingly different. The Soviets hoped the West would unilaterally reduce defence budgets and remove any obstacles to Soviet acquisition of high technology, with which to build up the already excessive military strength of the USSR. They hoped the West would give permanent – that is, *de jure* – recognition to the post-war frontiers of Europe: in other words, to Stalin's conquests and annexations. Their ultimate hope was that a European Security Treaty would be concluded, leading to the dissolution of NATO and the Warsaw Pact. Once NATO was dissolved, the Americans would withdraw their forces from

Europe and the Soviet forces would be free to intimidate and if necessary occupy Western Europe. To see things this way in any West European country in 1970 was to court unpopularity and such labels as 'right-wing' or better still 'extreme right-wing'; whereas the analysis was simply a recognition of realities.

Proposals for a European Security Conference (leading to a Security Treaty) had long been prime objectives of Soviet foreign policy. They had first been tabled in Berlin in 1954. In April 1971, the Soviet Communist Party held its 24th Congress in Moscow, and Leonid Brezhnev rehashed the old proposals. On past occasions the West had rejected them. This time it responded. The main reason for this favourable response was the new West German Ostpolitik already described. The road to 'détente' was now open.

ON 1 MARCH 1971, a long interview I had given to Joseph Fromm appeared in *US News and World Report*. The theme was terrorism and Communist intentions. On reading this interview, a Frenchman named Maître Jean Violet came to see me in my Piccadilly office, with an introduction from François Duchêne, my former *Economist* colleague and Director of the International Institute for Strategic Studies.

A small round man with a sallow complexion and intelligent dark eyes, Violet impressed me with the clarity and precision of his arguments – Gallic logic at its best – and with the breadth of his intellectual grasp of world problems. As Duchêne had put it, he represented a powerful consortium of French business interests. He did, but the most important element in his biography, which I learned later, was that for many years he had held the title of Special Advocate to the French intelligence service, the SDECE. As such, with a virtually unlimited budget, he had conducted psychological actions in furtherance of French interests. He suggested that the ISC should organise a conference, or a study group, to consider the problems inherent in the 'détente' process. He undertook to raise the necessary funds. I opted for the study group formula, having attended too many costly but unproductive conferences.

Jean Violet had done his homework before coming to see me. He gave me a pithy and provocative report, the outcome of a preliminary study group he had chaired himself.

Each member of the ISC Council received a copy of the Violet report. On the need for a study group, approval was unanimous. On the substance of the Violet paper, reactions were mixed. Professor Max Beloff, whom

I consider a forthright defender of Western values, exploded: 'We can't possibly be associated with extreme right-wing views like this.' I reasoned with him, pointing out that the Violet paper was factually accurate in all its details. It was merely a working document. The necessary nuances and modifications would be provided by the study group. Beloff calmed down, but his reaction had been an interesting example of the success of long-term Soviet propaganda, identifying anti-Communist views as 'right-wing', even among the most admirable supporters of the West.

The study group was duly constituted, and could not have been more authoritative. Our Soviet specialists, Leonard Schapiro and Hugh Seton-Watson, were members, as were Max Beloff and Brigadier Thompson. Two renowned outside specialists also took part: Robert Conquest, author of the ultimate study of Stalin's purges, *The Great Terror*, and Leopold Labedz, editor of *Survey* (and long associated with the Congress for Cultural Freedom). Whitehall had allowed one of its own best experts, Malcolm Mackintosh, to participate; and Adam Watson, not long out of Whitehall, was there. A distinguished academic of Yugoslav origin, Ivo Lapenna, contributed a section on the Soviet concept of international law.

The youngest member of the group was Robert Moss, an Australian academic and journalist. In 1969, Moss, then twenty-two, had come to see me, with an introduction from his father-in-law, Geoffrey Fairbairn, another member of the ISC's Founding Council.

The study group met at intervals between July and November 1971. In September, its relevance was demonstrated when the government of Edward Heath expelled ninety Soviet diplomats and officials, and pro-hibited the return of fifteen others. All 105 of these officials had been identified as spies, either for the KGB or the GRU. A Whitehall friend of mine had brought me a detailed analysis of Soviet spying activities and techniques, which I fed into our discussions.

The expulsion of the 105 Soviet spies still stands as a record for mass espionage expulsions in the West. The decision to expel them had been strongly advocated by the newly appointed British ambassador to Moscow, Sir John Killick, who was a talented and unusually forthright diplomat. His views had been unconditionally endorsed by the Foreign Secretary, Lord Home.

The Whitehall material contained hitherto unpublished background about Oleg Lyalin, a recent defector from the KGB whose disclosures had enabled the British security services to compile or verify the list of Soviet secret agents. He had also provided evidence of Soviet contingency plans for sabotage.

The report of the study group, *European Security and the Soviet Problem*, was published in January 1972. It ranged wide: over Russia's global policy; over Soviet subversive techniques, including systematic disinformation and espionage; disarmament proposals; and the weaknesses of both sides in the great confrontation. It made an immediate, but also a lasting, impact not only in Britain but internationally.

In Paris, Violet had launched a new quarterly review, *Le Monde Moderne*, which reproduced the entire text in translation. The funds for this project, and indeed for our study group's special report, had been provided by the late Carlo Pesenti, the Italian industrialist and financier, who was reputed to be the richest man in Italy. Violet introduced me to Pesenti, a man of great charm and restless energy. A creative insomniac, Pesenti slept no more than two or three hours a night.

Predictably, there was no shortage of dissenting voices. One of the interesting ones was that of Lord Chalfont, whom Harold Wilson had put into the House of Lords as his Minister of State for Disarmament. Although no longer in office, he had not yet shed his allegiances and wrote that our report was 'a classic exposition' of the attitudes of 'right-wing politicians'.[1]

However, nothing the ISC could do, with its modest means and non-official status, was going to arrest, or even substantially slow down, the process of 'détente'. All we could hope to do was to draw attention to the perils facing the Western Alliance. As individuals, some of us could help in other ways, not to stop the unstoppable but to avoid some of the worst pitfalls of 'détente' looming ahead.

Another of Violet's initiatives at that time was undertaken from Brussels. The operator Violet had chosen was an eccentric man, with the delectable name of Florimond Damman. Having made a small fortune from property deals, he ran a tiny but effective outfit with the grandiloquent name of the *Académie Européenne des Sciences Politiques*. The three of us – Damman, Violet and I – drafted an appeal for 'Peace without Frontiers', in which we defined *our* concept of a true détente.

We envisaged the situation that now prevailed between France and the German Federal Republic. Three times in a lifetime, the French and Germans had been at war: in 1870, in 1914, and in 1939. Now there was unimpeded freedom of movement between the two countries for people, goods and ideas. There was no censorship on either side. A French man could marry a German girl, or vice versa, without let or hindrance. You could buy German publications in France and French ones in Germany. If, we argued, such a situation could be brought about between the Eastern bloc and the West, there would indeed be a true détente.

The appeal, despatched to distinguished people in Western Europe from the Académie in Brussels, collected many hundreds of signatures in favour of 'Peace without Frontiers'. It is no exaggeration to claim that this initiative led to the Western insistence on 'Basket III' in the Helsinki discussions. Basket III was the third of the packages of themes for discussion at the proposed European Security Conference. It dealt with human rights, freedom of information, and cultural exchanges. It was the most fundamental and therefore the most important of the 'baskets'. If 'détente' did not include such freedoms, it would not be a true détente. Basket III was a point of reference to bring the Soviets to order.

VIOLET AND I now planned a still more ambitious exercise than the *European Security and the Soviet Problem* report. This time we would analyse the crisis in Western societies in the light of Soviet subversion. In September 1972, I assembled another group of experts. Some of the original ones were there, but so were others, including two journalists, Iain Hamilton and Anthony Hartley, because of their special knowledge, respectively, of the Irish problem and of French affairs. The former British ambassador to Cuba, Adam Watson, was also present. I noticed, as did others, that his heart did not seem to be in the exercise. Time and again, as the discussions progressed, it became clear that either he did not understand the phenomenon of Soviet subversion, or would prefer, for reasons unstated, not to expose it. Shortly after our report appeared, Adam Watson resigned from the Council and went to Paris to run the International Association for Cultural Freedom, the successor to the Congress, but no longer linked to the CIA.

This time, the Whitehall input was even more substantial than with the previous study group. It included comprehensive details of the Soviet KGB and GRU presence throughout Western Europe. The only country missing was Britain itself, partly no doubt for reasons of national security, but mainly because of the still recent expulsion of the 105 Soviet spies. Without revealing the name of my informant, or his department, I made it clear to the participants that the material provided came from an official source.

For France, the figure we gave of KGB/GRU personnel was 118, and for West Germany 82. Clearly, however, the German figure was mislead-ingly low, because most of the Soviet bloc espionage in the Federal Republic was handled by East Germans, both for obvious reasons of language and for their facility to merge into the background. Even a small country like Switzerland harboured eighty-seven Soviet spies.

We went on to analyse Soviet objectives in Western Europe: the acquisi-tion of Western technology on easy credit terms; the extension of Soviet influence over both domestic and foreign policies; economic damage through organised industrial unrest; the fostering of divisions within the Western Alliance. We gave further details of Oleg Lyalin's revelations. These, however, had not been provided by Whitehall, but had been picked up from the French press, which had not been inhibited by British Minis-try of Defence regulations. The most sensational of Lyalin's revelations were these: detailed Soviet plans for sabotage in Britain, including the destruction of the nuclear early-warning system at Fylingdales in York-shire, and of the long-range communications establishment at Orfordness in Suffolk, and even for the poisoning of London's water supply.

Our report, *The Peacetime Strategy of the Soviet Union*, was published in March 1973. It provided individual country studies of Soviet subversion covering the United Kingdom, France, West Germany, Italy, and the United States, with shorter entries for smaller countries. It was probably the most comprehensive compilation of facts and analysis to have been presented in public.

In Paris, *Le Monde Moderne* carried the entire text. One of the most famous political figures in France, the former Prime Minister Antoine Pinay, by then over eighty but still wonderfully energetic, was so fired with enthusiasm on reading the report that he came to London to present it in person to Prime Minister Edward Heath.

Both of these ISC special reports became required reading in Western intelligence and security services, and defence colleges and establish-ments. They also made me, more than ever, a prime KGB target.

DURING THIS TIME of false 'détente', major developments were happening in the secret war. In Britain, the Information Research Depart-ment was seriously weakened. In Chile, a dangerous subversive centre was defeated. In the United States, the covert action capacity of the CIA was emasculated. I was involved in all these events, the culmination of which – in all three countries – came in 1973.

The Heath years (1970–4) had begun spectacularly well, with the expulsion of the 105 Soviet agents. During the same period, however, the Labour Party was being taken over by the extreme Left. In the days of Attlee and Bevin, Labour had been the scourge of the Communists and a bulwark against Soviet expansionism. In 1970, spokesmen of the Communist Party of Great Britain (CPGB) spelt out their aims with cynical frankness. These were the Moscow-line Communists: they announced their intention to gain control of key trades unions, and through them of the Labour Party itself.

There was much confusion, then and later, over the role of the proliferating 'Trotskyist' and 'Maoist' groups and mini-parties. The fact that the 'official' Communists spent a good deal of energy denouncing the 'Trots' was indeed confusing. In fact, Trotskyists, Maoists, Fidelistas were all Communists, and it would make little difference, except in the degree of the inevitable atrocities, whether the CPGB, or one of its supposed rivals, such as the Workers' Revolutionary Party or the International Marxist Group (Trotskyist) or the Communist Party of Britain (Marxist-Leninist), which was Peking-line, ever came to power. There was no danger that any of these groups would be *elected* to power. The problem was that the voters might unwittingly vote Communists into power in the belief that they were voting for good Social Democratic members of the old Labour Party. Had this happened – and it very nearly did – the outcome would have been some kind of 'People's Democracy' on the East European model. The Trotskyist mini-parties would simply have been liquidated, or absorbed into the resulting governing group.

In this worsening situation, IRD had played an important role, by disseminating accurate background papers on the CPGB, and on the other Communist groups. My own relations with the Department were excellent, after an unsatisfactory period during the late 1960s, when those in charge had curtailed various activities, including one of IRD's important publications, the *Religious Digest*.

During that period, it had been decided to sever all relations with two major continental networks with which I had been associated. One was the Hague-based INTERDOC group. The other was admittedly more controversial. This was a private but highly effective French group controlled by a friend of mine, the late Georges Albertini. If high intelligence, courage and initiative had sufficed, Albertini would probably have had one of the outstanding political careers of his time. When he died, in mid-1982, *Le Monde* carried a lengthy obituary which said it all in the headline: 'GEORGES ALBERTINI – UN GRAND DESTIN MANQUÉ'.

Albertini was irremediably tainted by a Fascist and collaborationist background. Despite his great qualities, he lacked critical judgement at times of crisis. He was also short of luck. As a very young man, in the 1930s, he had been a Socialist, joining the entourage of the Prime Minister of Popular Front days, Léon Blum. He had then switched to the Fascists, as many others had done, and joined the group of Marcel Déat (who had also been a Socialist, but had turned to Fascism, largely because of despair over the failures and inefficiency of the parliamentary system of France's Third Republic).

When the war came, Déat and the young Albertini had become collaborators. More precisely, Déat collaborated with the Nazis when they invaded France, while Albertini joined the Vichy government as a member of the Secretariat of Marshal Pétain's Premier, Pierre Laval. This was indeed the choice of the overwhelming majority of the French people, who had rallied to Pétain as the hero of Verdun in 1917 and the one man who could save the country after its catastrophic defeat by Hitler. Only a tiny minority had chosen the lonely path of resistance advocated by General de Gaulle.

After the liberation of France by the Allies, Albertini paid dearly for having made the wrong choice. He was jailed for two years for collaboration. From my SDECE friend, Antoine Bonnemaison, I learned that he was initially condemned to death but reprieved.

After his release, he changed his views by 180 degrees, in economics as well as politics. He dropped socialism in favour of enterprise and the market economy. From Vichy and collaboration, he became an ardent Gaullist. For many years, he held two jobs. In the mornings, he was political adviser to the merchant bank and business consortium, Worms. In the afternoons, he crossed the Boulevard Haussmann to run his fortnightly *Est & Ouest*, the most authoritative publication in the French language on the problems of Communism. Having accurately predicted the seizure of the Suez Canal by Colonel Nasser in 1956, well ahead of the event, he saved millions for the shareholders of the Compagnie Universelle du Canal de Suez, and his morning job was safe for life.

There was more to him, however, than this combination of jobs. He had built up a huge network of informants and helpers and was increasingly consulted by those in the high offices of state to which he had ceased to aspire. Moreover, he and Georges Pompidou had been at school together, and during the Pompidou presidency and beyond he was a true *éminence grise* for the Elysée.

In return for all information and the contacts he gave me, I made sure that he received the IRD output, of which he made good and effective use. When a new head of IRD took over in the 1960s, however, this contact was officially broken on the ground that Albertini was a Fascist. Indeed, he had been, but he no longer was.

There was no question of restoring these official contacts, however, once they had been broken. In any case, INTERDOC's value had decreased sharply after the advent of Willy Brandt as Chancellor of the Federal Republic. As for Albertini, whom I met frequently in Paris or London, I made sure both that he received IRD material likely to be useful to him, and that I made good use of his own information and influence.

As a sign of renewed mutual confidence, IRD commissioned the Institute for the Study of Conflict to produce a manual of counter-insurgency, which appeared in March 1973 and consisted of a series of seven separately numbered 'Counter-Insurgency Studies'.[2] This enabled IRD to distribute the studies selectively, according to the character of the government at the receiving end.

The studies were not secret, but each was marked 'for official use only'. They were attributed to the Institute and contributed significantly to the international reputation of the ISC.

IRD had always had its enemies within the Foreign Office, however. With some logic, many high officials objected to its involvement in domestic affairs. To this there was no ideal solution. Logically, a counter-subversion organisation should have been run by the Home Office, but it had been obvious to Christopher Mayhew and others at the time the IRD was created that the Home Office lacked the necessary expertise, since the major source of subversion was the Soviet bloc. A more important consideration was the cost of the IRD, which had been allowed to grow virtually without control. It employed 400 staff, which made it the biggest department in the Foreign Office, and absorbed a yearly budget of £1 million.

When Oliver Wright became 'Chief Clerk' at the FO, in charge of Administration and Personnel, he decided that the time had come for substantial economies. Until then, IRD's budget was covered by the secret vote, and therefore not published. In earlier years, under the protection of secrecy, IRD had undoubtedly spent wildly. A previous head of IRD had developed the habit of recruiting staff on the basis of chance meetings at cocktail parties.

The case for cuts was strong. At this time, the Under-Secretary in charge of IRD and other research departments was Norman Reddaway, a skilful practitioner in the art of unattributable information. There was much heated discussion, at the end of which it was decided that IRD should come off the secret vote. This automatically created the problem of absorbing the existing staff under the open vote. As many as one hundred personnel were taken into the Foreign Office but many others went into the Research Department (mainly concerned with historical background). The effect was that all the non-attributable material had to be made attributable. By definition, this cut out a great deal of the current production.

Had I been consulted about these developments (about which I only learned after the event), I would certainly have supported cuts of, say, fifteen per cent. In fact, the savings totalled sixty per cent. It was a kind of administrative massacre, with broken careers, the disappearance of many specialists who would never be replaced, and general demoralisation. There is no evidence that this self-inflicted wound was itself subversive in intent. It stands, however, as a perfect example of unintended consequences.

FOR MANY YEARS, the Labour Party had done its own 'policing', by maintaining a list of 'proscribed organisations', which included the CPGB and its various front groups, along with the Trotskyists. The list was constantly revised. Any Labour Party member who joined any 'proscribed' organisation faced expulsion.

In 1973 – the year of the IRD massacre – the proscribed list was dropped, opening the floodgates to subversive penetration of the party. For the previous four years, the leadership of the two biggest trades unions had been in pro-Communist hands, with Jack Jones heading the Transport and General Workers (TGWU) and Hugh Scanlon in charge of the Engineers (AUEW).

The CPGB's policy of penetration was spelt out in a pamphlet entitled *Time to Change Course*. Its author, Jack Woodis, was a member of the CPGB's National Executive Committee. More significantly, Woodis was head of the party's International Department: the British arm of Moscow's own ID, successor to Lenin's Comintern. The way he put it was:

The fact that the Trades Unions are the mass basis of the Labour Party provides the key for progressive change in that Party ... Moving unions to the Left is

a first step to moving the Labour Party to the Left. And a victory for the Left
of the Labour Party is a vital part of the process of securing election of a new
type of Labour government.

By the spring of 1972, I had decided that a special study on subversion
in industry had become necessary; the stark fact was that the trades unions
virtually *owned* the Labour Party. The funds available to the ISC at that
time were too slender to do the job properly, and I therefore decided
to bring out a pilot study with the aim of raising more money. The secret
services with which I was associated were in no way involved in this
exercise, and there was therefore no point in my mentioning them to
the people I approached.

The first of these was Nigel Lawson, whom I had known when he
succeeded Iain Macleod as editor of the *Spectator*. In *The Times* of 24
May, he had written an article headed 'Communist Influence on Industrial
Strife', which showed that he understood the situation.

Lawson took on the job and produced an admirably concise report
which we issued in November 1972 under the title 'Subversion in British
Industry'. We printed only thirty copies. The report was not for the wider
public: the target audience was industry itself. The captains of industry
were the most closely affected by what was going on under their noses,
but were proving either apathetic or timid, or both.

The Lawson report unlocked doors, gave courage to the timid, and
opened purses. I was much helped by two well-placed allies: John
Dettmer, Chairman of the long-established Economic League, and Michael
Ivens, Director of Aims of Industry. One of our converts was John
Whitehorn, Deputy Director-General of the Confederation of British
Industry (CBI).

When the money came in, we convened a study group which met for
three months in the autumn of 1973. For such a controversial subject, we
needed representatives of both the trades unions and industry, as well
as specialised academics. The most active and committed of the latter was
(the late) Dr K. W. Watkins, who had made the traumatic journey from
membership of the CPGB to anti-Communism.[3] There was no point in
inviting one of the Communist trade union leaders; nor in trying to find
an anti-Communist one. On Ken Watkins's advice, we invited a non-
Communist leftist: Alan Fisher, of the National Union of Public Employees
(NUPE), sometimes called 'the union of the underpaid'. Industry was
represented by Edward Robertson, head of the labour relations depart-

ment of the CBI. To carry credibility, the study group would have to consider the non-political as well as the political causes of unrest. Two rapporteurs were therefore needed. For the non-political bulk of the report, I chose a gifted ex-reporter from the *Observer*, Eric Clark, who went on to make a name as a writer of suspense novels. For the controversial last section (the object of the exercise), I took Michael Ivens's advice and gave the task to Frank Broadway, a former industrial editor of the *Statist*.

There was bound to be a clash at the end when the study group turned its attention to subversion. In a loud, hectoring tone, Alan Fisher told us that if we were going to waste time discussing nonsense, he wanted no part of it. The study group had turned into a political meeting. Without waiting for counter-arguments, he walked out. Robertson of the CBI followed suit, having made it clear that quarrelling with trade union leaders was not one of his ambitions. Neither of them returned. Incidentally, each had received a fee of £500, paid in advance by the ISC; but neither offered even a partial refund...

There was a curious sequel. The next day, Alan Fisher was a scared man as well as an angry one. A double leak had occurred: the working draft of the final section, on subversion in industry, had been reprinted verbatim in *The Times*, and also in the *Morning Star*. I rang Fisher, who admitted that the leak must have occurred in his own office. On arrival that morning, he had found his copy of the draft on his desk. Though the envelope was marked 'Confidential', somebody else had opened it. The *Times* version was signed by its industrial correspondent, Paul Routledge, who had never hidden his sympathy for the extreme Left; which, I add, in no way affected the professional quality of his reporting.

By then the confrontation between the Heath government and the National Union of Mineworkers (NUM) was in full swing. The Prime Minister had introduced an ambitious Industrial Relations Act. The point of the NUM strike was to defeat it. Constitutionally, Heath did not need to go to the country for another sixteen or seventeen months. But he could not allow the miners' challenge to go unanswered, and called a general election.

Just before polling day, the Institute's report, *Sources of Conflict in British Industry*, had been published with unprecedented publicity. We had hawked the text around. *The Times* expressed interest but clearly the editor, William Rees-Mogg, could not carry his staff with him and his tentative offer was dropped. To our surprise, David Astor bought it for the *Observer*, thereby 'buying' a revolt from his staff. A whole page was devoted to the controversial last section of the report. Congratulations on my 'uncanny sense of timing' reached me from friends and strangers. I basked in this euphoria, but the timing was in fact fortuitous.

I was in Washington on 28 February 1974 when Britain went to the polls. For Harold Wilson and his Labour Party, by now deeply penetrated, it was a narrow victory. The country had lost confidence in Heath and his Tories, without wishing to be ruled by a party now calling for 'irreversible' socialism – in a manifesto almost identical to that of the CPGB.

There was a secret consequence, which carried the disarming of IRD a stage further. Until the election, the Department had been issuing regular and accurate reports on the rival Communist parties and on the various Trotskyist groups. As soon as the news of Labour's narrow victory came in, IRD suspended all its reports on subversion in Britain. The decision was taken by the mandarins, thus pre-empting any directives from 10 Downing Street.

CONFLICT IN INDUSTRY was not the only cause of conflict between the Institute for the Study of Conflict and the media in that troubled year. Another was a special study entitled 'Soviet Objectives in the Middle East', which embroiled us in an unpleasant dispute with *The Times*. We had assembled the usual formidable array of academic and other expertise to look at the situation in that area after the fourth Arab-Israeli War of October 1973, with specific reference to Soviet involvement in, or exploitation of, the conflict. To save time as well as money, Professor Leonard Schapiro, as Chairman of the group, asked me to be the rapporteur.

The study group met only once, in a room at the Reform Club, on 19 January, a Saturday. Our usual procedure was followed. Namely, having completed my draft, which reflected the views of all participants, I circularised it to each of them for their comments. When all the comments had arrived, I incorporated those that seemed relevant into a final draft, which again went to all concerned for any further comments they might have. The published text thus reflected a consensus of the views and expertise available.

In a special article in *The Times*, its Middle East specialist, Edward Mortimer, whose leftist views were public property, charged me with having passed my views off as those of the study group. Schapiro drafted a dignified and factual letter of rebuttal which, initially, Rees-Mogg declined to publish. Some acrimonious exchanges followed, and Rees-Mogg was persuaded to publish the letter.

By now, I had got used to the fact that anything carrying my name seemed automatically to provoke attacks and controversy; whereas the same views expressed by other people usually passed unchallenged. When the views expressed were my own, I had no objections; I did object to being attacked for merely expressing the collective views of a distinguished group of specialists.

THE DESTABILISATION of the Allende regime in Chile was probably the last successful covert action undertaken by the CIA before the disaster of Watergate. I played a modest part in it, willingly and in what I considered a good cause. The presidential election of 1970 had brought the Socialist candidate, Salvador Allende, to power, but on a minority vote of 36 per cent in a three-cornered contest. Allende's Popular Unity coalition included the large and well-disciplined Communist Party and the extreme Movement of the Revolutionary Left (MIR). The least 'left' of the three was in fact the Communist Party. The Communists, however, were strictly in line with Moscow, and had a clearer idea of strategy than their coalition partners. Allende gave the Communists the ministries of Labour and Finance, while the Economics portfolio went to an independent Marxist who worked closely with the Communists.

Through the Agency, I met an impressive, highly intelligent Chilean businessman, Héctor Castrillo (not his real name), who was on a visit to London. He spelled out the Communist strategy in great detail. The Party had moved swiftly to force the private sector out of business. The main weapon used by the Communist minister was a 1933 law providing for the appointment of an official administrator – known as an *interventor* – in businesses known to be losing money. To make sure that target businesses did indeed show a loss (thus 'justifying' the use of the 1933 law), three techniques were being used.

One was the lock-out of management after the seizure of factories by the workers. After a week or so, an *interventor* was appointed. Another technique was to send revenue auditors and inspectors to investigate banks and businesses. Even minor technical irregularities provided the pretext to appoint an *interventor*. Then there was a longer-term technique, available through the Finance Ministry's fiscal powers and control of prices and income. All firms were ordered to grant an immediate wage rise equivalent to the previous year's inflationary rise in the cost-of-living index, which stood at 36 per cent. At the same time, all prices were frozen. Thus, many small firms were driven out of business. On the fiscal side, twenty-one new taxes were imposed, the primary object being to finance an increase of 33 per cent in state expenditure.

These measures were drastic enough, but there was an officially encouraged breakdown of law and order. The President banned the use of force by the security forces, dissolved the riot police, and released MIR terrorists jailed under the preceding Christian Democratic administration. The released *Miristas* were later formed into a Palace Guard to protect the President.

President Allende also encouraged large-scale seizures of land. Dispossessed farmers organised their own resistance movement and an incipient civil war developed. Training facilities for the extreme wing of the Socialists were provided by the Cubans and North Koreans, and for the *Miristas* by the Soviet KGB.

I used Castrillo's revelations, which proved entirely accurate, in an article distributed by Forum World Features.[4] At this early stage of the Allende revolution, the role of the Soviet Union had not yet become clear. I soon learned that Cuba's centre for revolutionary activity throughout Latin America, which had been located in the Paris embassy, was transferred to Santiago. Fidel Castro's new embassy in Chile largely consisted of members of the Soviet-controlled Cuban DGI, or of Fidel Castro's rival Directorate of National Liberation.

The Communist plan for the takeover was in fact largely wrecked by the irresponsible violence of the other coalition partners. Inflation soared, reaching 1000 per cent, and unplanned strikes took their toll.

The next move from my CIA friends was to suggest that there was a need for a book on Chile. We agreed that the obvious place for it was in World Realities, the series of short books I had launched in 1969, under my editorship (see Ch. VII). The author I proposed to commission was Robert Moss, whose qualifications were ideal.

Before turning to journalism, Robert had lectured on Latin American history at Australia's National University in Canberra. He knew Spanish and had already been to Chile for *The Economist*. Robert was enthusiastic, and FWF, to which he was a regular contributor, met his travelling expenses.

It was agreed that he should not be told of the CIA's interest and involvement in this project. There were valid reasons for this. Had he known, there would have been one of two consequences. Either he would turn down the assignment, or he would accept but his presentation would inevitably be affected by the knowledge.

It was essential to a successful outcome that he should do the job as an objective (though not impartial) observer. Had I had any doubts about his commitment to the Western, democratic cause, I would have looked elsewhere.

Robert Moss wrote most of his book in 1972, but added an introduction to it immediately after Allende's overthrow. It was published in late 1973 by David and Charles, who had taken over the series from Secker & Warburg (and were equally unaware of the CIA connection). The title was bland: *Chile's Marxist Experiment*. As with Robert's later non-fiction books, it combined vivid reporting with sound scholarship. It was well received, and played its part in the necessary destabilisation of the Allende regime. In due course, several years on, it raised a storm of protest and denigration, to which I shall return.

In the end, a strike of a special kind, masterminded by Héctor Castrillo, cleared the way for Allende's overthrow. His master stroke (which was also the CIA's) was to immobilise all transport lorries. With the country at a standstill, the armed forces intervened on 11 September 1973. Allende died, probably by his own hand, and the long dictatorship of General Augusto Pinochet began.

THE WATERGATE AFFAIR, which brought down President Richard Nixon, does not belong to these memoirs, but some of its consequences do. Nixon had made history in several ways: by visiting Communist China in 1972; by recognising America's defeat in Vietnam; and by signing nuclear arms limitation treaties with Brezhnev. Watergate prevented him from following through on his controversial East–West policy. The aftermath included the severest 'own goal' in the secret war.

Egged on by unelected 'investigative' journalists, the Senators and Congressmen destroyed the intelligence-gathering capacity of the CIA, the FBI, the police, and the customs department. 'Destroyed' is hardly too strong a word. Two new laws did much of the damage. The Privacy Act made it illegal for the FBI or any other government agency to keep files on individuals or organisations, thus protecting terrorists as well as political subversives. Before the Privacy Act, and its companion, the Freedom of Information Act, the FBI had two or three thousand regular informants; after, the number shrank to a couple of dozen.

The Soviet spies in the United Nations and on Capitol Hill could now function with impunity, freed by law from the curiosity of the FBI or the CIA's counter-intelligence department. The Federal Loyalty Program, vetting admissions to the civil service, was discontinued, so that any subversive could find a way in.

On the covert action side, any CIA plans now had to run the gauntlet of Congressional Oversight. Moreover, any enemy of the US could gain access to many (though not all) secret files under the Freedom of Information Act.

The KGB had plenty to laugh about.

NOTES

1 *New Europe*, May 1972. Chalfont went on to become a courageous and outspoken opponent of Soviet Communism.

2 The titles of the 'Counter-Insurgency' series were: *The Roots of Insurgency; Indicators of Insurgency; Guidelines for Emergency Laws; Counter-Action and the Army's Role; Psychological and Information Measures; Reconciliation and Reconstruction;* and *The Rehabilitation of Detainees.*

3 The other academics were Professors A. J. M. Sykes (Sociology, Strathclyde); I. R. Ilersic (Social Studies, Bedford College, London); and Raymond Thomas (Business Administration, Bath).

4 'The "Santiago Model" for Revolution', FWF London, 30 January 1971.

IX

The crisis of the 1970s

IN THE SPRING of 1974, two ideological defectors from the American intelligence community brought out a book entitled *The CIA and the Cult of Intelligence* (Jonathan Cape, 1974). Their names were Victor Marchetti and John D. Marks. Marchetti had resigned from the CIA in 1969 in the wake of the New Left's wave of protests; Marks resigned the following year from his post in State Department intelligence.

Purchasers of the book may have felt cheated, for there were dozens of blank spaces. At that time, the CIA was still strong enough to take legal action to prevent undesirable revelations. The deleted passages included references to the origins of FWF, and (I was told) my name was mentioned, among others.

That was the prehistory. At about the time the Marchetti–Marks book came out, I had resigned as Chairman of FWF, for a reason of my own that had nothing to do with the book. I was simply overburdened. With Iain Hamilton as Director, the service no longer needed me. Iain was fully 'conscious' and in touch with the CIA officers in London, as indeed I still was. When I left, Iain took over as Chairman, and another tough, able Scotsman, Alan Brown, came in as editor. Brown had no 'need to know' about the CIA link.

A year went by. Then the CIA learned that Marks and Marchetti were about to release the suppressed material, in London. It was decided to close down FWF. The reason given was that a report to Mr Whitney had shown that the service was never going to pay its way. Nor indeed could it, since the main markets had been excluded for policy reasons from the outset.

The news came as a shock to Hamilton and the FWF staff, but it was undoubtedly the correct decision for the CIA to take, in the light of what happened next.

The crisis began with an article headed 'CIA Makes the News', in London's fun revolutionary weekly *Time Out*, in its issue of 20–26 June 1975. The article quoted from an alleged CIA internal report, said to have been prepared for its Director, Richard Helms, in 1968, and tracing the origin of Forum World Features as an offshoot of the Congress for Cultural Freedom.

FWF was said to have provided the United States with 'a significant means to counter Communist prop and has become a respected feature service well on the way to a position of prestige in the journalism world.'

Time Out correctly identified John Hay Whitney as the proprietor and myself as 'the top man on the London side', until 'at least 1974'.

An article on the same lines followed, in the *International Herald Tribune* (*IHT*) of 4 June, by the London correspondent of the *Washington Post*, Bernard Nossiter. In a letter to the *IHT* I described the article as 'a curious mixture of fact and fantasy'. Replying to me, Nossiter said:

> At the time I wrote, I had not run down the source of Crozier's current employment with the Institute for the Study of Conflict. Since then I have learned from *responsible officials* that ISC is also the creature of an intelligence service, British this time [emphasis added].

Who were these 'responsible officials'? I put this question a day or two later over lunch at the Oxford and Cambridge Club to the then head of MI-5, Sir Michael Hanley, and the head of its counter-subversion department, Dirk Hampden. When I remarked that this was obviously a KGB exercise, Hanley dismissed my remark as 'just surmise'. That afternoon there were red faces at MI-5 when the picture library found a shot of a known KGB man, Evgeny Kryukov, having lunch with a previously unidentified man who turned out to be none other than Bernard Nossiter. Kryukov's cover job was as the London correspondent of the Moscow journal *Socialist Industry*. An easy job: he had never been known to file a story.

The number Michael Hanley had given me to contact him now went dead and I had no further contact with MI-5, ever.

Some months later, the well-known *Daily Express* specialist on defence and intelligence, Chapman Pincher, revealed Nossiter's acquaintance with Kryukov. The identity of his 'responsible officials' having been blown, Nossiter took this Russian bull by the horns and admitted that this man Kryukov was indeed a contact, indeed more of a friend than a contact, since they often played tennis together.[1]

I had hoped the matter would die down, but was soon disabused. This was the beginning, not the end, of what I call 'the Great Smear Campaign' – a protracted operation, in which elements of truth (for example, the CIA connection) mingled with wild falsehood and unwarranted conclusions. Twenty-five files vanished from the offices of the ISC, containing some 300 documents running to 1500 pages. In two further articles, in August and September 1975, *Time Out* stated that these papers had arrived unsolicited through the post.

Both articles carried cartoons depicting me as Superman, first flying out of the Pentagon, laden with dollars in money bags, then landing on the House of Commons, laden with *Conflict Studies* for the MPs.

I sacked a member of the ISC staff for lunching *Time Out* reporters in defiance of a written order. I later learned that a Soviet intelligence officer, Lieutenant-Colonel Gregory Yakovlev (of GRU or military intelligence), had been dropping in at the ISC offices for informal chats with him.

The *Time Out* reporters were Phil Kelly and an American called Steve Weissman. I learned later that Weissman had been on the staff of *Ramparts*, the Californian magazine which had first exposed the CIA's links with the Congress for Cultural Freedom (see Ch. VI).

The campaign spread in waves. First an article would appear in *Time Out* or compatible journals such as the *Leveller* or *Militant*. There would be a follow-up in the *Guardian* or *Observer*. The climax always came at Question Time in the House of Commons, when one or other of the tight little band of fellow-travelling MPs would place pointed questions about ISC and its alleged links in Whitehall – with the police, the Army, the Ministry of Defence, the Foreign Office, the Home Office, or the secret services. The MPs included Stan Newens, Jo Richardson, Joan Lestor, Frank Allaun, and Joan Maynard.

Many years later, a senior KGB defector in London identified all those I have named as 'confidential contacts' of the Soviet embassy. This was, of course, in no sense a criminal offence on their part. All embassies have 'confidential contacts'.

Soon the campaign spread abroad. The operation was on such a scale that the organisation handling it could only be the KGB. I learned from the same source that the distribution of selected documents to international recipients is a standard monthly requirement for the KGB Rezidentura. Eventually, selections from the ISC documents appeared in no fewer than sixteen countries, as far apart as India in the east and Canada and the US in the west. It does not follow, incidentally, that the publication outlets selected by the KGB for this campaign knew that they were involved in a KGB exercise. Some would know, others not. I am not saying, for instance, that *Time Out, Militant* or the *Leveller* were conscious of acting as KGB 'transmission belts'. The role of intermediaries in such operations is important for success.

The most important clue to the KGB connection was the frequency with which the name Philip Agee started to appear. Agee was one of the CIA's first ideological defectors and had been working closely with Fidel Castro's KGB-controlled secret intelligence service, the DGI.

Agee had come to live in London. His close associates included some of the writers most persistently involved in the smear campaign, such as Martin Walker of the *Guardian*, Phil Kelly, Weissman, and another American, the young journalist Mark Hosenball, who was on the staff of *Time Out*.[2] It was known that Agee was having frequent contacts with the KGB in London. In the summer of 1976, he had spent time in Moscow discussing plans to expose the CIA throughout the world. His motivation appears to have been a mixture of ingredients, including opposition to the American role in the Vietnam War and the influence of a left-wing woman named Muriel whom he planned to marry when his own divorce was confirmed; although the plan misfired.[3]

Throughout the campaign, a heavily infiltrated Labour Party was in power in Britain. Fortunately, most of the key posts, including the Home Office (Merlyn Rees), Defence (Roy Mason), and Foreign Affairs (first Anthony Crosland, then Dr David Owen) were held by 'moderate' social democrats.

Although I bore the brunt of the campaign, the ultimate target was of course the CIA itself, in the wake of the Watergate Affair and President Nixon's resignation.

Nor was I the only target in Britain. My associates Robert Moss and Iain Hamilton were also under attack. Robert's book on Chile under Allende, published three years earlier, was singled out. He was a 'natural' for the smearers. He was rumoured (correctly) to have drafted Mrs Margaret

Thatcher's 'Iron Lady' speech of 19 January 1976, denouncing the ambition of the Soviets to dominate the world.

On 20 December 1976, the *Guardian* carried a front-page story alleging that Robert Moss had written *Chile's Marxist Experiment* on commission from 'a CIA-funded company', Forum World Features. Similar stories appeared in the *Daily Mail* and in a BBC interview with Martin Walker. The wisdom of not revealing the CIA connection to Robert Moss was now vindicated. Being quite unaware of the Agency connection, and therefore innocent of any propagandist intent, he had reported the truth as he had observed it. He issued writs and obtained apologies.

As for Iain Hamilton, not only had he succeeded me in charge of FWF, he had later accepted my invitation to join ISC as Editorial Director. His value as a target had thereby increased. In late July 1976, an iron bar was hurled through a window of his Highgate home – nearly opposite the huge Soviet trade mission complex. Later, arsonists gutted the house while he and his wife were away.

At about that time, the offices of *Encounter* magazine were ransacked, after a left-wing journalist had telephoned to ask for details of alleged links between *Encounter* and the ISC.

In November 1976, the Home Secretary, Merlyn Rees, decided to deport two of the Americans involved in the campaign: Philip Agee and Mark Hosenball. Nowhere was any indication given that the deportations were connected with the campaign against myself and my associates, although I have to assume that there was indeed some connection.[4]

Of the two deportees, Agee was by far the more important. A four-page letter from the Home Office delivered to his Cambridge home charged him with having 'maintained regular contacts harmful to the security of the United Kingdom with foreign intelligence officers'.

The time had come for me to strike back. I gathered all the relevant documents about FWF and my part in it, and sent them to Peter Preston, editor of the *Guardian*, in effect daring him to publish them. On the last day of the year, the *Guardian* gave me a whole page. Every letter I had sent was reproduced in full and my introductory narrative was printed without changes. The bottom column inches were devoted to a glossary of names and bodies mentioned, most of the entries factually accurate.

This was a victory and a turning-point. The truth about my troubled relations with the Congress for Cultural Freedom, and of my assertion of independence, was told; but not the whole truth of the still secret role of the CIA. This was many years before a British Cabinet Secretary popularised the phrase 'economical with the truth'.

IN LATE NOVEMBER 1975, Ross McWhirter, one of the famous twins who created the *Guinness Book of Records*, was shot dead by the Provisional IRA. For some time, Ross and I had been meeting with a small group of like-minded friends, concerned about the relentless spread of subversion. Ross had launched an appeal for £50,000 to establish a reward fund for information leading to the arrest of terrorist bombers. His murder was the IRA's vengeance.

In the wake of it, Norris McWhirter played a leading role in setting up the National Association for Freedom.[5] I was one of the founder members, with Lord De L'Isle as President, Michael Ivens of Aims of Industry, and Robert Moss, who became the first editor of the Association's journal, the *Free Nation* (later renamed *Freedom Today*). To avoid the delays implicit in formal Council meetings, a small group of us decided to function as an informal action committee, without reporting to the Council. Bill De L'Isle presided, and the other members were Winston Churchill, MP, John Gouriet, a former Guards officer and merchant banker, Robert Moss, and myself.

The sudden, unheralded resignation of Harold Wilson as Prime Minister, in mid-March 1976, nearly precipitated a major British constitutional crisis. We at The Freedom Association were worried by the possibility that his successor might be Michael Foot, with his retinue of extreme Left supporters.

Our informal action committee decided that we should urge the Queen to act. On 15 April, the *Free Nation* carried an unsigned lead article I had written headed 'Affront to the Queen'. We pointed out that the Queen would be within her rights in refusing to see Foot and ordering a dissolution and fresh elections. We carried two authoritative supporting articles. One was by Lord Blake, Provost of Queen's College, Oxford; the other, unsigned, was by a recently retired counter-subversion chief of MI-5.

This editorial treatment deeply shocked some members of the Council, including Sir Robert Thompson, the counter-insurgency specialist and founder member of the Institute for the Study of Conflict. Those of us most directly involved in this particular decision, Norris McWhirter, Robert Moss and myself, remained unrepentant.

*   *   *

THERE WERE FIERCE debates in the House in February and May 1977. In the February one, a prominent Conservative MP, Stephen Hastings, drew the Home Secretary's attention to an ITV 'World in Action' programme, 'which seemed specifically designed to further the interests of Agee and Hosenball together with their British supporters without a serious or fair attempt at achieving a balance'. Having watched the programme, I knew what he meant. Steve Weissman, Phil Kelly and others were paraded as witnesses of objective truth, repeating charges against me and my associates which went unchallenged by witnesses for our side.

I offered our version of the story, first to the *Daily Mail*, which was not interested, then to the *Daily Telegraph*, which accepted it but did not in the event actually publish it. We learned later that it was to have been the 'lead' of the paper. It was 'on the stone' ready to go when the printers threatened to strike if it was used. Editorial cold feet followed. The story was hurriedly withdrawn and killed and that first edition went to press late.

The Freedom Association President, Lord De L'Isle, who was as courageous in civilian life as on the battlefield where he had won his Victoria Cross, accompanied me to the Fleet Street office of his fellow Old Etonian, Lord Hartwell, the editor-in-chief, whom we tried to persuade to 'publish and be damned'. Hartwell was evasive: in those distant, pre-Wapping days, press barons did not tangle with trades unionists.

Wetness reigned. The Left went unopposed and hardly a voice was being raised on our side. The only recourse left seemed to be the *Free Nation*, organ of The Freedom Association. I re-wrote the story, with as much of the KGB angle as I could piece together, and the full story appeared in January 1977, under the headline: 'KGB AND THE BIG SMEAR JOB'. No writs were issued.

Agee and Hosenball were duly deported. The KGB and its British instruments had lost that battle. Sad to record, however, they went on to win a victory infinitely greater than the defeat they had sustained. In the last wave of the initial campaign, the Foreign Office and its temporary political chiefs tacitly conceded defeat.

FOR THE SOCIAL democratic majority within the Parliamentary Labour Party, this was a traumatic time, with Labour constituencies increasingly penetrated by Communists, mainly of the Trotskyist kind. The Foreign Secretary, Anthony Crosland, the ideologist of the Labour Party in its optimistic post-war phase, had stood firm.

As the smear campaign against me had gathered strength, he had requested background material on me from the head of MI-6, Maurice Oldfield. The latter responded with a memorandum on my past informal contacts with the Secret Intelligence Service. Crosland, however, died suddenly in mid-February 1977. Maurice Oldfield told me later that the memo had in fact strengthened Crosland's resolve.

I doubted whether this implied that Crosland actually approved of my activities. More likely, he may have feared public disclosures of my White-hall contacts. Maurice told me that after Crosland's death the memor-andum on my activities had been retrieved, by means which he left unstated. I never set eyes on it.

At any rate, until Crosland's death, every Parliamentary Question about the ISC had been stonewalled in the best Whitehall fashion. But the tide turned shortly after David Owen had taken over from Crosland. There was a sad irony in the fact that Owen's Junior Minister, Evan Luard, in his time as a don at St Antony's College, Oxford, had commissioned a contribution from me to a symposium on the Cold War. Now, the Cold War forgotten, he turned hostile. In the House, faced with yet another Question about the ISC, he dropped the standard 'No comment' and simply declared that he would look into the matter.

He sent for the list of recipients of material from the Information Research Department, saw my name on it, and alerted Dr Owen. Apparently alarmed, the future defector from the Labour Party took the momentous decision, in May 1977, to close down the Department. Thus the Labour Government had destroyed the only active instrument of counter-subversion in the United Kingdom (as distinct from the passive observation of MI-5), as a sop to the Left. The KGB had won, possibly when it least expected victory.

Aware of the agonising reappraisal in Whitehall, I had already written to the Foreign Office to resign my consultancy, drawing attention to the paradox that the IRD, set up by the Labour government of Clement Attlee to combat Communism, was now being destroyed by the very forces against which Labour had fought.

I learned later that my letter had been shown to the Prime Minister, James Callaghan. If he made any comments, they did not reach me.

In January 1978, the *Guardian* and the *Observer* carried detailed accounts of the life and death of IRD.[6] The secret of IRD's real objectives had been kept for thirty years.

The *Guardian*'s account, by David Leigh, one of my activist enemies, contained the following passage:

> ... Labour Ministers became aware of IRD's approved list of contacts. They
> ... were alarmed ... with the political complexion of a handful of them
> including Mr Brian Crozier, director of the Institute for the Study of Conflict
> ... Mr Crozier, asked about this episode, refuses to discuss it with us. 'I regard
> the *Guardian* as a hostile newspaper,' he says.

Leigh had truthfully reported my words, but not all of them. I had
asked him how old he was. Taken aback, he said 'about thirty'. 'Then, Mr
Leigh,' I said, 'you are too young to remember when the *Guardian* was
a good newspaper.'

The alarm David Leigh had reported appeared to have been due to the
fact that I had stuck to Labour's original purposes, which the Labour Party
had abandoned.

IF A MERE mention of the role of the monarchy in a political establishment could cause alarm, the possible need for intervention by the Army
discussed in the *Free Nation* was enough to shock the conventional and
the secret services, and was thought best left unmentioned, even in whis-
pers. There was no constitutional provision for their playing any part in
politics, except at the behest of the government of the day. The Army,
for instance, had been given the job, more than once, of keeping essential
services going during a strike.

During this critical period of 1975–8, I was invited several times, by
different Army establishments, to lecture on current problems. These
invitations were not, to my knowledge, concerted. But the fact that they
came from different places during that period did suggest some kind of
malaise within our armed forces – similar in kind, though certainly not
in degree, to the mood within the French Army in 1958.

Specifically, the invitations came from: the Staff College at Camberley;
the Joint Warfare Establishment at Old Sarum, near Salisbury; Army Headquarters, Wales, at Cardiff; and the Territorials at Harrogate, Yorkshire.

On each occasion, I tested the military mood in an oblique way,
borrowing an argument from my French friend, Colonel Bonnemaison.
'Foreign ministries,' he had said, gravely, 'are concerned with the transient
affairs of the State; secret services with the permanent interests of the
nation.'

There was a profound truth in this dictum. In the last resort,
would men whose careers had been devoted to detecting and combating

subversion stand idly by while the enemy took over, in the name of a
factitious legality?

If this was true of security and intelligence services, then it seemed to
me that it had to be true of the armed forces, whose *raison d'être* was
to defend the nation against its enemies. It became clear at these military
meetings that this was indeed the view of the professional soldiers I was
addressing; although none of those present would have expressed such
views in public.

At the end of each lecture, I quoted Bonnemaison's dictum, without
attribution. In all places but one, it was greeted with applause, followed
by words of support in the eating intervals. At Harrogate, my audience
consisted of about eighty regular Army officers, with some 200 part-
time Territorials (by definition, patriotic volunteers) responsible for
signals and communications throughout the United Kingdom. There,
the audience rose as one man, cheering and clapping for fully five
minutes.

At Camberley, I was not the only speaker. With me were John Gouriet,
campaign director of The Freedom Association, and Ralph (later Lord)
Harris, Director of the influential Institute of Economic Affairs. There, the
reaction to the Bonnemaison dictum was more muted. Over lunch, several
senior Army officers told me they were glad I had brought the subject
up. However, the Commandant, General Sir Hugh Beach, who was not
present at the lunch, was displeased. He wrote to Gouriet to complain
that he had found Ralph Harris's approach to economic problems too
'monetarist' for his liking. As for my talk, I had embarrassed him by
evoking the possibility of military intervention.

I wrote to him, enclosing a copy of my book *A Theory of Conflict*
(Hamish Hamilton, 1974) and saying I was sorry I had caused him embarrassment, but ı had felt the subject should not be evaded. To my surprise,
he wrote to me (on 25 November 1975) to say, among other things:

> Action which armed forces might be justified in taking, in certain circum-
> stances, is in the forefront of my mind at present and I do hope we may have
> the chance of carrying the debate a stage further.

We never met again, but this letter from a high officer widely regarded
as a 'wet' had at least established that the possibility of military intervention to save the threatened realm was not a fantasy.

                         *   *   *

ONE EVENING IN early May 1975, an unknown voice telephoned me at home from America. It belonged to David Martin, who invited me, in the name of the Internal Security Subcommittee of the US Senate, to fly over the following week and be the 'keynote' witness in hearings on international terrorism. David Martin was the Subcommittee's senior analyst. He met me at Dulles airport and on the drive to Washington told me more about his job and about his own background. A one-time Trotskyist, his knowledge of the Communist world was wide and deep. A Canadian by birth, he had served in Britain and the Middle East during World War II, both in the Royal Canadian Air Force and in the RAF. In Cairo he had become acquainted with the Soviet spy network run by the British Communist James Klugmann (see Ch. I).

The tactical object of the exercise in which I would be the temporary star soon became apparent. Faced with an unprecedented wave of terrorist attacks on American diplomatic personnel, of bombings at home and of skyjacking, the US administration had at last decided to 'do something'. A Cabinet Committee for Combating Terrorism had been set up, chaired by a Foreign Service official, Robert A. Fearey, who had also been appointed Special Assistant to the Secretary of State in a coordinating role to deal with terrorism affecting US personnel abroad. Fearey thus presided over an effort in which other arms of the State, including the FBI and the CIA, were also involved.

It might have seemed logical for Fearey to be the 'keynote' witness, but Martin and the other able professionals who ran the Subcommittee had different ideas. The senior man among them was the Chief Counsel, J. G. Sourwine. The point was not to hear what Fearey had to say, but to condition Fearey to face realities.

Fearey had all the charm and urbanity of the trained diplomat. His problem was a total lack of experience in the fields of terrorism and security, which indeed he frankly recognised. The Cabinet Committee for Combating Terrorism had been set up on the order of President Nixon in September 1972, but Fearey's appointment as coordinator had been made only a few weeks before the hearings. The Committee's brief was absurdly narrow, with terrorism defined as 'violent attacks or threats by politically motivated or mentally disturbed individuals or groups against innocent bystanders who fall under our [i.e., US] particular responsibility'. By this definition, the massacre at Lydda airport in 1972, in which twenty-five tourists had been killed and seventy-eight wounded by Japanese terrorists, would not constitute terrorism, since the victims did not fall

under US responsibility. The same would apply to the killing of eleven
Israeli athletes at the Munich Olympic Games by the Palestinian 'Black
September' group, and to many other terrorist incidents.

My role, although it was not spelt out, was to define various types of
terrorism and above all to produce the evidence (which the State Department was anxious to conceal) of the key role of the Soviet Union and its
satellites in the recruiting, training and financing of terrorist gangs. The
tactic worked. Not only were my speech and answers to questions written
into the record, but so were extensive extracts of my Institute's publications. The official White Paper of the Senate Committee on the Judiciary
(the parent body of the Subcommittee) was dated 14 May 1975.

When Fearey's turn came, he began with some complimentary words
about me ('His name is well known to me and the fact that he is appearing
today spurred me to reacquaint myself with his excellent writings'). It
was embarrassing, after that, to hear Fearey being mercilessly grilled by
Mr Sourwine, to expose for the record the weaknesses in the official
approach to terrorism.

To be fair, Robert Fearey learned fast. In March 1976, he presided over
a major international conference on terrorism in Washington, in which I
made the keynote speech. Other speakers included friends such as Robert
Moss and 'Jupp' Horchem, who was still running the Hamburg branch of
the German security service; the young British academic Paul Wilkinson
(later Professor at Aberdeen, then St Andrews universities); the well-
known American journalist and polemicist Arnold Beichman; and Brian
Jenkins of the Rand Corporation, a leading exponent of the 'statistical'
(that is, non-ideological) school of students of terrorism.

Unusually, for this kind of occasion, I was cheered all the way to the
rostrum. Later, I was booed by the large contingent of 'liberal' writers
and sociologists in the audience. One of the 'cheerers' introduced himself
to me. He was Edward V. Hickey, who was running the security apparatus
of California under Governor Ronald Reagan. A tall, strong figure,
intensely loyal to Reagan, Ed Hickey later served as counsellor at the
American embassy in London. When Reagan became President, he
appointed Hickey as Special Assistant for Security at the White House.

IN MAY 1975, a few days after the Subcommittee hearings, the ISC
hosted an international conference at Ditchley Park, near Oxford, which
yielded another Special Report, *New Dimensions of Security in Europe*.
We had sent a helicopter to pick up the aged President Pinay, together

with two major figures in Italian industry: the cement king Carlo Pesenti, and Cefis of Marconi. Cefis was monolingual, and I had the arduous task of sitting between him and Pinay and interpreting from and into French and Italian.

Later, when the conference chairman, Sir Ralph Murray, lately retired from the Foreign Office, invited Cefis to speak, Pesenti offered to translate his speech, passage by passage, into French (one of the two conference languages). I soon noted that what Pesenti said bore only a distant resemblance to what Cefis had been saying. I challenged him, good-humouredly. Pesenti didn't deny my charge. His arm draped around Cefis's waist, he said, disarmingly, 'This is what he really meant to say'! Cefis just smiled benignly.

AT HELSINKI IN JULY 1975, the protracted international negotiations on European Security culminated with a massive document styled the Final Act. Although the Final Act was by no means a complete success for the Soviet Union, it did provide a prime example of the fundamental role of deception in Soviet negotiations. The KGB defector, Stanislav Levchenko, who was stationed in Tokyo, revealed that a representative of the Administrative Organs of the Central Committee had come to Tokyo to address him and his colleagues. The man claimed that the Helsinki Agreements were 'one of the Soviet Union's greatest triumphs since World War II'. He went on:

Poor fools! It will take years for them to understand. We will sell their books, magazines and newspapers, to foreigners in hotels reserved for foreigners, and we will burn the rest.[7]

Years later, Levchenko revealed that the man was actually Vladimir Kryuchkov, at that time Head of the First Chief Directorate, in charge of operations beyond the USSR. This was the man appointed by Mikhail Gorbachev as the new Chairman of the KGB, who went on to join the hardline coup of August 1991.

NOTES

1 *Washington Post*, 21 March 1976.
2 Some of the journalists involved in the campaign went on to make legitimately respected names for themselves. I am thinking, in particular, of Martin Walker's coverage of events in the Soviet Union, and Mark Hosenball's American coverage for the *Sunday Times*, after his deportation from Britain. In an earlier generation, Arthur Koestler outlived his early Comintern involvement and built up a deserved celebrity status.
3 See Philip Agee, *On the Run* (Bloomsbury, 1987), Ch. 1.
4 Over lunch with me in 1990, Merlyn Rees appeared unaware of the connection, and attributed his decision solely to Agee's contacts with the KGB and the Cuban DGI.
5 Later changed to 'The Freedom Association', because of ill-intentioned attempts to link the 'National' in the original name to the neo-Fascist National Front.
6 See the *Guardian* and the *Observer*, 27 and 29 January 1978 respectively.
7 John Barron, *KGB Today: the Hidden Hand* (Hodder & Stoughton, London; Reader's Digest Press, New York, 1983), pp. 146–7.

X

A *shield for the lady*
(1976–9)

THE LADY TOOK notes when I first met her. I found this flattering.
I was also surprised, as we were in the middle of dinner in excellent
company when she produced her notebook. I soon learned that her
appetite for facts and views was inexhaustible, as was her energy. Both
qualities would in time serve her country. That evening, Tuesday, 9 March
1976, they served the legitimate ambitions of the first woman Leader of
Her Majesty's Opposition, elected to that post by an overwhelming majority of Tory MPs, just over a year before.

Our host was Bill De L'Isle who, with Norris McWhirter, also present,
had been urging Margaret Thatcher to meet me for some time. I needed
no urging. The other guests on that memorable occasion in Lord De
L'Isle's London residence in Eaton Place were John Gouriet and Robert
Moss. Apart from the guest of honour, all of us that evening were founder
members of The Freedom Association.

Mrs Thatcher was listening and writing because I was telling her things
nobody had yet mentioned to her, about Soviet subversion in the United
Kingdom and worldwide, about the penetration of our trades unions and
of the Labour Party, still in power at that time. All her experience so far
had been in the adversarial give-and-take world of party politics, in the
House of Commons. Her experience of the outside world, of foreign
affairs, of secret intelligence and security, was virtually nil.

Gouriet saw us as her 'liege men'. My view was less romantic. I thought
it vitally important that she should be extensively briefed on these matters
before she became Prime Minister. None of us present that evening

doubted that she had it in her to win. We were determined to make sure she did, and we wanted her to be well prepared for the greatest problem she would face on reaching 10 Downing Street.

On leaving, we shook hands and she invited me to see her from time to time to continue our conversation. Thereafter we had many meetings, either at the Thatchers' London home at 2 Flood Street, Chelsea, or in her room in the House. Later, they continued, usually at Chequers, but sometimes at 10 Downing Street.

Mostly, we met alone. In the early days, however, I was often accompanied by a well-known (some would say notorious) ex-senior man in Britain's Secret Intelligence Service, Nicholas Elliott. Son of a Provost of Eton, Elliott's main claim to fame was that he was the man who unmasked and confronted the master spy and traitor 'Kim' Philby; and to notoriety, that he allowed Philby to get away.

In 1976 and 1977, Elliott and I were involved in two secret counter-subversion exercises: one of them national, the other international. The originator of the national one was Stephen Hastings a distinguished Conservative backbencher. The initiative for the international effort came from me.

Chronologically, the domestic operation came first. Stephen Hastings's idea was to set up a secret advisory committee to brief Mrs Thatcher and her closest colleagues on security and intelligence. We called the committee 'Shield'.

Shield's first move was to commission an extensive report on the current state of subversion and on the existing official agencies that were supposed to handle the problem. The report, which ran to about 100 pages, was drafted by a former senior member of the Secret Intelligence Service: an old and trusted friend of Stephen Hastings and myself. After revisions by Stephen, Nicholas and me, the final draft was ready in May 1977. It was comprehensive and accurate.

Why were we doing this? Memories are short, and I imagine most adults at that time had no idea that the situation was as grave as we knew it to be. Some knew but were too timid to do anything about it. Others did not want to know.

The problem was subversion: the deliberate undermining of the State and society. Subversion is an insidious, man-made disease, a creeping paralysis in which the State's defensive organs are invaded and neutralised, until they cease to function: the political equivalent of AIDS.

In Britain, as in other affected countries, the ultimate aim was to turn the country into a 'people's democracy' on the East European model.

It is easier to write about such things now when the truth about these regimes, and about the mother model of them all – the Soviet Union – has come into the open. But in the 1970s, all Western countries were at risk, to some degree. In Britain in particular the problem had become more threatening. The main reason was simply that the trades unions and the Labour Party had largely been taken over by the subversive Left. Many other areas of life were affected: the schools and universities, the media, the Churches.

The consensual view of such problems, where they were recognised, was that a pluralist democracy is by its nature self-correcting, so that there is no need to take any special action. There is some force in this argument, but our view then was that the situation was abnormal and the self-correcting mechanisms of free elections could no longer be assumed to work. Therefore, we reasoned, this kind of optimism was not enough.

The unions were by far the biggest source of the Labour Party's funds, and since the biggest unions were controlled by the subversive Left, there was little the moderates could do about it. Moreover, at this time, the subversives were rapidly taking over Labour's constituency organisations. To wait for the self-correcting processes of democracy might be to leave it too late. We felt more positive action was needed.

THE SHIELD COMMITTEE was necessarily small, secrecy being a paramount consideration. The facts I give here have not, until now, been published.

Shield divided naturally into two segments: the active and the passive; or, alternatively, the givers and the receivers. On the giving side, apart from Stephen Hastings and myself, we had Nicholas Elliott and the late Harry Sporborg, of Hambros Bank. Sporborg, who died in 1984, had served with distinction as deputy head of the wartime Special Operations Executive (SOE), the secret agency that operated in German-occupied France and other countries. Of Norwegian origin, he could not have been more British, from his Rugby and Cambridge intonation to his quiet, underplayed sense of humour.

With the resources of the Institute for the Study of Conflict at our disposal, we produced some twenty papers on various aspects of subversion. The researchers were two younger men Peter Shipley and Douglas Eden (see Chap: XI). The papers were always made available immediately to Margaret Thatcher and, on request, to other members of the committee on the 'receiving' side. Apart from Mrs Thatcher, there were three of them, all members of her shadow cabinet: Lord Carrington, William (later Lord) Whitelaw, and Sir Keith Joseph.

The contrasting attitudes of the 'receivers' were interesting and, in one case, disquieting. Willie Whitelaw, bonhomous and self-deprecatory, the ultimate squirearch (and, later, Mrs Thatcher's skilled fixer), seemed only physically present: a bulky presence, to be sure, but not a participating one. Keith Joseph, civilised, studious, earnest of mien, was deeply interested: out of his depth but eager to learn.

The odd man out was Peter Carrington. As Defence Secretary in the Heath government, as a former High Commissioner in Australia, and (by then) as shadow Foreign Secretary, he had a fairly wide knowledge of foreign affairs. Pragmatists, by definition, find it hard to understand a rigid ideological challenge, and Carrington was a self-declared pragmatist. I had met him several times, and had been susceptible to his undoubted charm. Alone of the receivers, he was systematically hostile to our ideas, and even more to our proposals.

On Tuesday, 18 April 1978, Carrington shocked us all. The lead story in *The Times* that day was headed: 'MRS THATCHER WARNED IN SECRET REPORT OF DEFEAT IN CONFRONTATION WITH UNIONS'. In a secret report to Mrs Thatcher by a high-level Tory group led by Lord Carrington, she was advised that a future Conservative government would be unable to defeat certain powerful trades unions in a direct confrontation. As Secretary of State for Energy, Carrington had played a leading role (said *The Times*) in handling the emergency created by the mineworkers' strike which brought down the government of Edward Heath in February 1974. Here he was telling the future Prime Minister that she would have to cave in if similarly challenged.

That morning I wrote to Mrs Thatcher:

The story in *The Times* today came as a disagreeable shock . . .

As you know, [we] spent a good deal of time and effort preparing a paper on the same theme, on the assumption that this was in the area reserved for Shield . . . the paper went to Peter C [Carrington] and of course to you. It would have been useful to know that he was exploring the same theme with others – and incidentally coming to conclusions diametrically opposed to ours.

It is very easy to prove that victory is impossible. This could have been done with persuasive finality in June 1940.

I advised Mrs Thatcher to destroy my note, but I kept a copy for myself. She did not reply. By the time the second great challenge from the mineworkers (now led by Arthur Scargill) came in 1985, Carrington was out of office. She stood firm and defeated the challenge.

THE PUBLIC IMAGE of Mrs Thatcher in later years, and especially after her second election victory, is of a masterful (or, as her enemies might put it, an imperious) leader, full of self-confidence and authority. There was never any doubting her determination, but she was far from self-confident in those early days. Indeed, she was cautious to the point of diffidence. In the circumstances of that time, that was hardly surprising. She was the first woman elected to the leadership of one of the two main governing parties. Although her victory was clear in the ballot of 11 February 1975 (with 146 votes to Whitelaw's 79 and three others trailing well behind), the party had not yet united behind her. The defeated former leader, Edward Heath, went into his marathon sulk. Uncertain of herself, she surrounded herself with her defeated rivals, including Whitelaw, Sir Geoffrey Howe, and James Prior, and a number of others who came to be known as 'wets'. These and others were in her shadow cabinet at the time I met her, and became senior ministers in her early Cabinets.

I considered it one of my own prime tasks (as distinct from Shield's) to strengthen her self-confidence and to suggest ways in which to cultivate and consolidate a public image of clear-headedness and resolution. To this end, at one of our private Flood Street meetings, I handed her a programme of 'Psychological Action'. This was in no sense a gimmick. It was a practical technique originally formalised by my close French friend, Maître Jean Violet. In fact, I had been working on much the same lines, and it was a case rather like Molière's Monsieur Jourdain, who was delighted to learn that he had been speaking prose all his life without knowing it.

What I had done was to borrow Violet's tried and tested principles, and adapt them to current British needs. Properly applied, this can be devastating. The essence of the technique is to find short, sharp answers to three questions:

- What do people want?
- What do they fear?
- What do they feel strongly about?

At that time, in the 1976–8 period, what the voters wanted was: safer streets; a wider choice of jobs; freedom of travel (meaning, primarily, unrestricted access to foreign currency); more spending money; easier mortgages; and more freedom of choice, for instance in education. What they dreaded was: trade union power; government bullying; 'Russia', meaning primarily Soviet military power and the threat of nuclear war; and, in a hazy way, political violence with something nasty at the end, such as 'Fascism', military rule, and concentration camps. There was curiously little understanding of the real problem, which was not Fascism but Communism. The fact that few people understood this was itself part of the problem.

Psychological Action has nothing to do with the intellect, and everything to do with gut emotions. Having made a list, the next step is to find the right things to say to carefully selected groups of voters. Take the trades unions. At that time, their power was at its peak. With that power went arrogance. The crunch had come and gone in 1969, when Barbara Castle, Wilson's Secretary for Employment, produced a White Paper, entitled *In Place of Strife*, which proposed a twenty-eight-day conciliation pause in unofficial strikes. Even that relatively timid proposal was too much for the powerful union barons who gave the orders in those days. After prolonged debate inside and outside Parliament, Wilson caved in. Henceforth, the TUC gave the orders, and the government passed them on to the people.

That uniquely undemocratic device, the trade union block vote, prevailed unchallenged (as indeed it still did in early 1993). The real masters of public life were men like Jack Jones, who ran the then immensely powerful Transport and General Workers' Union (TGWU) and Hugh Scanlon, President of the Engineers' Union (AUEW). Neither was a member of the Communist Party, but their words and actions were consistent with Party policies.

In terms of Psychological Action, therefore, I proposed a list of selected questions to be put in political speeches. Here are some of them:

- Do you like paying the political levy? (Meaning, did trades unionists approve of having a portion of their pay packet diverted to supporting the Labour Party? The point was that support for Labour was taken for granted. You *could* opt out of the levy, and mark yourself as out of step. You did not opt *in*: the union did that for you, without your consent.)

- Do you think it right that people like Jones and Scanlon should tell the government what to do?
- Is it right that Trots and Commies should order you to strike?

And there were judiciously chosen side arguments, such as:

- The trades unions are pricing Britain out of the market and you out of a job.
- American workers are three times as well off as you – because of free enterprise.

The paper I gave Mrs Thatcher was very short. She read it attentively, then sprang to her feet, walked to a cupboard, and said, as she unlocked and relocked it: 'From now on, Brian, these are *my* ideas.' I did not object. Many, though not all, of the points made surfaced in her speeches and those of her followers in the run-up to the next elections.

The value and impact of such exercises can never be measured scientifically, and public opinion polls, however sophisticated, are not a branch of science. But I like to think this one in particular was useful at the time, if only to clarify issues and concentrate minds.

The Shield approach was strictly within the framework of democracy and liberty, including a strong element of what has since become known as 'Thatcherism': a free market, and a marked reduction in the scope of government interference in people's lives. We also called for secret and compulsory balloting for executive office in the trades unions and the outlawing of the closed shop.

In some respects, therefore, we anticipated certain great and much-needed reforms of the Thatcher era. Our most important and fundamental recommendations, however, remained unimplemented, though not exactly unheeded. I deal with this point later.

The international initiative mentioned earlier was launched in early 1977, to deal with a worsening situation. Things were bad enough in Britain, but far worse in the United States and far from healthy in West Germany, France, Italy, and other West European countries. Something bigger than Shield was needed to deal with the wider threat from the Soviet Union and its worldwide subversive network.

In the US, the KGB had been presented with the biggest windfall in its history of systematic aggression against what was still called 'the main enemy' or 'the main citadel of capitalism': the Watergate affair.

Let the KGB speak. A *Time* magazine cover story on the CIA on 5 February 1978 included the following passage:

> A Soviet KGB agent told a *Time* correspondent in Cairo last week: 'Of all the operations that the Soviet Union and the US have conducted against each other, none have benefited the KGB as much as the campaign in the US to discredit the CIA. In our wildest scenarios, we could never have anticipated such a plus for our side. It's the kind of gift all espionage men dream about. Today our boys have it a lot easier, and we didn't have to lift a finger. You did all our work for us.'

Had I spoken those words, I would doubtless have been charged with paranoia. Down to 'lift a finger', they have the ring of truth. The last sentence is a neat piece of deception. The windfall was genuine. However, having been presented with it, the KGB naturally exploited it for all it was worth, mobilising all its available skills and 'assets': meaning the fronts and agents of influence whose purpose was to advance the Communist cause by weakening America's will and capacity to resist.

The stark fact was that the entire security apparatus of the United States was in a state of near-collapse. A true anecdote illustrates the problem. One of my best sources, who had been a very senior Agency man in charge of counter-subversion in Western Europe, told me he was summoned to Langley by Admiral Stansfield Turner shortly after he took over as Director of Central Intelligence under President Jimmy Carter in 1977. Virtually in one breath, the Admiral had congratulated him on the 'superb' job he had done, and added: 'Therefore, I'm afraid you'll have to go.'

Taken aback, my friend asked for an explanation, which Turner gave readily. 'You see, you are an anti-Soviet specialist. We don't need anti-Soviet specialists any more.'

My friend was one of some 400 CIA Soviet experts fired by Turner: about 50 per cent of 820 personnel forced into early retirement at that time. In his account of this major pruning, Admiral Turner makes a convincing case for the view that the CIA was seriously overstaffed. But he has nothing to say about the virtual elimination of the Agency's analytical and operational capacity to deal with the Soviet problem.[1] This catastrophic decision completed the self-emasculation of American intelligence.

To be fair to Admiral Turner, the mass redundancies were strictly in line with President Carter's policies and reflected the post-Watergate situation.

The underlying argument was that the CIA's problems had been caused by HUMINT: Human Intelligence. The safest antidote was seen to be SIGINT: Signals Intelligence. The National Security Agency (NSA) offered SIGINT in abundance. Satellites did not talk to journalists or plot against the President. SIGINT did have one drawback, however. As Nicholas Elliott put it (doubtless quoting somebody else): 'The spy in the sky tells you how many missiles the Soviets have, but not what they intend to do with them.'

The question was whether something could be done in the private sector – not only in Britain, but in the United States and other countries of the Western Alliance. A few of us had been exchanging views, and decided that action was indeed possible. I took the initiative by convening a very small and very secret meeting in London. We met in the luxurious executive suite of a leading City of London bank on the morning of Sunday 13 February 1977. Our host, a leading figure in the bank, took the chair. Three of us were British, four were American, with one German. Ill health prevented a French associate from attending; Jean Violet was with us in spirit.

Apart from the banker and myself, the other Briton was Nicholas Elliott. The German was a very active member of the Bundestag, whose career had started in diplomacy. He had a very wide understanding of Soviet strategy, on which he wrote several first-rate books.

The Americans included two able and diligent Congressional staffers, and the Viennese-born representative of a big Belgian company. Also there was the remarkable General Vernon ('Dick') Walters, recently retired as Deputy Director of Central Intelligence, and later to re-emerge in public life as President Reagan's ambassador, first to the UN, and later to the German Federal Republic.

Dick Walters, like myself educated in France and England, was a formidable linguist, able to switch without accent into eight or nine languages. As such, he interpreted for several US Presidents. Ronald Reagan would send him on confidential missions all over the world.

I proposed the creation of a Private Sector Operational Intelligence agency, beholden to no government, but at the disposal of allied or friendly governments for certain tasks which, for one reason or another, they were no longer able to tackle. I must make it clear that *these tasks did not include any acts of armed force or physical coercion*.

Our main concerns would be:

- To provide reliable intelligence in areas which governments were barred from investigating, either through recent legislation (as in the US) or because political circumstances made such inquiries difficult or potentially embarrassing.

• To conduct secret counter-subversion operations in any country in which such actions were deemed feasible.

There were no dissenting voices, although there was much discussion about the areas for action: the 'requirements', in intelligence jargon.

It was agreed that no outsiders should be made aware of the existence of the organisation, except if, in the judgement of one of us, the person was deemed a suitable candidate for recruitment. In the interests of security, I proposed that the organisation should be nameless. Some months later, however, a distinguished Argentine associate of ours, a former Justice Minister (and anti-Peronist) named Jacques Perriaux, suggested to me that we should call ourselves 'The 61'. Why '61'? I asked. 'Because the Fourth International split,' he replied.

The reasoning was abstruse. There had been four Internationals, of which the third was Lenin's Comintern. The Fourth International was the Trotskyist one, and when it split, this meant that, on paper, there were five Internationals. In this numbers game, we would constitute the Sixth International, or '61'.

On this tenuous basis, the organisation was known, among its members, as 'The 61', and members or conscious contacts were known as 'numerical'.

One of the security problems we faced, and discussed that morning, was fund-raising. Nicholas Elliott and I undertook to find the money. The task was daunting, for how does one raise money for a secret agency without running the risk that some of the people approached would talk about it? In the event, however, we had no leaks from the business world.

Our initial estimate of financial needs was too high: not for the requirements, but for the realistic limits of generosity on the part of the necessarily small number of sources we approached. We agreed on a target figure of $5 million a year, which may sound a lot, but was trifling in the face of the enemy's enormous resources.

NOTES

1 Stansfield Turner, *Secrecy and
   Democracy* (Sidgwick & Jackson,
   London, 1985), pp. 196–8.

XI

Shield and beyond
(1976–82)

THE WORK of the Shield committee fell into two broad categories. One was strategic: it concerned the state of Britain's existing counter-subversion machinery, proposals for fundamental change, and contingency planning for a major crisis – a widespread paralysis caused by political strikes and riots – which Margaret Thatcher might well face when, as we trusted, the Conservative Party won the next general election.

The other category was tactical: to provide short, factual and accurate research papers on the Communist connections of Labour MPs and trades unionists in the increasingly critical industrial scene, especially in late 1978 and early 1979. This time of strife and sordid chaos came to be known as the 'winter of discontent' and was the undoing of the increasingly complacent Prime Minister, Jim Callaghan.

AT THAT TIME, we were not concerned, except tangentially, with the correct economic and social prescriptions for the chaotic legacy that awaited Margaret Thatcher when she came to power. Such issues were under constant discussion at the Centre for Policy Studies, which she and Keith Joseph had launched, on the advice of Alfred Sherman, a thoroughly reformed ex-Communist and a brilliant 'ideas man'.

Our self-imposed task was narrower but more fundamental: a question of survival in a nation in which the dominant role, increasingly, was played by extreme Left Labour MPs and constituency managers, and by trades unions whose long-term goal, whether consciously or not on behalf of the Soviet Union, was to transform Britain into another East Germany or Czechoslovakia. Without the will and a correctly motivated intelligence and security apparatus with appropriate legal powers, the subversives would win, if not now then next time round.

Between May 1977 and July 1979, Shield produced no fewer than fifteen strategic papers, recommending counter-action to meet the subversive challenge and defeat it. There were proposals for reorganising the intelligence and security services; on public order in the event of widespread and organised rioting; and three papers on contingency planning for a Conservative government, kept up to date with the deteriorating situation.

On 19 June 1977, I drafted 'A Strategy for Victory', which I defined as 'the total defeat of the country's enemies, eliminating all risks of their recovery in the foreseeable future'.

In this, as in the other Shield papers, our proposals were all either within the existing law, or subject to precise amendments through Parliament. Nor was our concern only with the challenge from the extreme Left, although this was by far the most dangerous. The public order paper, for example, condemned 'neo-Fascists such as the National Front'. The terms 'extreme Left' and 'extreme Right' are in any case misleading. Fascists and Communists have common origins and both are totalitarian (or totalist, as I prefer to call them). Norris McWhirter's favourite image was of a horseshoe, in which the two ends (Fascist and Communist) almost touched.

One of our primary aims was to examine the existing security machine, spot its weaknesses, and make proposals for improvement. Our first attempt, the major paper of May 1977 on subversion, had proposed the reorganisation of the intelligence and security services. We recognised that MI-6 (foreign intelligence) was basically in good shape, whereas MI-5 (security) was not.

We had pointed to one of the major causes of weakness within MI-5. In a directive of September 1952, quoted in Lord Denning's report on the Profumo affair in 1963, the Director-General of the Service is instructed (rightly, in principle) that the Service 'should be kept absolutely free of any political bias or influence' unless 'an important public interest bearing on the Defence of the Realm . . . is at stake'. In his comment, Lord Denning ruled out prying into any man's political opinions, 'except in so far as they are subversive, that they would contemplate *the overthrow of the government by unlawful means*' (my emphasis).

Personally, I admire Lord Denning, but in this instance his Lordship

had not really grasped the meaning of subversion. The ultimate sophisti-
cation of subversion is to take over the government, not by unlawful but
by *lawful* means. The takeover would be no less permanent.

In that initial paper, therefore, we had proposed an urgent redefinition
of the terms of reference of MI-5; along with fresh directives to both
Services enabling them not merely to report on subversion, but to go
over to the counter-offensive. For MI-6, too, the counter-offensive angle
was emphasised. For example, it wasn't enough to tell the government
what the Soviets and Cubans were up to in Angola and Mozambique: the
point was to find ways of getting them out. East European resistance to
Soviet hegemony should also be found, and internal disruption would
be fomented within the USSR; all this twelve years before the great
upheavals of 1989.

During this troubled period, Shield's 'tactical' papers came in profusion. One, dated April 1978, gave details of joint Labour–Communist
activity. Today it makes quaint reading. On 6 February, for instance,
Sydney Bidwell, MP, had written to the *Morning Star* to express support
for Communist policy to solve 'the crisis of capitalism'. True, that was a
decade before Mikhail Gorbachev and the collapse of Communism.

On 21 February, Ron Thomas, MP, and Eddie Loyden, MP, had jointly
written an article for the *Morning Star* pressing for trade union rights
for the armed services as 'an essential step toward the democratisation
of Britain's armed forces'. (Translation: to neutralise the armed forces in
the event of a pro-Communist takeover.)

The expansion of *Militant*, organ of the so-called Militant Tendency
within the Labour Party, to sixteen pages drew quotable congratulations
from Frank Allaun, Sydney Bidwell, Eric Heffer, Arthur Latham, Eddie
Loyden, and 'Tony' Benn.

In November that year, we identified forty-eight Labour Party prospective parliamentary candidates with extreme Left views and connections.
There is nothing wrong with the 'know thine enemy' principle.

In another paper, dated 26 February 1979, we gave details of various
Labour groups which had been campaigning for the overthrow of the
Shah of Iran. Now, with the Shah driven into exile, they welcomed the
advent of Ayatollah Khomeini but called for a 'genuine socialist revolution'
in Iran. True, the Ayatollah had not yet disillusioned his leftist admirers
with his death sentence on Salman Rushdie.

As the great industrial crisis deepened early in 1979, so our Shield
papers multiplied. By then, water supplies were being cut off, sewage

went untreated, ambulance workers and nurses were on strike, and refuse lay uncollected. Then came the lorry drivers' strike.

On 15 January a Shield paper traced the origins of the strike to Alex Kitson, General Secretary of the Scottish Commercial Motormen's Union. Kitson, a member of the Labour Party's National Executive Committee (NEC), was well known for his pro-Soviet sympathies, which had been given ample airing on Radio Moscow in December 1977.

On 17 January, a further paper analysed the potential consequences, which included the possible use of troops for essential services. Five days later, we issued a follow-up, pointing to the picketing by the National Union of Mineworkers, and the (Trotskyist) Socialist Workers' Party. In a further paper, on 29 January, Shield dwelt on the extremist influences within the National Union of Public Employees (NUPE) and COHSE (Confederation of Health Service Employees). Together, NUPE and COHSE catered for a mass underclass of the lowest-paid union members in Britain.

In a longer paper dated 12 February 1979, Shield looked at the strike policy of the Communist Party, and tentatively concluded that the aim might well be the defeat of the Callaghan government, to be replaced by a 'broad Left' coalition.

Outwardly unflapped by all this drama, Jim Callaghan returned in mid-January from a relaxing tropical summit in Guadeloupe to tell reporters that he could see no crisis. From the wings, Norman Tebbit, at that time establishing a reputation for straight speaking, said: 'He was puffing and posturing in the sunny Caribbean while Britain shuddered to a freezing, strike-bound halt.'

NOT ALL PROBLEMS came from the Left. Not all Conservatives automatically accepted Margaret Thatcher's views or her leadership. I was bothered, in particular, by the attitude of Peregrine Worsthorne, as expressed in his widely read column in the *Sunday Telegraph*. In July 1977, he was losing no opportunity to snipe at her. For instance, in the issue of 17 July, in a column entitled 'Fallacies of Freedom', he attacked her for her habit of speaking about freedom instead of attacking what he saw as the current 'lack of government', with the Labour Party still in power.

I had first met Perry in March 1956, at a seminar on Indochina at St Antony's College, Oxford. We were both founder members of the National Association for Freedom, and I could therefore assume a certain ideological solidarity with him. At that time, however, he still espoused a traditional form of Toryism. Mrs Thatcher's radical approach and forthright manner apparently jarred on him.

I had more time than usual on my hands; or should I say 'my feet'? I was recovering from an operation to my left foot, involving the severance of a ligament, and took advantage of my enforced leisure to write to Perry:

BC to Peregrine Worsthorne:
It seems to me that you are confusing two things: you talk about 'lack of government' when you should be talking about *bad government*. . . .

Mrs Thatcher is absolutely right to talk of 'setting the people free' in economic terms, and what she says is in no way incompatible with good government, that is with bringing inflation under control and protecting the international value of the pound; strengthening the police force; and strengthening our defences.

. . . I agree with you that there has been a spectacular decline in respect for authority over the past twenty-five years. The reason, in my view, lies mainly in the decreasing readiness to *govern*, that is to protect the people against crime, the nation against its enemies, and your money and mine. . . . What I am suggesting is that there is an instinctive and growing public contempt for those in power when they overtax those who put them there while allowing the value of money to dwindle; when they allow crime to get out of hand; when they permit trades unions to become more powerful than Parliament or the Law; and when they so reduce our defences that if, say, the Russians wanted to walk in there is precious little to stop them. . . .

Personally, I think that Margaret Thatcher offers the only real hope of returning to good government and bringing back freedom. It would be a pity if you were to continue to undermine her chances with the kind of arguments you used in yesterday's paper.

I hope you will forgive my frankness. I shouldn't be writing in this vein if I didn't think your views important.

Peregrine Worsthorne to BC, 26 July 1977:
I was delighted and chastened to receive your letter. . . .

The point of my article was to consider what should be the Conservative rhetoric in the present situation. My own view is that no good can come from encouraging the public to believe that a nineteenth-century attitude to freedom has much relevance to the current difficulties.

I suspect that in the early days of the next government, Mrs Thatcher will be compelled to behave in a way that will be strongly anti-libertarian, and because of this assumption, she is most ill-advised at this stage to emphasise so strongly her commitment to individual freedom.

These are difficult questions, and I would not wish to be dogmatic.

I sent this correspondence to Mrs Thatcher, who wrote to thank me. I cannot presume that my letter to Worsthorne influenced him, but he did become one of her staunchest supporters, throughout her eleven years at 10 Downing Street. Sir Peregrine Worsthorne, as he became, was knighted in the departing Prime Minister's resignation Honours List.

AS THE SITUATION worsened, the inner group of Shield (the 'givers') realised that reformed directives and terms of reference, however desirable, were not going to be enough. The inner group met frequently; the full committee only occasionally. We talked it through, and decided that what was needed was a new coordinating body, responsible directly to the Prime Minister, and with a clear mandate for counter-action. An analogy suggested itself, especially to the one among us – Harry Sporborg – who had served on it: the wartime Special Operations Executive.

The parallel was not exact, of course. Historical parallels rarely are. But there was enough substance in it to prompt the name of the new body we were proposing: the Counter-Subversion Executive (CSE). It was natural that we should entrust the drafting to Harry himself. The outcome was 'The Mechanism Paper', the third draft of which, dated 17 May 1978, was adopted for distribution. The function of the CSE was defined as 'not only to counter anti-British subversive activity both in the United Kingdom and in other parts of the world, by all clandestine means both offensive and defensive, but also actively to conduct a clandestine offensive against Soviet power'.

On the basis of Sporborg's text, the committee asked me to draft a further and more elaborate paper, the title of which was 'Tasks of the Counter-Subversion Executive (CSE)'. A final draft, dated 8 June 1978, was distributed to all members of Shield.

Some weeks later, the full Shield committee met in the boardroom of a City bank. Mrs Thatcher, keen and alert, presided. Hers was the 'receiving' side. On her left was Sir Keith Joseph who, I noted with interest, had brought with him a copy of my new book, *Strategy of Survival*. He had marked one or two passages on which he raised questions with me before the meeting began. On her right was Willie Whitelaw and, beyond him, Lord Carrington. We the 'givers' faced them across the table. On my left was Harry Sporborg. On my right were Nicholas Elliott and Sam Hall. Thus, Sam Hall was as far as he could be from Peter Carrington.

Perhaps this was as well, as the meeting degenerated into a slanging match between them. The third Old Etonian present, Elliott, tried a conciliatory role, without making much impact. Carrington's main objection was to our proposals for the location of the CSE. The problem was secrecy. Even a small group, such as we were proposing, would find it difficult to pass unnoticed, if only because of its potential power. The mandarins would sense the existence of an alien body.

The CSE paper had left the question open. I asked for reactions to its functioning in the margin of the Foreign Office, as IRD had done, but Carrington, who saw himself as Foreign Secretary in the forthcoming government, would have none of it. There was indeed little logic in handling subversion from a foreign affairs ministry, but then that was what IRD had done, successfully enough within its limits.

Mrs Thatcher intervened, to propose that the CSE should in effect be a small intelligence committee serving the Prime Minister, and accommodated either in the Cabinet Office in Whitehall, or at 10 Downing Street itself. But Carrington objected to this as well, and the meeting ended on a less than harmonious note.

Harry Sporborg saw some sense in Carrington's objections, and on 22 August he wrote a constructive letter to Stephen Hastings, with copies to Nicholas and me. His idea was that the CSE should simply be an ultra-secret appendage of MI-6, settling discreetly into a West End building already used by the Secret Intelligence Service, and moving the present occupants elsewhere, so that nobody would notice.

It was not until some time later that the truth gradually dawned on us. It was not the secrecy aspect that Carrington really objected to. That was just an excuse. He was against the idea itself. He did not *want* a Counter-Subversion Executive. The future Prime Minister did, and Whitelaw and Joseph went along with it. Carrington was against the whole thing. And it was his view that prevailed.

ON TUESDAY 8 May 1979, less than a week after Margaret Thatcher's first electoral triumph, I was chairing a small international meeting at the Churchill Hotel in Portman Square, when an unexpected call came. The caller was a senior member of the Joint Intelligence Committee and he

needed to see me urgently. It was 5 p.m., and he had tracked me down
after trying my office and home.

I adjourned the meeting for one hour from 6 p.m. and the man joined
me in the bar. We had been lunching together two or three times a
year. On one such occasion, I had started to tell him about the Shield
committee, and he had stopped me short: 'I'd rather not know, Brian, if
you don't mind,' he had said.

Now, as he pointed out, the situation had changed. He had been summoned to meet the new Prime Minister the following day, and he wanted
to know the whole story. Over a couple of whiskies apiece, I gave it to
him.

For us in the inner group of Shield, however, this was a time of
deepening frustration, turning to gloom. We met three times in May and
June, on the last occasion to consider a new 'strategic' paper prepared
for Shield that month by a senior officer of MI-5 who had just retired.
This was a penetrating dissection of the Security Service, and specifically
where it had gone wrong. The picture that emerged was of an
intellectually weakened organisation no longer prepared to take Marxist-
Leninist influences seriously. Too much time and resources were devoted
to the trailing of foreign spies (which, it was argued, could be left to the
police Special Branch) and too little to domestic subversion. This report
was intended for the (new) Prime Minister and was duly passed on to
her, though to little effect, if any.

There was indeed no sign of life, yet, from the new incumbent at No. 10.
And then, in the first week of July, a formal invitation came to each of
us: lunch at Chequers on Sunday 15 July.

It was my first visit to the Prime Minister's country residence. Denis
Thatcher greeted us and introduced us to their son Mark, then the lady
made her appearance. She could not have been warmer or more friendly.
We sat on the terrace, over pre-lunch drinks. It was a bright summer's
day and the roses were out, in profusion. Harry Sporborg, very formal,
addressed her as 'Prime Minister', and she corrected him with a smile.
'Margaret, please, to all of you,' she said, beaming.

Nothing of much substance was said. The message of the occasion,
unspoken but clear, was: 'Thanks, but no thanks.' Shield was dead.

THE FACT THAT Shield no longer existed did not mean that the
challenge of subversion had gone away. The London end of The 61 simply
took over Shield's work.

We infiltrated one mole apiece into the Militant Tendency, the most threatening of the Trotskyist groups, and into the Campaign for Nuclear Disarmament (CND). Both operations were successful.

Our man's secret report on Militant reached me in October 1979. It was precise, revealing and worrying. It went a good deal further than the Labour peer, Lord Underhill, had been able to go in the Underhill Report on Militant, which Harold Wilson, in his second incarnation as Prime Minister, had shelved rather than face the problem of taking action. The hidden core of Militant was a highly organised and disciplined Marxist-Leninist party calling itself the Revolutionary Socialist League. When Militant emerged, it claimed that the RSL had dissolved itself, but in fact it had gone underground, thus constituting a secret revolutionary party. This fact was not known to MI-5 at the time of the 1979 general election.

The effectiveness of RSL was out of all proportion to the membership, which at the time of our report had reached 1569. Each member contributed a basic £2 a week, thus raising an annual fund of more than £160,000. In fact, a few richer members contributed much larger sums, so that the annual income exceeded £230,000.

The RSL was headed by a National Committee with sixty-six full-time agents, operating in nineteen designated areas of the UK. The real leader was Peter Taaffe, editor of *Militant*; but the original inspiration came from Ted Grant, born in South Africa, who had settled in Britain in the 1930s. During World War II, he had advocated infiltration of the armed forces, notably of Montgomery's Eighth Army from 1942 on.

Re-reading the turgid theoretical texts of the RSL/Militant[1], one is tempted to laugh at its pretensions. Were these just 'fun' revolutionaries? Alas, no. In isolation, they were the stuff of satirical comedy. But they advocated 'entryism' into the Labour Party, and practised what they preached. Their programme forecast the failure of Mrs Thatcher's economic measures and an attempted U-turn in less than two years, whereupon Mrs Thatcher would be dropped. The right wing of the Labour Party was doomed, and the Tribunites, under Tony Benn, would take over. They, too, would fail, as their programme was essentially reformist. With trade union support, Labour would become a Marxist-Leninist instrument for the socialist revolution. One thing they had not counted on: Mrs Thatcher was made of sterner stuff than Edward Heath. As she said, 'the lady's not for turning'.

It was clearly important that the Prime Minister should see our mole's report. Nicholas Elliott and I discussed the matter, and we agreed that we should ask to see her. I rang 10 Downing Street and was put through to her. She immediately agreed to see us, but said it would have to be at Chequers, and she did not wish Willie or Keith or Peter, or even Stephen Hastings, to know.

I could see the point of not telling her Cabinet colleagues, Whitelaw, Joseph and Carrington. As for Stephen Hastings, though he had kept his seat, he was still a backbencher. I should have liked to have consulted him on this and other matters, but deferred to her wishes. He knew nothing, therefore, of the long series of meetings at Chequers.

She read the mole's report attentively and commented that MI-5 had not reported on similar lines. At our next meeting, however, she told us that the Security Service had caught up with us. But she did not say how.

Because the machinery of counter-subversion had not been revived, the problem was as intractable as ever. I had learned from a reliable source that Shield's proposal for a 'Counter-Subversion Executive' had in fact been submitted to the Cabinet Secretary and rejected. The grounds given were weakly bureaucratic: the cost of creating a new department; and (doubtless the decisive objection) the probability that the idea would run into determined opposition in Whitehall.

In a 'personal and secret' memorandum to the Prime Minister in October 1981, I recorded my awareness of the situation, which Mrs Thatcher had not mentioned during our visits. I went on to argue that the need had never been greater 'and is indeed growing in the face of international terrorism, the spread of extremist Communist groups (mainly of the so-called "Trotskyist" variety), the incipient threat from neo-Fascist groups, and the efforts of the Soviet Union to penetrate the media, and exploit pacifist, religious and environmentalist sentiment . . . to undermine NATO'.

In the light of Whitehall opposition, I proposed instead a 'minimal cost' alternative: the appointment of a Coordinator, whose job would be to ensure that the resources and expertise of the existing departments (the Security Service, the Secret Intelligence Service, the Ministry of Defence and the Information Department of the Foreign and Commonwealth Office) were used to the best effect.

I raised this proposal with Mrs Thatcher at our next Chequers meeting, on 2 January 1982. On 4 January, she summoned the Secretary to the Cabinet, Sir Robert Armstrong, and instructed him to discuss require-ments with his colleagues and report back. He did so, at leisure over the next few months.

At the end of July 1982, my understanding was that Sir Robert had recommended that she should appoint an 'Information Coordinator', whose function would be to coordinate the counter-subversive capacities of the relevant services, including the police Special Branch, in close liaison with our own organisation. I learned later, however, that my information was wrong. There was indeed an Intelligence Coordinator, but his role was simply to coordinate the intelligence from MI-5 and MI-6, for the benefit of the Joint Intelligence Committee. There was no formal provision for coordination with us, although the informal link continued.

I HAD LONG nursed the idea that, with the Labour Party apparently irremediably tainted, the solution to a subversive Opposition which might come back to power could only lie in the creation of a non-subversive alternative party of government. Nor was I alone in this manner of thinking.

British readers at least are familiar with the sad, sometimes farcical story of the Social Democratic Party (SDP), the personality clashes between David Owen and Roy Jenkins, the unhappy merger with the Liberals; in short, the collapse of what had seemed a promising realignment of British politics. And yet, the true story of its prehistory has not, until now, been told, although its rival leaders have given their versions of the story in lengthy memoirs that came out within weeks of one another in 1991, while this book was being written.[2]

In fact, the inspirers of the SDP were two young academics, and the idea matured through meetings in my office. The academics were Douglas Eden and Stephen Haseler, both of whom taught Politics at London polytechnics, Eden at the Middlesex and Haseler at the City of London.

I first met Douglas Eden at one of the early sessions of the National Association for Freedom, with Ross McWhirter in the chair. The NAF was supposed to be strictly non-party, and the presence of a long-time Labour man, as Eden was, emphasised this aspect of its work. Later, when the issue of freedom came to be more closely identified with Mrs Thatcher's leadership of the Conservative Party, the dividing line between the NAF and the Tories became blurred.

A strongly built man with large black eyes, Eden had a powerful analytical intellect. He was, to me, an interesting and rare example of assimilation. I had assumed that he was an Englishman, and specifically a Londoner, but he told me, a year or so after we met, that he was a New Yorker by birth and early upbringing. I had detected no transatlantic tones in his speech.

I already knew his close associate Stephen Haseler who, incidentally, had an American wife. The three of us met a number of times in my office, while I was running the ISC and later. The theme of our discussions was invariably the accelerating takeover of the Labour Party by the Marxist-Leninist Left. Haseler had written an important book on it in *The Death of British Democracy.*[3]

Eden and Haseler had already done something about the problem, as co-founders of the Social Democratic Alliance (SDA), which concentrated on political work at the municipal level; all three of us agreed that something bigger was needed: a Social Democratic *Party*. The objective was simpler to define than to accomplish, as we were all aware. It was to create and build up an alternative to the Labour Party, in the hope that the non-Marxist majority would transfer their allegiance to the new party, thus isolating the revolutionary Left and cutting it down in size. On my side, this was entirely a personal initiative. My CIA and SIS connections were irrelevant, and I did not mention them.

For my part, except for a short (six months) and regretted membership of the Liberal Party after its unexpected victory at Orpington in 1962, I had always and deliberately kept out of party involvements. My personal aim in 1962, as in the late 1970s, was to help to mould a party of the centre-Left that would act as a magnet both to the voters and to the disenchanted moderates in the Labour Party. I soon realised that the Liberals had no understanding of the real issues and were unlikely to learn. A Social Democratic Party in the late 1970s seemed more promising.

On a small scale, I was able to help the Social Democratic Alliance financially. At that time, the SDA had some 700 members, nearly all of them municipal councillors all over the United Kingdom. It was a good start, a hard core for the national party we envisaged. The rest was up to Eden and Haseler, who did the basic work of proselytising and organising.

A key question was the leadership. We all agreed that the most promising choice, in terms of political weight and experience, was Roy Jenkins, who at that time was in Brussels as Commissioner of the European Community. His term was due to expire in 1981. One Sunday, Douglas Eden came to my home to report that he and Haseler had gone to Brussels to talk to Jenkins, who had decided in favour of the proposed new party. At the end of February 1981, four Labour moderates – Jenkins, Shirley Williams, David Owen, and William Rodgers – met in Dr Owen's Docklands home and issued what became known as the Limehouse Declaration, announcing the creation of a Council for Social Democracy. They went on to form the SDP, and were duly expelled from the Labour Party. Our idea had borne fruit.

The prehistory I have recounted does not appear in either the Jenkins or the Owen memoirs. The fact that I was involved was of course not conveyed to them, as it would have been a premature kiss of death. However, it is surely surprising that neither man acknowledges a debt to Eden or Haseler. Roy Jenkins does not mention either of them; Owen does, fleetingly, but only to say that:

> ... The Social Democratic Alliance, led by Stephen Haseler and Douglas Eden, was on the point of being proscribed by the NEC [National Executive Committee of the Labour Party] and they were pressing Roy Jenkins to ally himself with them....[4]

This was hardly the point of the Eden/Haseler approach to Jenkins.

Apart from the personal differences between Owen and Jenkins, and the complications of the link with David Steel's Liberal Party, the deeper reason for the fiasco of the SDP experiment, in Eden's view and in mine (I did not discuss it with Haseler, who had gone to America for an academic stint), lay in Roy Jenkins's unwillingness to use the party for the purpose for which it had been created. His aim was not to split the Labour Party so much as to split the Tories, by attracting moderate, anti-Thatcher MPs. He comes close to saying as much in a passage about the Prime Minister's dismissal of various 'wets' from her government, listing as examples Norman St John-Stevas, Ian Gilmour, and Christopher Soames. He goes on:

> The question was whether this would lead to a significant break from the Conservative Party towards us. My view is that this was as near as it could be to happening on a small scale, and that, had the small break occurred, the instability of the atmosphere was such that it might have spread quite wide. However, the more significant fact is that it did not happen. We recruited a significant number of Tories in the country, some of whom had been active in local government or party organisation. But at Westminster we stopped at one MP. Christopher Brocklebank-Fowler, the member for North-West Norfolk, had joined us a few weeks before the launch of the party.

This was a silly idea, if only because moderate Conservatives do not necessarily think of themselves as Social Democrats. The point was to woo true social democrats away from the stranglehold of the Leninist extremists who had taken over major unions and were dictating Labour's programme. What was needed was a non-extremist, left-of-centre party to replace the corrupted party that would have horrified Clement Attlee, Hugh Gaitskell and Ernest Bevin.

There was another ideological blind spot. Shirley Williams thought of herself as a 'democratic socialist', and Owen seemed to equate that term with 'social democrat'. Neither seemed conscious of the contradiction at the heart of 'democratic socialism', for socialism, even if achieved by democratic means, is by its nature irreversible; as the doctrinaire socialists who drafted Labour's 1974 manifesto well knew. That manifesto called for 'a fundamental and irreversible shift in the balance of power and wealth in favour of working people and their families'. The key word, 'irreversible', is the ingredient that is incompatible with democracy. There is no such contradiction in the formula of 'social democracy'.

DURING THIS TROUBLED period, I decided, with the backing of the ISC Council, to tackle the fourth and in some ways the trickiest of the four major areas of subversion in the United Kingdom: television. We had already tackled the other three – industry, education, and the economic system – and stirred up the expected controversy with our Special Reports.

The point was not to produce a comprehensive study of the comparatively new subject of television, but to look at its role in the coverage of national and international news, with special reference to controversial aspects such as terrorism, the Cold War, and political strikes.

We stuck to our usual and proven formula: an expert study group, to include a knowledgeable rapporteur who would express his own views forcibly but in the context of a report accurately reflecting the views of the other participants. Clearly, this was not going to be easy. I would have to persuade certain key television 'personalities' to take part, in the knowledge that if they spoke out, they might well jeopardise their careers. In the event, this did prove a major problem, which indeed almost wrecked the whole project.

My first move, in May 1977, was to set up a study group. I discussed the idea with Brian Connell, a television professional whose views on subversion in the media had drawn fire on himself and indeed had, in effect, forced him out of his old job in London to a new post with Anglia Television in Norwich. He responded positively and accepted the fee of

£1000 I had offered, a substantial one at that time. To complete the hard core of professionals, I also invited Robin Day and Michael Charlton. Day (later Sir Robin) was at the height of his fame as a forceful interviewer, which would inspire the title of his 1989 memoirs, *Grand Inquisitor*. Years earlier, Robin Day had stirred considerable controversy with an article in *Encounter*, 'Troubled Thoughts of a Television Journalist', in which he had commented on the apparently unavoidable distortions of the medium.

Michael Charlton, like myself a long-time expatriate from Australia, went on to crown a distinguished career in radio and television with his book *The Price of Victory* (BBC, 1983), an important oral history of post-war diplomacy based on the author's interviews with key players, including Winston Churchill and the Belgian statesman Paul-Henri Spaak.

Other members of the study group included Sir Geoffrey Jackson, a former British ambassador in Uruguay, who had been kidnapped by the Tupamaros terrorists in 1971 and held in solitary confinement for eight months.

Charlton was the first to drop out. He attended the first meeting, then vanished without a parting word. Unfortunately, this was the only meeting I myself was able to attend, because of my fund-raising travels, and I had left the job of coordinating and organising the whole project to Iain Hamilton. The full conference was held on 21–23 April 1978, in the ideal setting of W. H. Smith's training centre at Milton Hill House, near Oxford. The participants were a roll-call of those inside the medium, or affected by it, or concerned with the consequences.

In the chair was Sir Edward Pickering, a former editor of the *Daily Express*, in his capacity as Vice-Chairman of the Press Council. A forthright yet conciliatory personality, he was the ideal choice. In addition to Connell and Day, the media professionals included Richard Francis, the BBC's Director of News and Current Affairs; Christopher Capron, editor of the BBC's current affairs programme 'Panorama'; and Colin Shaw, Director of Television in the Independent Television Authority.

Among those seriously affected by television coverage, we had Sir Robert Mark, lately retired as Commissioner of Metropolitan Police; Sir Kenneth Newman, at that time in the thick of terrorism as Chief Constable of the Royal Ulster Constabulary; and Colonel Colin Mitchell, who had commanded the Argyll and Sutherland Highlanders in Aden, and had been an MP from 1970 to 1974.

Our ISC Council was of course well represented at the expert level, with the two Thompsons, Sir Robert and Brigadier 'Sheriff'. Sir Robert Thompson, in particular, set the tone of the debate on the basis of his experience in Vietnam and as an adviser to the White House and the National Security Council, with the words: 'The Vietnam War was lost on the television screens of the United States.'

Ideological allies of ours were present, such as Norris McWhirter and Michael Ivens of Aims of Industry; but so were opponents, such as Anthony Howard, a former editor of the *New Statesman*, and Keith Kyle of Chatham House. There were non-media specialists as well, including the constitutional lawyer Professor Claire Palley, at that time 'Master' of Darwin College at the University of Kent; and Dr Anthony Flood, a consultant psychiatrist.

Not surprisingly, it was the most animated and one of the best conferences the ISC had hosted. The trouble began when it was all over and the Special Report came to be written. When Brian Connell's draft reached me, I read it several times and found it very disappointing. I wrote to Connell on 30 June 1978 to say so and explain why:

> ... it is a faithful account of what went on at the Conference, but this is of little or no interest to those who were not actually there – i.e. the public, the press and Parliament. My colleagues share my view that as it stands, it is hardly worth publishing.
>
> The real problem, as I see it, is that you haven't treated the subject in the way we had agreed. My own clear understanding was that you would write a paper representing essentially your own views, but in the light of, and benefiting from, the discussions in the study group and in the full conference. ...
>
> I am not sure what to do about it. I would be prepared, as a very last resort, to write the report myself. But I am very reluctant to do so, if only because it makes no sense to retain the services of a man of your experience and special knowledge and of Iain Hamilton as well, if in the end I have to do the job myself.

Understandably, my letter came as a shock to Connell, who replied on 3 July:

> I have received your belated bombshell ... with distinct dismay. ... My own participation as 'rapporteur' defines my function. I cannot suddenly become a committed polemicist. ... I really feel that I have pushed my participation in this operation to the limit of the position I can defend. I have spent 15 years as

an anti-Communist Trojan horse inside the television fortress. It is not and has not been a comfortable situation to maintain and I have had to fight off two determined efforts to get me extruded permanently from the ITV network.

I discussed the problem with Iain Hamilton. There seemed no way out other than writing the introductory chapter myself. I did, pulling no punches. One defect of television, to which various speakers had drawn attention, was its inevitable one-sided approach, especially on terrorism. We would be shown any high-handed behaviour by the British Army in Ulster, or the US Army in Vietnam; but no corresponding shots of IRA knee-cappings, or the bayoneting of pregnant women by the Vietcong.

Then there was the (morally worse) problem of a positive discrimination within the television establishment in favour of giving a disproportionate amount of screen time to the extreme Left. This was a particularly difficult question as the best way of demonstrating the truth of this assertion was to point out that virtually no time was allocated to the (Fascist) National Front, whereas Communists and their Trotskyist variant had considerable exposure. The problem about this easily demonstrable fact was that merely to point it out was to run the risk of such charges as 'right-wing extremist' or 'pro-Fascist'. *The point, however, was not to call for more time for Fascists, but less time for their moral equivalents on the Left.*

With the examples of Connell, Day and Charlton in mind, I wrote:

> To do the job properly [i.e., considering the problem of television coverage of conflict] the layman will have to call in the professionals. But they, on their side, have a problem that is peculiarly their own: their careers are in television, and they cannot entirely ignore the views of their colleagues (which may themselves be the targets of criticism), their place in the organisational hierarchy, or their own career prospects.

In this context, as I had already discovered, we were in a 'no-win' situation. Having written the introduction which I wished Brian Connell could have felt able to write, I sent it to members of the Council and of the study group for their comments. Robin Day, heavily involved in his own work, did not reply until the end of July, when he wrote to me, by hand and from his home. He requested that the study group should be referred to as the 'advisory study group'. He insisted on a separate note before my introduction, to include the following disclaimer:

In preparing for the conference the Institute was assisted by an advisory study group whose function was to advise on subjects for discussion and possible participants. Members of the advisory study group, it must be emphasised, have no responsibility for the contents of either Mr Crozier's introduction or Mr Connell's report.

More delays. We were now in the August holiday season, and material that had been sent to the printers had to be retrieved and edited. In the end, the project that had begun in the spring of 1977 did not reach fruition until November 1978. By then, the British public and press had other things to think about than the fairness or otherwise of television coverage: Labour's winter of discontent had started. Sad to say, but not by then unexpectedly, the Special Report, *Television and Conflict*, despite the famous names and the controversial theme, attracted little attention.

A relevant case was that of Bryan Magee, MP, who in no way could be described as an extremist.

Iain Hamilton and I had both thought that Magee should be invited to the conference. Since Hamilton and Magee were friends, Iain wrote to him. Replying on 15 February 1978, Magee said:

> ... since you're an old friend, I can tell you also that I'm leery of having anything – anything formally, politically – to do with your lot. Everything that comes from over there on the subject of social democracy in general and the Labour Party in particular is so inane that I've come to think of you (plural) as being some kind of political equivalent of Mary Whitehouse.

Iain was as puzzled as I was on reading these lines, and inclined to think that Magee must be mixing us up with something else. I therefore wrote to Magee a few days later, to say:

> The discrepancy between what we actually are and what you perceive us to be is so great that I hope you won't mind this attempt, in the friendliest possible spirit, to get things straight.

I suggested one of two possible explanations: that this was a case of mistaken identity; or that Magee was judging us not by what we are and do but by what others say we are. I pointed out that, because of our 'charitable' status, we had not published anything specifically on the Labour Party, apart from occasional passing references and footnotes. I went on:

There is another possibility – that you may be confusing this Institute with my own views as its Director. [Quoting from p. 167 of my forthcoming book, *Strategy of Survival*, of which Magee had received a copy:] 'My views are indistinguishable from those of the Social Democratic Alliance – a body founded by Gaitskellite members of the Labour Party. . . .' Indeed, I can't think of anything in the recent writings of disillusioned Social Democrats, such as Woodrow Wyatt, Paul Johnson or Reg Prentice, with which I would in any way disagree.

That 'did it', but not in the way Iain and I had hoped. Bryan Magee wrote back immediately. Quoting my reference to Wyatt, Johnson and Prentice, he went on:

If I were writing to Iain I would say I regard such views as bonkers. To a stranger, not wishing to offend, I say that these evince a radical and profound incomprehension of the Labour Movement and are in any case contradicted by manifest facts. Because of my personal concern for Reg [Prentice] I had some arguments with him about them before he left the Labour Party. Apart from some such personal concern, they seem to me beneath serious discussion.

By 1982, even Bryan Magee had grasped what was happening in the Labour Party. In his turn, he resigned from it and joined the Social Democratic Party.

NOTES

1 Notably *British Perspectives 1979*, a fifty-two-page report which reached us in draft form.
2 Roy Jenkins, *A Life at the Centre* (Macmillan, 1991), pp. 535 et seq; and David Owen, *A Time to Declare* (Michael Joseph, 1991), pp. 420 et seq.
3 Stephen Haseler, *The Death of British Democracy* (Elek, London, 1976). Similar diagnoses were made almost simultaneously by Robert Moss, in *The Collapse of Democracy* (Temple Smith, London, 1975), and Woodrow Wyatt, in *What's Left of the Labour Party?* (Sidgwick & Jackson, London, 1977).
4 David Owen, op. cit., p. 471.

XII

Trial run (1977–80)

OUR SECRET OPERATIONAL organisation, The 61, was involved in various danger-spots in the late 1970s, notably in South America and Iran. It was a kind of trial period: the issues were worthy, I believe, but the results mostly negative.

In all three countries of the *Cono Sur* (Southern Cone) – Argentina, Uruguay, and Chile – the military had taken over after major outbreaks of terrorism. Argentina, in particular, had been in the grip of the worst terrorist threat of the twentieth century. In all three countries, the military overreacted in the cruel Hispanic tradition with unpardonable brutalities and abuses of human rights. Understandably, these abuses were denounced in the UN, in our elected assemblies, and by human rights organisations, such as Amnesty International. In London and Paris, in Washington and New York, there were demonstrations against the juntas, but none for the victims of terrorism. Frustrated by the turn of events, the Soviet Union had deployed its vast propaganda apparatus. Vietnam had ceased to be an issue, with the victory of the Communist side. Another issue was needed, and the *Cono Sur* provided it.

The Western media's reporting of these situations was, in my view, seriously one-sided. This was particularly true of television. Rightly, the abuses committed by the juntas were covered. But the situation that had caused them to intervene sometimes went unmentioned, as did the role of the Soviet Union and its Cuban satellite.

A parallel suggests itself. To condemn military abuses of human rights (real though they were), without matching concern for the many victims of terrorism, is like condemning the RAF's obliteration of Dresden without mentioning the Nazi Blitz on London or the bombing of Coventry.

In all three countries, my main concern, when addressing the armed forces or advising the security services, was to advocate the use of some of the non-violent, psychological techniques with which we had been experimenting in Europe. Cautiously, in Argentina, I criticised the arbitrary actions (*arbitrariedades*) of the military. In Chile, I spent several days closeted with the dictator, General Augusto Pinochet, for whom I had drafted (in Spanish) fifteen clauses for a new Constitution. Fourteen of them were in the final document.

IRAN WAS OF increasing concern to The 61. The Imperial Throne was under siege from an alliance against nature between Shi'ite fundamentalists and Marxists. Apart from unsubtle repression by the Iranian secret service, the SAVAK, and by the armed forces, little was being done to break the unholy alliance. SAVAK was unversed in the arts of psychological action. From his exile in neighbouring Iraq, the Ayatollah Khomeini, a fundamentalist zealot, sent inflammatory messages, many on cassette, which brought vast and excited crowds into the streets.

Jean Violet was particularly insistent that I should go to Tehran and talk to the Shah. General Douglas Brown, a robust, outspoken man who managed the Dulverton Trust in London, alerted a well-placed friend in Tehran. The unexpected intermediary was General Alan Fraser, at that time South Africa's Consul-General in Iran. The only non-Afrikaner to have held the post of Chief of Staff of the South African Army, Fraser was a personal friend of the Shah.

A tall man with a white military moustache, Fraser met me at the airport and drove me to the Hilton Hotel. Next morning, at exactly 11 o'clock, the appointed time, we were ushered into the Shah's study in his summer palace. Having introduced us, Fraser then merely listened to our conversation.

I was impressed by Reza Pahlavi's courtesy, intelligence, and readiness to listen. However, I detected in him a marked reluctance to believe some of the things I was telling him. This was understandable. He was surrounded by court sycophants and susceptible to the blandishments of Western ambassadors.

I recalled the successful joint operation by SIS and the CIA in 1953, which had put him back on his throne after his brief exile in Rome. There could be no repetition of this happy ending, I told him. The CIA had virtually collapsed and its operational capacity had been reduced to zero. And there was no prospect that the British would act alone.

He was clearly sceptical. He had been seeing a lot of the American ambassador, William Sullivan. Despite the ambassador's persistent warnings about the Carter Administration's concern over human rights in Iran, these conversations had convinced the Shah that somewhere, out of sight, the Central Intelligence Agency was being rebuilt. 'They will not let me fall,' he said.

He did not mention the British ambassador, Sir Anthony Parsons, who has since admitted that he was taken by surprise by the Shah's over-throw.[1]

'I am sorry, Your Imperial Majesty,' I declared, respectful of protocol, 'but please believe me: the CIA is now totally impotent. There is no chance at all that you will be defended if events are allowed to get out of hand.'

SHORTLY AFTER my visit to Tehran, I spent, through my Pittsburgh friend Dan McMichael, an hour or so with Prince Turki bin Feisal, of the Saudi royal family. I briefed him about The 61 and about my conversation with the Shah. He invited me to come to Riyadh, suggesting a date later in May. On the 24th, I wrote to him, suggesting that a date in June or July might be more suitable. He did not reply, and I did not make the journey. However, I learned later that he had played a part in subsequent events.

As the fundamentalist agitation mounted in Iran, the Shah may have thought that perhaps, after all, the shadowy organisation I had told him about might be useful. He sent an emissary to Riyadh, where Prince Turki (I learned later) spoke favourably of us.

Other influences also came into play. On 4 July 1978, the Chief of Britain's Defence Staff, Marshal of the Royal Air Force Sir Neil Cameron, wrote this note to me:

> I left your splendid book with the Chief of the Defence Staff of Iran when I was visiting there last week, and no doubt it will find its way into the hands of the Shah, with whom I had an audience. I found your book absolutely first class and do congratulate you on it.

I had met Cameron when addressing the Royal College of Defence Studies. The 'splendid book' he referred to was *Strategy of Survival*, which had appeared in March that year and attracted a good deal of attention.[2] In fact, I had presented a copy to the Shah on taking my leave of him with Alan Fraser. I dare say the Chief of the Iranian Defence Staff did as he was bidden and it is possible that the Shah, on receiving a second copy, may have dipped into it.

A more likely influence was that of Alan Fraser who, on 27 July, had written me a long and disturbing letter. He had raised with the Shah the question of financial assistance for our group, in return for our advice and expertise on combating the wave of subversion that threatened to sweep him off his throne. He said:

> The object of this letter is to tell you why I think it important that someone like Sir Robert Thompson should come out to assess the Iranian scene. Such an assessment coupled with what I have to say may point to a need for you to review the priorities for action outlined in your book. I believe that to bolster the Shah is becoming an urgent need.
>
> The riots throughout Iran over the last few months have been serious – and there was another nasty one in Mashad two days ago. . . . Mashad, as you know, is the holy of holies and the riot, coming as it did close to the end of the month of Ramazan [Farsi version of the Arabic Ramadan] – when Mashad's population swells from its normal 1 million inhabitants to upwards of 2.5 million of devout, fanatic, self-flagellating and fasting pilgrims – could mean that more trouble is imminent.

A month later, through the Iranian embassy, the Shah invited me to return, this time with a team of advisers. Violet hired a Mirage executive jet for our journey, although his ill health prevented him from joining us. With me on the flight from Heathrow on 3 September were Sir Robert Thompson (as Fraser had requested) and Nicholas Elliott. We made a brief landing at a small airport near Clermont in central France, to pick up our friend Antoine Pinay, who had known the Shah for many years, and whose presence would add authority to our little team. We flew low over the stark landscapes of Turkey and Iran, and on landing were taken immediately to the summer palace.

This time, the Shah gave us two and a half hours of imperial time. We were all struck by his curious apathy. The only reaction was an occasional raising of an eyebrow and widening of the eyes. Was it because he was still in deep shock as the result of the recent terrorist incident at Abadan when 430 people had suffocated or been burnt to death in the Rex cinema? This was our tentative surmise. We had no idea at that time that the man we were briefing was dying of cancer.

That evening was reserved for a working dinner with General Oveissi, Commander of the Tehran garrison, and two of the top officials of SAVAK, General Motazed and the head of the research department, a man named Kaveh. Some weeks earlier, in a vain attempt to defuse the situation, the Shah had sacked the chief of SAVAK, General Nassiri, and sent him to Pakistan as ambassador. Oveissi did not come, however: he had more important matters to attend to, namely the mounting street disorders.

I had brought with me some tentative drafts for leaflets designed to sow discord between the Shi'ite fundamentalists and the Communist Tudeh ('Masses') Party, by drawing attention to the persecution of Muslims in the Islamic republics of the Soviet Union, including Azerbaijan along the Iranian frontier. The SAVAK people promised to study the drafts, and listened respectfully while Sir Robert Thompson talked of his counter-insurgency experience in Malaya and Vietnam.

The following day, the caretaker Prime Minister, Jaafar Sharif-Emami, offered his resignation, which was refused. Four days later – by which time we were safely back in England – martial law was proclaimed after 2000 people had been killed in clashes between the rioters and the forces of order.

Seven weeks later, an urgent message came from Tehran. Very late in the day, it seemed, our mission had been successful. The Shah had now decided that he needed our services. By then, however, the situation was getting out of hand. The Ayatollah Khomeini, having settled at Neauphle-le-Château, outside Paris, by courtesy of President Giscard d'Estaing, was sending ever more inflammatory messages to the religious masses in Iran. His words, relayed by the BBC's Farsi service, were whipping up an uncontrollable wave of anti-Shah hysteria.[3]

In November 1978, the Shah sent the top civilian in the SAVAK hierarchy to London to see me. I arranged for him to be closeted with Robert Moss for a whole week. He had brought a pile of secret reports in Farsi, which he translated for us, and other documentary evidence of Soviet involvement with the Shah's enemies. This included copies of *Navid*, a well-produced publication believed to be printed on modern presses in the Soviet embassy. *Navid* carried forged 'Army declarations' against the Shah, and articles calling for a Muslim-Marxist revolutionary front.[4]

The outcome was a *Conflict Study* dated November 1978, 'The Campaign to Destabilise Iran', by Robert Moss. Shortly after the study had appeared, the Iranian chargé d'affaires informed me that the Shah had authorised a first annual payment of £1 million to The 61 for a psychological action operation on the lines we had suggested to him.

The welcome news came too late: the Shah was driven into exile before he could make the first payment.

By then, in any case, Iran was a lost cause. We might, I believe, have been able to help if the Shah had responded to our proposal in May. By September, it was probably too late. By November, it was a hopeless case. For one thing, the chances of American intervention were nil. Jimmy Carter's policies had played a major role in unseating the Shah.[5] The attempt by an American task force to rescue the fifty-three hostages from the US embassy in Tehran in April 1980 might have changed the outlook for the better, had it succeeded. But it ended in fiasco when a helicopter of the assault force collided with a tanker aircraft on the ground in the Iranian desert. If anything, the spectacular success of the British SAS assault on the terrorist-held Iranian embassy in London in May depressed American morale still further. Whatever happened, from then on the US was going to be passive.

Despite these discouraging circumstances, my colleagues and I felt that there remained at least a fighting chance of a coup to overthrow Ayatollah Khomeini's fledgling regime. The outbreak of the Iraq–Iran War encouraged this view.

Much seemed to depend on the longevity of the Ayatollah, who was seventy-nine when the Shah fell in mid-January 1979. From a Western point of view, the advent of an Islamic fundamentalist regime in what had been a friendly country was, in any case, highly unwelcome.

I discussed the matter with an Iranian businessman long established in Britain, and he suggested that I should go to Cairo for an exploratory talk with the Shah's widow, Farah Diba. After a spell in Morocco, the Shah and the ex-Empress had accepted President Anwar Sadat's offer of hospitality. He had put a palace at their disposal.

Between the ex-Shah's death in Cairo's Maadi military hospital on 27 July 1980 and the following November, I made three trips to Egypt. Farah Diba proved to be as beautiful as the media had portrayed her, but emaciated, doubtless as a result of the stresses of the past year. She carried herself with dignity. At her request we spoke in French. After an hour or so, she called in her son, the Crown Prince, who made a good impression on me. She had understandably mixed feelings about the Gulf war between Iraq and Iran, which had broken out a few weeks earlier. Saddam

Hussein had started it by his unprovoked invasion of Iran. She hated the regime of the mullahs, but the patriotic strain in her did not want Iraq to win. The long and bloody war ended in stalemate in August 1988.

Farah Diba had offered to arrange a meeting with President Sadat, and did so. I saw him at his Cairo residence on 10 November 1980. The President was dressed in khaki army fatigues, without insignia of rank. His manner was simple and unpretentious.

I was aware of Sadat's extremist past, including his one-time Nazi connections, his phase of terrorism, and his subservience to Nasser. Nevertheless, I admired the man, not least for his courage in going to Jerusalem to see the Israeli ex-terrorist and Prime Minister, Menachem Begin. The Camp David Agreements, although open to criticism, stood as President Jimmy Carter's only achievement of substance in foreign affairs. But the key role had been Sadat's. He restored Egypt's shattered national prestige by standing up to the formidable Israeli armed forces in 1973. Having done so, he held out the hand of peace in defiance of his own and other Arab fanatics. The man I met was sober and reasonable, youthful follies far behind. He had none of the paranoid charisma of Nasser.

Much of our talk was a monologue from Sadat. Understandably, he was pleased with the peace process with Israel he had initiated in November 1977: 'There will be no more wars between our two countries. The peace process is irreversible, but Jerusalem and the issue of autonomy cannot be left out of it. Begin still holds the ideas that he brought with him when he came over from Poland forty years ago. . . .

'My view is that we are going to have to wait for [King] Hussein. In the end, the Palestinians themselves have a veto. The key to Hussein is Saudi Arabia, and Iraq: that is why he took the Iraqi side in the present fighting.'

We had agreed that our talk was strictly 'off the record' (and it has remained so until now, a decade after his death). He went on in the same outspoken vein.

'Gaddafi is a mental case. Initially, he stayed with me here in Cairo, I regarded him as a son. Now, nobody can predict what he will do next. Why did he have to buy 3000 tanks?

'Some years ago, when I estimated the value of his arms deal with Russia at $12 billion, my estimate was scorned in London and in Washington, but I have been proved right. The point was that there was a down-payment of $800 million, so it was fairly easy to work out the total.'

On the Iraq–Iran War: 'I knew in advance of Saddam Hussein's intention to attack Iran. He went to Saudi Arabia to seek the advice of King Khaled, who gave him the green light. Khaled told the Americans, who also gave Saddam Hussein the green light. But the Americans did not bother to tell me. I found these things out through my intelligence service system.

'I am not a conceited man, but I believe I am capable of calculating the political consequences accurately, and I was certain from the start that the Iraqis would fail.'

On Iran: 'The Shah should never have left Iran. The Iraq war has proved that Khomeini has deprived the country of its security, represented by the Shah's armies. While the Shah was there, he and his armed forces kept Iraq away from Iran's borders.

'After the war it will be seen that the Khomeini regime is obsolete.'

Sadat's most startling comments were about the Romanian despot, Ceausescu. 'My friendship with him goes back to contacts under Nasser. When I was elected in 1970, he invited me to stay with him. He suggested a reconciliation with Israel. Begin was to visit him, and I welcomed the idea. However, I did not tell him what my precise plans were, because I was not yet ready. I went from Romania to Tehran, and on the journey I worked out the details. But again, I did not tell either the Shah or King Khaled whom I also visited.

'There were two questions in my mind:

'One: is Begin genuinely in favour of peace?

'Two: is he strong enough to face the Knesset and the nation?

'I thought him conceited and arrogant. It would have been easier with Ben Gurion, or with the old lady [Golda Meir]. But I didn't know Begin. Later, Ceausescu had six hours with Begin. After that, he told me that he could answer me and that Begin was genuinely in favour of peace, and strong enough to carry it through.'

On relations with Saudi Arabia: 'The Saudis tried to choke Egypt and bring her to her knees. It was up to them to open diplomatic relations. I am in no hurry. I have a philosophy: if my enemy tries to hurt me, he hurts himself. I was not hurt, but I cannot forgive them for hurting Egypt. Let us resume our big Arab family.'

Earlier in our talk, Sadat had praised President Carter for his work in achieving the peace treaty with Israel. His parting remark to me was all the sharper. 'The US is the richest and greatest power in the world. How could it take the initiative to let the Shah fall?' How indeed?

On my return to London, I sent a 'secret' report on my meeting with Sadat to Mrs Thatcher and President Reagan.

* * *

IN FOREIGN POLICY, apart from the Camp David accords between Sadat and Begin, the performance of the Carter Administration was disastrous. Although the Soviet-Cuban axis had been defeated in southern Latin America, Nicaragua and Grenada came into the Soviet peripheral empire in 1979. The admittedly unsavoury Somoza dictatorship was brought down by the Marxist-Leninist Sandinista Front, under Cuban control.

A CIA report, sent to me by a senior member of The 61 in the Pentagon, gave detailed evidence that the Sandinistas' final offensive had been planned in detail by the Cuban General Staff. In overall charge was the Cuban General Zenen Casals, whose battle experience had included a spell in Cuba's semi-colony, Angola. The arms, from the Soviet Union, had been delivered by Fidel Castro.

This evidence was of course available to President Carter, but he decided not to publish it. I passed it on to Robert Moss, who used it in his column in the *Daily Telegraph* (6 August 1980).

The CIA report, dated 2 May, was classified 'SECRET: No Foreign Dissemination'. It described Cuban plans to use Nicaragua as the model for similar revolutionary uprisings in Guatemala, El Salvador, and other Central American countries. Early in 1980, Nicaragua's new regime sent a secret delegation to Moscow, where close inter-party links were established between the *Frente Sandinista* and the ruling CPSU.

After Grenada came into the Cuban/Soviet orbit through a coup in March 1979, it was rapidly turned into a base for operations elsewhere in Latin America. A similar coup also took place that year in the Seychelles in the Indian Ocean. The Soviet empire was growing fast.

NOTES

1 Anthony Parsons, *The Pride and the Fall: Iran 1974–1979* (Jonathan Cape, London, 1984). In the spring of 1978 he wrote: '. . . I still did not believe that there was a serious risk of the Shah being overthrown' (p. 67). In late September: 'I was still confident that the armed forces would do their duty. . . .' (p. 77). Nor was the Foreign Office alone in not anticipating the Shah's fate. The US government was equally unprepared. Oliver North, the National Security man involved in the 'Iran-Contra' affair in the 1980s, reported in his book *Under Fire: An American Story* (HarperCollins, 1991) that the running down of the CIA's agents under President Carter had left the US government unwarned about this and other vital matters, so that '. . . we were shocked when the Shah was overthrown and our embassy was captured' (p. 48). (See Ch. XIV for a further discussion of the North affair; the collapse of the CIA is discussed in Ch. X and elsewhere. It remains surprising that the US, especially, had no idea that the Shah's rule was under urgent threat whereas our fledgling 61 knew what was happening.)

2 *Strategy of Survival* elaborated on a theme discussed in a special issue of *Conflict Studies*, 'Security and the Myth of "Peace": Surviving the Third World War' (ISC, October 1976). The book, addressed to a wide audience, was a short history and analysis of Soviet expansionism. On 14 March 1978, a Conservative MP whom I had not met, Victor Goodhew, stood up in a House of Commons defence debate and called on the Secretary of State to present every member of the Cabinet with a copy. It went into a number of languages (including Japanese) and became an international bestseller.

3 In subsequent exchanges with me, the BBC strongly denied that it had played any such role, but those at the listening end were emphatic that the declamatory tone adopted by the BBC's Farsi speakers when merely reading the Ayatollah's daily 'bulletins' had greatly contributed to the impact of his revolutionary propaganda.

4 The Soviet defector Vladimir Kuzichkin, who was stationed in Tehran during the Iranian revolution, plays down the KGB's role in his book, *Inside the KGB* (André Deutsch, 1990). For example, he does not mention *Navid*, and gives the impression that the KGB was almost passive during this period. Personally, I still accept the authenticity of the evidence made available to us at the time.

5 See Michael A. Ledeen and William H. Lewis, 'Carter and the Fall of the Shah: the Inside Story' in the *Washington Quarterly*, Spring 1980.

XIII

'Palace coup'
(1979)

BOARDROOM REVOLTS adorn the business pages of the press nearly every week; palace coups are less numerous, if only because there are fewer States than companies. What happened to me in 1979, however, was closer to a palace coup than to a boardroom plot.

In the late spring of 1979, I became aware of a kind of unease at the Institute. It was hard to define, like one of those baffling toys with a pattern that changes when you move it. Two members of the Council of the Institute were dropping seemingly contradictory hints. On the one hand, they were saying, the Institute was too closely identified with me. Most people called it 'Brian Crozier's Institute', not the Institute for the Study of Conflict. On the other hand, I was not devoting enough of my time to running the ISC. I was travelling too much, giving too many lectures, writing too many articles and books. At times, they were saying, the ISC seemed rudderless.

It is hard to please all the people all the time. My lectures did not bring me much money, but they did keep the Institute in the public eye. The main point of my travels was to raise funds. Prestige produced money, and more and more of it was needed, both because the Institute was expanding and because inflation eroded scarce reserves.

These were my counter-arguments, but they made little impression. The true reasons had to be different. The pattern changed: I was a political activist, and the attacks on me in the press and on the ISC in Parliament were beginning to worry some people. I found this surprising, as the Council had remained solidly loyal when the Great Smear Campaign was at its height in 1975 and 1976. Since my full page in the *Guardian* (see Ch. IX), the smearers had been much quieter.

Who were these worriers? The most vocal of them was Vice-Admiral Sir Louis Le Bailly. A delightful man, Lou Le Bailly had been Director-General of Intelligence at the Ministry of Defence from 1972 to 1975. I had known him during this period and had invited him to join the Council on his retirement. He sat on the shadowy board which interviewed candidates for the Security Service. Each time the board met, he said Sir Michael Hanley had made his standard remark: 'The trouble with Brian is that you never know what he's up to.' I had always treated this oft-repeated comment as a mildly flattering little joke. I should have known better.

The other worrier was Professor Leonard Schapiro, my co-founder in the sense that he had gone along with my ideas in 1970. Unlike the voluble Lou, Leonard was monosyllabic and impenetrably taciturn. It was difficult to know whether he was dropping a hint or merely conveying somebody else's misgivings.

Partly for security reasons, partly because I did not want to involve the ISC Council in my extra-curricular activities, I had not taken any member of it into my confidence about the creation of The 61. I can only assume some indiscretion within Whitehall, presumably from one of the few officers of SIS who were aware of it: Lou and Leonard both had intelligence contacts. So did Professor Hugh Seton-Watson, but he had never dropped hints. There was, of course, a highly visible side of my political activism, and it was on this that the hints were focusing. The message, never spelt out, seemed to be: 'Was it right that I should be expressing my views so forcibly and in so many places, about the Soviet Union and about subversion?'

To my mind, there was no incompatibility. It was because my views were well known that I attracted the necessary funds for the more sober activities and publications of the ISC.

The crisis began in obscurity and ended in mystery. About seven years elapsed before I pieced together the curious details.

On the first day of August 1979, Lou asked to see me. He seemed less relaxed than usual. He told me he had just come back from Pittsburgh, where he had been 'summoned' to see Dan McMichael, the administrator of the Scaife Family Charitable Trusts, major financial contributors to the Institute. The reason for the invitation, he said, was to discuss the problems of the ISC. This seemed odd. Although Lou Le Bailly had been one of the most energetic and enthusiastic of our Council members, he had never been involved on the fund-raising side. His message to me was of paralysing obscurity. Our American supporters, it seemed, had developed misgivings about my 'other' activities. Were they not increasingly incompatible with my role as Director of the Institute?

I could see no incompatibility, and said so. I had always been scrupulously careful to avoid involving the ISC in any party political activity, which would indeed have been incompatible with its 'charitable', tax-exempt status, under both US and UK law. True, the Institute had drawn attention to the penetration of the Labour Party, but in a strictly factual and analytical manner. As for my extra-curricular activities, to the extent that they were public, they were directly linked to successful fund-raising. I had never mentioned The 61 to our friends in Pittsburgh, or even, at that stage, to the CIA friends I still saw informally . . .

So obscure, indeed tortuous, was the message from America that I spent most of the following Sunday writing a lengthy memorandum *to myself* in a vain search for the cryptic code. Having failed, I joined my wife Lila in Shoreham for the annual mixture of swimming and writing.

The blow fell on the Monday after our return four weeks later. This time, it was Leonard Schapiro who wanted to see me in my office, urgently. There, his craggy face as expressionless as ever, he said: 'I'm afraid Lou wants to resign.'

Without another word, he handed me Le Bailly's letter of resignation. I read it in bewilderment, but before handing it back I had a copy made. I am glad I did, as it is one of the strangest items in my collected papers.

It was dated 30 August 1979. For a letter of resignation, it was long-winded. Indeed, it had an epic quality, more suitable to an Homeric poem than to a declaration of intent. The key passages were these:

> It is not given to many of us to have Brian Crozier's facility with the pen or to have a book held up in Parliament with the advice that all MPs and every member of Parliament should read it . . .
>
> This of course is only a small instance of the debt we all, and many others outside the Institute, owe to our Director. But sadly, it is his immense and accelerating activity outside the strict duties of Director which cause me such deep anxiety for the future of the Institute itself.
>
> It has been said that 'no man can serve two masters'. It is also difficult for most men to ride two horses. I have come to the belief that, with the most

sincere and in many ways highly commendable motives, our Director is attempting the difficult and dangerous feat of doing both.

This great Institute which, with you, he bore and bred and which ... he has done so much to sustain is a charitable Trust with a Council of Management. And the Council of Management being responsible for the activities of the Director must, in this sense, be his 'Master'.

But Brian's other 'Master' is his own brave spirit, and in this role he is waging a personal crusade (for it is no less) against the forces of evil emanating largely from Russia, which are increasingly assaulting our society and our way of life. Inevitably, in this crusade, he deploys his own views (with many of which many of us would probably agree), but some of which, by their nature, are inimical to the objectivity of the Institute. ...

But the Institute only has one Director. And such is the force and power of his personality that while this crusade convinces many it also repels many; and some of these are men of great good will, patriotism and influence. All of this, in practice, means that to some, the writings and sayings of Brian Crozier are regarded as synonymous with the views of the Institute thus detracting from the credibility the Council, through its Director, seeks to establish amongst the very people who need to be educated and persuaded towards his views.

There followed a number of examples and anecdotes. Then:

I hope profoundly, for the sake of this Institute, that the Director will find it in him to abandon his crusade and concentrate on the Institute. ... If, happily, he should choose this course, I would still leave my resignation in your hands because I recognise that for all his friendliness to me in the past, the Director, after reading this letter, may well find it personally more agreeable to serve a Council of which I was no longer a part.

Should Brian ... pursue his crusade independently, then of course I would be content to stay on if you so wished.

Lou's letter did at least spell out possible reasons for his trip to Pittsburgh, but there were puzzling aspects to it. Why now? Why the urgency? I had already let it be known that I was planning to resign, although for sentimental reasons I wanted to delay my departure until June 1980, when I would have completed ten years' service. This would give me ample time to find a qualified successor.

On reflection, I could see that my high profile, as it had become, might indeed embarrass some members of the Council, although to my knowledge only the two hint-droppers had thought to complain about it. In fact, as I learned later, this was not the reason for Lou Le Bailly's initiative.

Having shown me Lou's letter, Leonard left me to think the matter over. That evening I telephoned him to say that, valuable though the Admiral was, I thought his departure would do less harm to the Institute than my own. To pursue Lou's own argument, those I 'convinced' provided funds for the Institute; would those I 'repelled' be equally generous if I stepped down?

Leonard's reply chilled me. Calmly, he said: 'Brian, I am bound to say that if Lou goes, so do I,' and he went on without raising his voice: 'Moreover, I think you will find that most other Council members will go too.'

Only then did I understand that I had a real crisis on my hands. When I pressed him for an explanation, Schapiro suggested that I should drop in for a chat at his Maida Vale flat on the coming Sunday.

I brought Michael Goodwin along. When we arrived, Lou was already there. Leonard had further shocks in store. The first was the revelation that Lou's resignation had not been spontaneous. Indeed, said the Professor, 'it was I who put him up to it'.

More bewildered than ever, I asked him what was the point of that?

'It seemed the easiest way of bringing the matter to a head,' he said.

'What matter?' I asked.

'It would be a terrible scandal if your other activities came into the open,' he replied. 'Especially for our academic members. An awful scandal. Their careers might be ruined.'

I pointed out that we had already been through a *real* scandal, with the Great Smear Campaign against me. Yet nobody on the Council had thought it necessary to resign, even though the campaign had dragged on for two or three years. If this real scandal had not upset our friends and colleagues, what was the point of getting worked up about a hypothetical 'scandal'? But Schapiro, nodding his head gravely, simply muttered: 'A terrible scandal. We simply can't expose our Council to this kind of thing.'

Without any further explanation, he spelt out an ultimatum. The full Council was due to meet on Wednesday, 12 September – three days later. Either I would agree to drop my political activities, in which case Schapiro hoped, as everybody else did, that I would stay on as Director. Or, if I insisted on carrying on, he would expect me to present my formal resignation to the Council.

I protested that my precipitate departure would demoralise the staff; that the Institute would soon be short of funds if I left; that I had intended to resign anyway the following June, and needed time to leave the Institute on a sound financial basis.

Le Bailly and Goodwin were just listening silently, Lou with a slight smile, Goodwin merely looking bewildered.

My arguments left Schapiro unmoved. 'I am afraid I have to insist on your resignation next Wednesday,' he said.

My first instinct was to fight, to canvass Council members, to address the full Council, to carry on with anybody who decided not to side with Le Bailly and Schapiro, and find others of equal standing to replace those of faint heart. But I quickly thought better of it. My 'other' work was more important than running the ISC.

I agreed to draft a statement, but suggested that it would attract less public attention if I 'retired' instead of 'resigned'.

The Chairman accepted this nuance.

I could see from Michael Goodwin's face that all that had been said was new to him. Now, I thought I detected a look of self-interest in his eyes.

Had any thought been given, I asked Schapiro, to a successor as Director? The Chairman pointed in Goodwin's direction: 'Michael can take over,' he said.

'Michael is an excellent administrator,' I commented, 'but even he would scarcely claim expertise in our field.'

Goodwin demurred. Averting his eyes, he said: 'Oh, I think one will manage all right.' My parting shot was: 'You realise, don't you, that you are condemning the Institute to a slow death, if not a quick one?'

The Professor was ready for that one: 'You may be right. But better by far that the Institute should die than that it should face a scandal.'

I left without shaking hands. Goodwin and Le Bailly stayed on.

I PRESENTED MY 'retirement' draft to Schapiro on the morning of the 12th. Two new faces were present at the Council meeting. One belonged to a new member, 'recruited' by Admiral Le Bailly: Air Chief Marshal Sir Christopher Foxley-Norris. The other was the guest of honour, Sir Robert Armstrong, who would shortly occupy the powerful post of Secretary to the Cabinet under Margaret Thatcher.

The statement attributed my decision to retire to other pressures in my life, which made it impossible for me to give my full attention to the ISC. It ended with a pledge to continue to raise funds for the Institute, in order to secure its financial future.

The statement was carried by the news agencies and appeared in newspapers in London and other capitals.

I HAD THOUGHT that this would be the end to the crisis. Instead, it was the beginning of another one, far deeper and more protracted.

The core of the new crisis was financial. In partnership with Georges Albertini in Paris, I had launched an experimental French-language edition of *Conflict Studies*, under the title *Le Monde des Conflits*. Seven issues had appeared, but the publication was not yet financially viable. At the time of my 'retirement', I had been negotiating with a French publisher.

The future of the French edition was no longer of concern to me, but the point was that, hitherto, I had subsidised the series out of my personal consultancy funds. The money spent, in French currency, amounted to about £35,000. Had I stayed on as Director, I would not have raised the issue. As I was being forced out, I thought it fair that the ISC should refund the money, which I could then use for The 61.

I raised the matter with Sir Robert Thompson, a founder member of the Council. A solution emerged. No money needed to change hands. Instead, I would continue to occupy my offices in a self-contained suite in the ISC's Golden Square premises. My secretary, Barbara Rose, would stay on, but her salary would be paid by the Institute, which would also meet my travelling and general office expenses. A careful audit would be made. Within a year or so, the ISC would have repaid its debt, painlessly to both sides. In return I would continue, as the 'retirement' press release had stated, to raise funds for the Institute.

Several members of the Council, in letters to me, expressed support for this proposal, and various optional titles were suggested, such as 'consultant', 'adviser', 'counsellor', and even 'chairman' (in succession to Leonard Schapiro).

Schapiro, however, vetoed all the proposals, including the refunding of the money owed to me by further fund-raising on my part.

I was losing patience with the Chairman. A further meeting was held in his flat. By now it was 28 October, a Sunday. This time, I brought Nicholas Elliott with me, after overcoming strong objections from Schapiro. Michael Goodwin was also present.

Although never formally connected with the Institute, Nicholas had in fact raised substantial sums for it. I had typed out a financial statement showing that in the years 1977–9, Elliott and I had raised a total of £447,000 of which £330,000 or 73.7 per cent had gone to ISC. The sums specifically raised by Nicholas Elliott had totalled £130,000, of which £115,000 had gone to ISC.

These were the facts. Did the ISC have any proven alternative fund-raisers? The only sensible course, I argued, was to use me as a consultant and allow me to continue to use my office until the money owed to me had been repaid.

If Schapiro rejected this solution, I thought the question should be put to an emergency meeting of the whole Council. One possible solution would be for Schapiro to resign on grounds of age (he was seventy-one, ten years older than I), and for Le Bailly to do likewise on the ground of inconvenience: by then, he had gone to live in Cornwall.

Elliott supported me forcibly; Goodwin sulked. Schapiro, fixing us with his glaucous eyes, merely remarked that if it came to it, the entire Council would walk out on me. My 'retirement' had been accepted. That was the irreversible fact.

IN A MEMO to me early in November, Michael Goodwin proposed a meeting in the presence of lawyers from both sides. He had made a provisional appointment for 11 a.m., Friday, 9 November, in the office of John Perry, of Knapp-Fishers. The date proposed did not suit me, and as Lila and I were about to go to Israel on a fortnight's holiday, I suggested that the meeting should be deferred until our return.

The blow came on the evening of the cancelled appointment. I had gone home earlier than usual. At about 4.55, a letter from Knapp-Fishers was dropped into my letter-box.

The time is relevant. The letter, on behalf of the Institute for the Study of Conflict, required me to leave my office, 'taking all your personal possessions with you', by 5.30 p.m. that day. Knapp-Fishers were prepared to grant me access to my office until 5.30 p.m. on Monday, 12 November, to remove any confidential papers, '*solely* for the purpose of collecting such confidential papers, *and* that you enter your office only in the presence of a senior employee of, or a Council member of, the ISC.'

If I failed to comply, legal proceedings would be instituted against me immediately.

The conditions were of course impossible. I was being given thirty-five minutes from the time of delivery of the letter to leave my home in NW11, go to Golden Square and clear my office. Moreover, Goodwin and his colleagues were well aware that on the Monday I would be in Israel.

I tried to 'do it my way'. I had a key to the building at 12a Golden Square. On the Sunday morning, feeling like a burglar, I opened the front door, took the lift, and tried to insert the key into my office door. Tried, and failed: the lock had been changed.

Before leaving for Israel, I wrote a letter to Schapiro which, had it been copied to any third party, would have been highly defamatory in law. As a former barrister, Schapiro would have been well aware of this, so I made it clear that I was not copying the letter for third parties.

A PROTRACTED legal wrangle followed my return from Israel. The other side denied that any money was owed to me and contested my title to control over the bank account opened to handle my consultancy funds. On hearing of the problem, General Douglas Brown made a generous offer on behalf of the Dulverton Trust. In 1978, on the initiative of Robert ('Bobby') Wills, Dulverton had made a grant of £50,000 to the ISC. Brown now proposed to Michael Goodwin that £35,000 of the same sum to be granted for 1979–80 should be used to pay off the Institute's debt to me, leaving £15,000 for the ISC. Presumably on instructions from Schapiro, Goodwin immediately turned down the proposal. Thereupon, Dulverton reduced the grant to £15,000. After some fifteen months of stonewalling, the Institute offered me £5000 in settlement of my claim of £35,000. Bored and weary by now, I countered with a claim of £10,000, then settled for £7500, which was duly paid.

Within weeks of my departure, the entire research staff of the ISC had been sacked. Not long after, the research library I had built up over many years was disposed of to an ex-servicemen's group in Aldershot, thereby ceasing to be available for its former clientele in London. There was a regrettable side effect: a major publication of the ISC since 1971 had been the *Annual of Power and Conflict*, widely consulted as an authoritative source on terrorist movements worldwide and their strategic relevance. The Annual appeared for only three issues after my departure. It is indeed impossible to produce a reference work of this kind without a functioning library.

I had other things to do than to spend precious time on investigating the circumstances of the 'palace coup'. On a *cui bono?* approach, I could hardly rule out a KGB hand, since the Soviets had tried to destroy me and the ISC during the preceding years. The fact that the whole affair had clearly been masterminded by Leonard Schapiro, one of the world's leading Sovietologists, suggested, however unlikely it might seem, that the distinguished Professor was himself a 'mole', working for the KGB. This hypothesis turned out to be untrue, however. So did another, equally improbable.

IN 1984, FIVE years after the event, one of my closest friends told me a startling story that seemed to account for all the facts. I know now that it was totally untrue, but it was so ingenious a piece of disinformation that it bears re-telling.

The essence of the story was that it was not the KGB but the *CIA* that had sought to destroy me. Could anything be less likely, and better calculated to put me off the scent?

Although fundamentally pro-American, I was explicitly and actively anti-Carter. Not only had I attacked Jimmy Carter's policies in my *National Review* and *Now!* columns and elsewhere, but I had also provided anti-Carter material to other journalists, American as well as British. My views would not have gone unnoticed at the Langley headquarters of the CIA. As the story went, Carter's Director of Central Intelligence, Admiral Stansfield Turner, had issued the order: 'That man must be stopped.' Whether he had done so on his own initiative or at the request of the White House, my informant knew not.

Turner (the story went on) had talked the problem over with Dan McMichael of Pittsburgh and put pressure on him to face the ISC with an ultimatum: unless I ceased my political activities, all funds from Pittsburgh would be cut off. Thereupon, McMichael had summoned Admiral Sir Louis Le Bailly to Pittsburgh and given him the ultimatum.

The story was the more convincing because of my own views of the way Admiral Turner was mishandling the CIA, which I had not expressed in writing but had not concealed in conversation (see Ch. X). At any rate, the Turner story kept me quiet for a while. At my suggestion, Elliott lunched Lou Le Bailly and tried it on him. According to his account, 'something like that' did happen.

Two or three years later, I was lunching with a guest at the Café Royal when I noticed my old friend Harry Chapman Pincher at the next table. I recognised one of his two guests from press and television: Admiral Stansfield Turner. With him was Mrs Turner. A moment later, Harry stood up with the Admiral, who, on learning who I was, wanted to meet me. I noted the guileless look in his eyes. He asked if he could come to see me in my office.

At this meeting, I confronted the Admiral with the story about his alleged role in my removal from the ISC, and could tell immediately from his unfeigned astonishment that he knew nothing about it.

In the interests of good relations with my friends in Pittsburgh, I had never mentioned the Turner version to them. I raised it on my next trip, in the presence of Dick Scaife. Again, I could tell from Dan McMichael's demeanour that he knew nothing about it. That afternoon, we spent two hours together going over the known facts. Dan assured me that he had only met Stansfield Turner once, at a dinner the Admiral had addressed in Pittsburgh.

He had *not* 'summoned' Lou Le Bailly: it was Le Bailly who had asked to see *him*. He had not covered the Admiral's travelling expenses. Lou had asked him whether political activities were in breach of the US law on tax-exempt donations (known as '501/C/3'). Asked for the background, Lou had said that 'a senior member of Mrs Thatcher's Cabinet' was seriously concerned about my activities and had asked him to find out whether some way could be found of stopping them.

Eight years after the event, various facts and incidents came to mind. Lou Le Bailly's political boss when he was Director-General of Defence Intelligence was the then Defence Secretary, Lord Carrington, whom Mrs Thatcher had appointed as her first Foreign Secretary after the Conservative victory in the general election of May 1979.

The man who had blocked Shield's plan for a Counter-Subversion Executive was Lord Carrington. The man whom I had criticised in my letter to Mrs Thatcher for his defeatist attitude in the event of another mineworkers' strike was Lord Carrington. In 1981, Lord De L'Isle, without consulting me but with the support of Norris McWhirter, had approached the Prime Minister to propose that I should be elevated to the peerage, with the object of providing her with an ally in the House of Lords, where anti-Thatcher sentiment prevailed. The proposal was turned down. When Bill De L'Isle inquired what had happened, he learned that the Foreign Office had raised strong objections to my name.

I wrote to the Prime Minister to ask what had happened, and received a hand-written letter from her which did not clarify the issue.

In a letter to me, dated 10 January 1980, a close American friend of mine – the late General Richard Stilwell[1] – told me of a dinner-table conversation he had had with Hugh (later Lord) Thomas, the historian.

Thomas, who had lately been appointed Chairman of the Centre for Policy Studies ('Mrs Thatcher's think-tank'), asked the general 'what I knew of the contretemps involving you. I said that the summary action to divorce you physically from the ISC premises remained inexplicable.' His comment was that he understood that ISC intended to become an arm of the Foreign Office – implying that this may have been the 'why' (but it sheds no light on the 'how'!).

A friend of Thomas's later told me that the Foreign Office wanted me 'out of the way'.

From the FO's standpoint, I can see excellent reasons for wanting me 'out of the way'. Collectively, this body of highly trained pragmatists, now headed by an intelligent pragmatist, was always open to the possibility of negotiations with Moscow, and against any long-term strategy of resistance to Soviet subversion and expansion.

There had been much low-key rejoicing over the Callaghan government's decision to kill off the IRD. With me at its head, however, the ISC was seen as a potential thorn in the Foreign Office's side, ever ready to expose and criticise appeasing words or gestures. With me out of the way, the Institute for the Study of Conflict could be made into a pliable adjunct to HMG's policy: an unembarrassing junior partner to the Royal Institute of International Affairs.

On the evidence, the mastermind was Schapiro, with Le Bailly as the instrument. In retrospect, I can only salute his skills.

NOTES

1 A four-star general, Dick Stilwell had served with distinction in Vietnam. Under President Reagan, he was appointed Assistant Defense Secretary. While in this post, he joined the inner group of The 61. (He was not related to General 'Vinegar Joe' Stilwell, who had liaised with Chiang Kai-shek during World War II: an assumption frequently made, to the annoyance of Dick Stilwell.)

Reagan meets 'The 61'

THE 61 HAD been born at the nadir of Western political leadership, especially in the US. Watergate had ended the presidency of Richard Nixon who, whatever his faults and errors of judgement, knew more about international affairs than any other post-war President, and had a special understanding of Communism.

Gerald Ford, a stop-gap President, had distinguished himself when, in a televised debate with his rival, Jimmy Carter, he had declared: 'There is no Soviet domination of Eastern Europe and there never will be under a Ford Administration.' This spectacular gaffe contributed to Carter's victory in the presidential race of 1976.

Under President Carter, however, the security situation continued to deteriorate, as much through gratuitous acts of appeasement as through the spectacular expansion of the Soviet peripheral empire under Leonid Brezhnev. Indeed, the appeasement contributed to the expansion.

In the US, however, as in Britain, there was a human ray of hope. The American one was named Ronald Reagan. I confess that at that time I shared the media consensus, especially in the US, that Reagan was a lightweight, a political simpleton, who as a politician carried no more weight than the star of B-movie Westerns he had once been. My instinctive preference for the next President was George Bush, with whom I had a long private talk during an international conference on terrorism in Jerusalem in July 1979, at which we were both speakers. However, the American friends whose opinions I most respected told me Reagan was the better choice, and events proved them right.

Bush had impressed me favourably with his knowledge of international affairs, but unfavourably by his over-confidence. 'I'll get the Republican nomination,' he assured me. 'It's in the bag.' It was not, and he would have to wait eight long years before obtaining it.

Although I knew several members of the Carter Administration, including his National Security Adviser, Zbigniew Brzezinski, and his Defense Secretary, James Schlesinger, and was received by each in the White House, I had no discernible influence on the Carter Administration, of which I became outspokenly critical.

When the presidential line-up for the elections of November 1980 was announced, I decided that, somehow or other, I had to meet Reagan and establish the necessary rapport with him, so that, in Washington as in London, I had access at the top.

My entry key was the delightful, and amazingly energetic, Aline, Condesa de Romanones, whom I had met some years earlier when I was her guest at dinner in her home in Madrid. Aline had joined the wartime Office for Strategic Services towards the end of World War II and had thus become one of the founder members of the CIA when it took over from the OSS. She had been serving in Spain and married the Conde de Romanones. She later told her own story in her bestselling book *The Spy Wore Red*.

In later life, Aline's Spanish was perfect, and she spoke her native American with more than a trace of Spanish sibilance. She spent much of her time on lecture tours of the United States. Her range of friends was awesome, and one of the many was Nancy Reagan. On 8 July 1980, I flew from Washington DC, to Los Angeles to see Ronald Reagan.

It was a hot day and he was wearing a cowboy shirt. We spent more than an hour in his study at his home at Pacific Palisades outside Los Angeles. At sixty-nine, he looked fit. The telephone rang once during our conversation, and he sprang to his feet to take the call.

The main point of the meeting was to brief him on The 61 and to offer its services to him when, as we hoped, he was elected the next President of the United States. As the former Governor of California, the largest and richest State of the Union, with a wide range of political contacts, Reagan was of course generally well informed. He mentioned that he had served on President Ford's Committee on Intelligence and thought it had done what was necessary, until Senator Church had spoilt it. (The Church Committee undoubtedly was mainly responsible for the emasculation of the CIA.) Despite this experience, there were, understandably, gaps in his knowledge of the security and intelligence situation, and in his appreciation of the enormous intensification of the Soviet threat at the time.

The *operational* capacity of the CIA had been paralysed by the savage and sustained campaign launched against it, and in the end by the Freedom of Information and Privacy Acts. This was equally true not only of the FBI, but also of the State police forces, the Customs Department, and the Internal Revenue Service in its law-enforcement capacity. Before Watergate, the FBI had had some 2500 informants scattered through the US. Now, there were barely three dozen.[1]

As Reagan knew, all recent testimonials before Congressional committees agreed that the flow of intelligence on which effective action depends had virtually dried up – for the simple reason that there was now no guarantee of confidentiality for the names of informants. Moreover, the security organs of the State were now forbidden to keep files either on individuals or on groups, so that the prevention of terrorism and other crimes had become virtually impossible.

Among other consequences of this situation, two points seemed particularly important. One was that the Federal Loyalty Security Program for entry into the American Civil Service had been abolished. This meant that there were now no vetting procedures for prospective entrants.

The other point was that the Subcommittee on Internal Security of the Senate Committee on the Judiciary had been disbanded. What this meant, quite simply, was that threats to the internal security of the US were no longer publicly examined in the Congress. This was bad enough, but we wanted to draw Reagan's particular attention to certain specific aspects of the problem. One anomaly was that the FBI was no longer allowed to function either in the United Nations headquarters in Manhattan, or on Capitol Hill, although neither area was out of bounds to the KGB. Indeed, the KGB was extremely active in both.

At that time, the intelligence functions of the FBI, in terms of counter-espionage and counter-action against terrorism, were increasingly being performed by specialised companies, groups and individuals in an attempt to fill – at least in part – the even more serious gap caused by the operational collapse of the CIA.

That, I explained, was where The 61 came in. We planned both to initiate secret operations in our various countries, and to coordinate the existing overt actions of the many private groups involved in the resistance to Soviet propaganda and Active Measures. At that time, we had no plans to operate as an espionage agency in the Soviet bloc countries. We felt that this was still a task that could be entrusted to our existing intelligence services, including the CIA. Our main mission was in the field of counter-subversion. Inevitably, we expected to pick up occasional items of secret intelligence. These we would pass on, at our discretion, to interested Allied agencies. We intended also to supplement the analyses made available to the American, British and other Allied governments by the official secret agencies. In many cases, these analyses would prove different. To this extent, they would provide an alternative assessment of current dangers for the special benefit of presidents and prime ministers.

Unlike existing agencies, we would not be hampered by prohibitions on functioning in our own or Allied countries. Security would be rigorously observed. In particular, the media, whatever they might guess or speculate upon, would never be told of our existence, or of the work we were doing. We would be concerned equally with home-grown subversion and the other kind. Soviet power and influence had been spreading, not only because of conscious efforts to that end by the KGB and its huge network of conscious ('witting') agents, but also spontaneously.

The prevailing ideology, among our intellectuals and media people, was heavily influenced, whether they knew it or not, by one variety or another of Marxism-Leninism. It was our job to counter this. Partly because of it, but also because the natural and commendable role of the press in a free society is to be critical of our governments, there was a tendency to give the other side (the Soviet bloc) the benefit of any doubt. There was no question, however, of interfering with freedom of the press or speech. The aim was to make alternative facts and opinions more widely available to our own leaders.

I had brought with me two or three issues of our monthly analysis, at that time still called *Transnational Security*, which was read regularly by Margaret Thatcher. Henceforth, I said, it would be available to Ronald Reagan, and we hoped he would find it useful when he reached the White House.

He leafed through the bulletin, and expressed interest. We agreed that for the time being it would be sent to him at his Pacific Palisades address, and later, by means to be worked out, to the Oval Office.

Reagan had been listening intently. On the CIA, he assured me that one of the first things he would do on coming to power would be to revive it.

The conversation broadened. Reagan told me he had met and greatly admired our Prime Minister. He had formed a poor opinion of his forth-coming rival, Jimmy Carter, when Carter was Governor of Georgia and he was still Governor of California. At the Conference of Governors, he said, Jimmy Carter never seemed to have anything of substance to say.

He had also got to know Nelson Rockefeller when the latter was Governor of New York State, and shared my view that Nelson was more intelligent than his banker brother, David. He was critical of the role of David Rockefeller's Chase Manhattan Bank in easing technology transfers to the Soviet Union. Reagan also mentioned, with mild distaste, the role of the Trilateral Commission (in which David Rockefeller, Brzezinski and, incidentally, Edward Heath and Willy Brandt were involved) in sponsoring Jimmy Carter as a potential presidential candidate.

The Governor ruled out a European trip before the elections on the ground that his detractors would present it as an attempt on his part to establish his credentials in foreign affairs. In fact, he made it clear that he had already had considerable experience in foreign affairs as special presidential envoy in various situations. As one example among many, he mentioned that President Nixon had sent him to Taiwan to explain American policy at the time of the Nixon–Kissinger visit to Peking, and to reassure the defeated Nationalist leader, President Chiang Kai-shek. Chiang, however, predictably gave him a frosty reception.

The conversation came back to security and the Soviet problem. I observed that the consequences of President Carter's initial declaration about losing 'our inordinate fear of Communism' had been disastrous. The Communist takeover of Nicaragua was only one example. When Mr Reagan reached the White House, he could make it clear that the US would no longer be bound by the undertaking given by President Kennedy to Khrushchev at the end of the Cuban missiles crisis of 1962 that the US would refrain from using force to overthrow Fidel Castro, in view of the many breaches of international agreements by the Soviet Union.

The Soviet brigade known to be stationed in Cuba, though militarily insignificant, was there in furtherance of the Brezhnev Doctrine (claiming the right to intervene with force, should 'socialism' be threatened in any member country of the 'socialist commonwealth'). Indeed, the US President should publicly declare that he was in no way bound to respect the Brezhnev Doctrine.[2]

We discussed the problem of Angola, where a Communist government installed by Soviet power was bolstered by Cuban forces, airlifted by the Soviet Union. Two-thirds of the country was in the hands of anti-Communist guerrillas, yet the US was forbidden to help the guerrillas under the terms of the so-called Clark Amendment, adopted in the wake of the US retreat from Vietnam.

Meanwhile, anti-Communist governments, such as those of Chile, Argentina, Uruguay, and South Africa, had been ostracised. The three Latin American regimes had admittedly been guilty of unpardonable excesses. Against this, they had been victims of perhaps the most vicious and concentrated wave of subversion and terrorism in modern history. As for Chile, the worst phase of repression had ended two or three years earlier, and the country's remarkable experiment in market economics deserved to be encouraged.

South Africa was a different problem. Its minerals were indispensable to the West. At that time (in 1980) the alternative to the existing regime seemed unlikely to be a Western-style democratic system, with 'one man one vote', but a Communist takeover, through the ANC and its close allies in the Communist Party of South Africa, one of the Comintern's earliest creations (1921), and closely linked with Moscow. Meanwhile, the South African government should be urged to remove anomalies in its treatment of the black and coloured populations.

Reagan did not comment on South Africa. On Chile, he said he planned an official visit to Santiago, and considered it a scandal that Chile – a 'friend and ally' – was being ostracised by the United States.

For me, the future President's most interesting remarks concerned his early career as a trade union organiser when, in the late 1940s, he became President of the Screen Actors' Guild. It was at this time that he became aware of the problem of Communist penetration. He recalled a quiet visit from a high official of the FBI. Not once did the man use the word 'Communist', but 'I got the message', said Reagan. He found himself Chairman of two Communist front organisations. When he realised what they were, he resigned. Thereupon, the two organisations were dissolved, as of no further interest to the Communists.

He mentioned the role of Lillian Hellman, the fellow-travelling playwright, during that period, and complained that the recent film of her life (with Jane Fonda and Vanessa Redgrave) was a travesty of the truth. All this, he said, had happened in 1947 – that is, a few years before Senator Joe McCarthy had come into the public eye.

I was fascinated to learn that Ronald Reagan and I had been 'sensitised' about Communism at approximately the same time.

After we had talked for more than an hour, Nancy Reagan came in. She had been shopping. Her husband introduced us, and she gave me an appraising look, as though to weigh up whether this visitor from London was going to be useful, or merely another intruder into Ronald's life. It was common knowledge how protective of him she was.

On leaving, I asked Reagan if he would receive me in the Oval Office. He hesitated, aware no doubt of the enormous pressures on his time that the Presidency would bring. He could have said that he would see how things worked out, or some other evasion, but he said he would.

'Is that a promise?' I asked.

He gave me his warm smile and said: 'It is.'

He kept the promise.

DURING THE PRESIDENTIAL ELECTION campaign, I kept in touch with Bill Casey, who was in charge of it in the latter stages, and with Richard V. Allen, who played a leading role in formulating foreign policy for the prospective President. I had met both men as part of the enormous network of contacts opened up by Frank Barnett, my unannounced visitor in Madrid.

Allen in particular had vitally important qualifications: a wide knowledge of international affairs in general, and of Communist affairs in particular, and a special interest in Germany. He had studied at Munich University; he had edited a volume of the Hoover Institution's invaluable *Yearbook on International Communist Affairs*; and he had written a penetrating monograph on the key Soviet concept of 'Peaceful Co-Existence'.

When Reagan won, on a landslide, he appointed Casey as his first Director of Central Intelligence (see Ch. VII), and Dick Allen as his first National Security Adviser. I had put both of them on the receiving list for *Transnational Security*, and both wanted to continue to read it after their appointments.

Possibly because of Allen's declared anti-Communist attitude, he was the target for a smear campaign before the election; a further round of attacks forced him out of office within a year. The incumbent National Security Adviser has a particularly punishing schedule and my meetings with him usually lasted, on average, about twenty minutes. On one unscheduled occasion, however, we had a talk lasting several hours, when we found we were on the same flight across the Atlantic. I was sorry to see him go, as our contact had proved useful to both of us.

I was able, for instance, to tip him off on the recent activities of forthcoming visitors to Washington. One example was the meeting Willy

Brandt and his *éminence grise* Egon Bahr had had with Boris Ponomarev, head of the Soviet International Department, before their trip to Mexico City (via Washington) in July 1981 for a North-South conference.

Replying on 30 June, Allen said: 'Thank you for your "heads-up" on the prospective visit of Bahr and Brandt. You can be assured that I will be alert to their suggested itinerary.'

DICK ALLEN'S OFFICIAL CAREER ended abruptly at the end of 1981, and he was succeeded by Judge William B. Clark, one of Reagan's Californian cronies, whom he had brought into his administration as Deputy Secretary of State (under General Alexander Haig, the former NATO commander-in-chief).

On his appointment, Judge Clark had only a hazy notion of international affairs, as the Senators who vetted him found out. However, he was a highly intelligent man, who learned fast, and a man of wisdom, who soon grasped the strategic plans I brought to him from The 61. Unfortunately, Judge Clark, too, ran the National Security Council for too short a time, for in October 1983 President Reagan appointed him Secretary for the Interior. He wrote and told me of his 'life long interest in our heritage of resources'.

I was sorry he had left, although I soon developed a productive relationship with his successors, Robert C. ('Bud') McFarlane and Admiral John M. Poindexter. Both men were intelligent and good listeners. I always found McFarlane highly strung, however, and I got the impression that the tensions of the job were too great for his temperament. In contrast, Poindexter was cool and collected. The careers of both men, of course, were blighted by the Iran Contra affair.

The 'regulars' on my White House visits included three other men of outstanding intellect and devotion: Richard Pipes, Ken deGraffenreid, and Sven Kraemer. Pipes, born in Poland, was on loan from Harvard, where he held the Chair of Russian History. Our exchanges on current Soviet affairs were the richer for our ideological compatibility. After two years in the White House, he returned to academic life and wrote a definitive history of *The Russian Revolution, 1899–1919* (CollinsHarvill, 1990). DeGraffenreid was Senior Director of Intelligence Programs; Sven Kraemer handled arms control matters within the National Security Council. Yet another 'regular' was Colonel 'Ollie' North, the central figure in the Iran Contra affair; I always found Ollie lucid and articulate but, I am sorry to say, he did not take me into his confidence about his execution of Casey's plan to raise money for the Nicaraguan *contras* through arms sales to Iran. Nor would I have expected him to.

An observation seems called for, however. Leaks of CIA plans had become almost an epidemic because of the requirement that plans for covert action be subject to Congressional oversight. This unfortunate consequence of the Watergate affair made covert action virtually impossible, and a tacit decision was made to transfer certain projects to the White House. This was sound in principle; but the White House staff was not adequate to provide the necessary logistical back-up. It was a vicious circle, as those involved would learn.

In general, I used the incumbent National Security Adviser to convey special strategic analyses and proposals to the President. For more politically sensitive letters to the President, my conduit was Ed Hickey, the President's Special Assistant for Security (see Ch. IX); and for more personal letters (for instance, after the near-fatal assassination attempt of March 1981) I wrote via Nancy Reagan, by means of a special code number on the envelope. As far as I am aware, there were no leaks from any of these quarters.

After his first election victory but before taking office, Reagan had appointed another of his Californian friends, William A. Wilson, to liaise both with the Pinay Cercle (see Ch. XV) and with The 61. The intermediary in this useful appointment was Aline de Romanones. In those early days, this arrangement worked well. In 1982, however, Bill Wilson was appointed US ambassador to the Vatican, which made it impossible for him to act as our intermediary. By then, however, my own White House network was fully functional.

For these early arrangements, and not least for introducing me to Ronald Reagan, Aline had earned our thanks.

NOTES

1 For a fuller account of this problem, see Brian Crozier, *The Minimum State* (Hamish Hamilton, London, 1979), Part II, Ch. 5, 'America's Death Wish'; see also David Rees, 'The Crisis in United States Intelligence', *Conflict Studies* 114, ISC, London, December 1979.

2 The Reagan government did (tacitly, not publicly) drop Kennedy's assurance over Cuba; and, without publicly denouncing the Brezhnev Doctrine, treated it with contempt by liberating Grenada in 1983 (see Ch. XIX).

XV

About and around 'The 61'

IN NOVEMBER 1979, with the ISC link severed, the initially small staff of The 61 moved into offices in Grand Buildings, Trafalgar Square. From there, in daily communion with Admiral Nelson on his column, I set about building up The 61: its funds, its human resources, its activities. We started off with a reserve of $30,000. Although we never reached our initial annual budget target of $5 million, at the height of The 61's activities in the mid-1980s we were spending around $1 million a year.

The prime purposes of The 61 were: to brief Western and friendly Third World leaders, and through them and in other ways to influence policy decisions in the light of the Soviet threat; and to counter the disinformation and propaganda of the Soviet International Department and its satellite network in the major Western countries. The 'bottom line' was simply to 'get things done'.

We were aware of the weaknesses of the Soviet camp, which was held together by force and fear, on the basis of a discredited doctrine. We knew the Western side, for all its faults, was the stronger. The need was to stiffen Western resolve, end appeasement, and go for victory in the Cold War.

The recipients of *Transnational Security*, the 'restricted' analytical newsletter I had shown Ronald Reagan, fell into three layers. The top layer, which included the President and Mrs Thatcher, consisted of the Western and friendly Third World leaders, selected politicians, and friendly secret services. In the second layer, as of right, were contributors to our funds. The third layer consisted of our own people: agents and associates in various countries.

This third category included a tiny number of trusted journalists, each on the clear understanding that they would not use anything in the bulletin for at least three weeks. The reason was obvious: the Prime Minister and the President, for instance, would soon lose interest in our material and in our private briefings and special reports if they found the same stuff at the same time in the newspapers.

The launching of the newsletter was one of my top priorities on moving into Grand Buildings; the 'pilot' issue had been distributed in October 1979 while I was still, on sufferance, in Golden Square. On the home front, we built up a reference archive of quotations from the already published words of hundreds of extremist politicians and trades unionists, as raw material for analytical reports in the Shield manner. In charge was a former MI-5 man who had brought me disquieting information about the paralysis of the Security Service in the late 1970s.

We made no charge for the bulletin or for special reports: this was a private, non-profit service, not a commercial venture. The basic production cost of each single copy of *Transnational Security* was about £25. Recipients were free to use any information therein (except for the journalistic embargo), but without attribution. Partly in the interests of fund-raising, the first few issues of the newsletter bore the attribution 'from BRIAN CROZIER and associates'. At this early stage, the idea of using my name was to reassure the sources of our initial funds that the money was indeed being used by me and the embryo organisation I had set up. I regarded it as a kind of guarantee, and a possible way of raising more money. I had allowed myself to suppose that the carefully chosen recipients would keep their copies to themselves or show them only to friends on a confidential basis. I now realised, rather late, that the use of my name was incompatible with our supposed secrecy, and therefore a mistake.

Indeed, the mistake led to the first of only two leaks in our ten years of active life, when a Spanish defence attaché in Bonn was recalled to Madrid at short notice and left a copy on his desk.

The first I knew of it was when references to the bulletin, which still bore my name, started appearing in left-wing papers, in a brief revival of the smear campaign. To this day, some leftist writers are convinced that the secret organisation which they assumed I was running was called 'Transnational Security'.

I turned this leak to our advantage by the simple expedient of removing my name from the cover of the bulletin (where it should never have been in the first place) and changing its title to the more anodyne *Notes and Analysis*. The leak thus turned into a useful piece of self-disinformation by our enemies.

The second leak was more serious and is dealt with further on.

ON REACHING 10 Downing Street, Mrs Thatcher, spurred on I believe by my account of the way Labour had killed off the Information Research Department, attempted to revive it, in the face of entrenched opposition from the Foreign Office mandarins. A new Overseas Information Department or OID was set up. To run it, the Prime Minister appointed a friend of mine from Cambodian days, Peter Blaker, who was now the Minister of State at the FO. Over lunch, I gave him, at least in part, the inside story of the demise of IRD. Unlike the IRD papers, however, the origin of the new service was stated on each paper issued. The 'unattributable' rule, which had proved so effective in the past, had gone.

Although the new OID papers were useful, as auxiliary material, they were far from making our own output superfluous. Unlike the official Western intelligence and security services, we were not hampered by constitutional limitations on the range of our inquiries. We were thus able to offer the Prime Minister, the President, and other recipients an alternative view of developments.

Our own network of informants, both paid and honorary, grew fast. As with official intelligence services, the main requirement for recruitment was *access*. We needed well-placed men and women, with access to leaders, to intelligence and security services, to selected politicians, to editors of potentially useful publications. All that was needed was for those selected from the contacts each had built up before and after the birth of The 61, to be conscious of our existence and goals. Those who needed money for the extra work we called for were put on our payroll; some were rich enough not to need remuneration, although only a few spurned the reimbursement of expenses.

As with the enemy services, we too had our 'unconscious' agents: men and women 'on our side' who did not need to know of our existence but were ready to help anyway.

In addition to our own network, we gained access to a number of existing networks, both private and official. In Germany, we had three prime sources. One was the ex-diplomat turned politician, Count Hans Huyn, a close friend of the Bavarian leader, Franz Josef Strauss, and a leading authority on Soviet policy. Another was the ebullient, ever-cheerful Hans-Josef ('Jupp') Horchem, at that time head of the Hamburg branch of the Federal security service, the *Landesamt für Verfassungs-schutz*. One of the world's leading authorities on terrorism, Jupp had written some of the most penetrating of the ISC's *Conflict Studies*.

The third source was one of the senior intelligence officials who had resigned in disgust when Chancellor Brandt emasculated the former Gehlen office (see Ch. VII). I shall call him Hans von Machtenberg. With him, into early retirement, he took a substantial network of agents, whose identities he had refused to disclose to his new political masters.

Hans lived near Pullach, in Bavaria, headquarters of the BND. There, with the approval and backing of Strauss, he secured financial backing to continue his work, in the private sector. One of his sources of funds had also helped us, and introduced me to von Machtenberg. I invited him to join our directing committee (which we called our 'Politburo'). There-after, he received our bulletin and a selection of our occasional secret reports. In return I received his regular intelligence reports in German, with full discretion to use them, unattributably.

OUR GERMAN NETWORK gave us some of our most spectacular successes (see Ch. XVI). Sad to record, however, a regrettable leak in October 1982 destroyed its value to The 61. The earlier leak had been caused by unintended carelessness; the new one by a serious error of judgement. Unknown to us, Hans von Machtenberg had been pass-ing on full reports of our secret meetings to the head of Bavarian State Security, Hans Langemann, in exchange for Langemann's own secret intelligence.

One day, Langemann had a crisis of identity. He wanted his work to be known to the wider world, and recorded his revelations on lengthy audio tapes. In a fit of ideological perverseness, he sold them to the extreme Left glossy magazine *Konkret*, which had gained notoriety in the 1970s when it channelled KGB money through the East German Stasi to fund the Baader-Meinhof gang (also known as the *Rote Armee Fraktion* or Red Army Group).[1]

The *Konkret* story was picked up by *Der Spiegel*[2], which sent a photographer to take pictures of me. As there was no way of stopping the projected story, I 'posed' for him. As with so many stories about the activities of groups with which I had been associated, this one came out as a mish-mash of true and false. There were long passages about the Pinay Cercle, to which of course I did belong.

Much has been written about the Cercle, from the outside, and much of it has been false or misleading. For example, it has been alleged that it was a forum for bringing together 'international linkmen of the Right', such as myself and Robert Moss, with secret service chiefs like Alexandre de Marenches, long-time head of the French SDECE, and Sir Arthur ('Dickie') Franks, sometime head of MI-6.[3]

There are pitfalls in writing about confidential matters from the outside, and drawing on similarly handicapped material. In fact, neither Marenches nor Dickie Franks ever attended a Pinay Cercle meeting during the years I was involved with it: between 1971 and 1985. There was a very good reason why Marenches would never have been invited. The inspirer and long-serving organiser of the Pinay Cercle was Jean Violet, who for many years had been retained by the SDECE as Special Advocate. As such, he had initiated many highly successful political actions, for which indeed he was awarded the Grand Cross of the French Legion of Honour.

Inevitably, he had made enemies. One of them was a close friend of the Comte de Marenches who, on being appointed Director-General of the SDECE in 1970, closed down Violet's office without notice. The two men – Marenches and Violet – never met (see Ch. XVII).

As for Dickie Franks, he never attended Cercle meetings, for the reason that Directors of SIS do not involve themselves in such private groups. So he was never invited.

It was not until the spring of 1993 that I learned the details of Jean Violet's real secret service role when General de Gaulle was in power. A background document was given to me by one of Violet's ex-colleagues. Ironically, a few years before Gabriel Decazes and I started spying on de Gaulle, Violet was masterminding a *Service Spécial* to promote the General's objectives in defence and foreign policy.

The document began with a paragraph of wistful praise for Britain's remarkable achievements in intelligence and clandestine action. But France, too, offered a precedent: Louis XV had set up a special service known to the few who were aware of it as the *Secret du Roi*. This service reported directly to the King, bypassing the Foreign Ministry of the day.

Only two people were aware of de Gaulle's latter-day model: General Grossin, the then head of the SDECE, and a certain 'Monsieur X'. It required no great deductive powers to assume that Monsieur X had to be Maître Violet, but Jean refused to comment when I asked him. My other source, however, confirmed my supposition. No wonder, in retrospect, that Violet's shadowy role and apparently bottomless purse stirred resentful envy among his colleagues and poisoned Alexandre de Marenches's mind against Violet, whom he had never met. By far the dominant theme in de Gaulle's foreign policy (as Violet interpreted it) was Franco-German reconciliation. A genius at (non-violent) operations of influence, Violet played an historically key role between 1957 and 1961 in bringing about this *rapprochement*, which is the real core of the European Community. He had developed a close friendship with Antoine Pinay, who had served as French Premier in 1951 under the unstable Fourth Republic. At a lower level, a complementary role was played by his SDECE colleague Antoine Bonnemaison (see Chs III and IV). Violet was the go-between in secret meetings between Pinay and the West German Chancellor, Konrad Adenauer, and his coalition partner Franz Josef Strauss. These paved the way for Charles de Gaulle's own encounters with Adenauer, which culminated in the Franco-German Treaty of January 1963.

When that goal had been achieved, de Gaulle told the *Service Spécial* that this was 'the most important fact that France and the world had known in centuries'. For a man as careful as de Gaulle in his choice of words, this was a measure of his gratitude to Grossin and Violet.

Another task of special importance to de Gaulle was, of course, Algeria. The Grossin–Violet strategy was to win over the twenty republics of Latin America, so that whenever the issue came before the United Nations, any anti-French resolution was bound to be defeated. During this early phase of de Gaulle's presidency, such resolutions were backed by the Soviet bloc.

The *Service Spécial* also cleared the way for de Gaulle's triumphal tour of Latin America in 1964. As a gesture of gratitude to 'Monsieur X', President Castello Branco of Brazil invited Jean Violet to an 'official' visit to his country.

The Pinay Cercle was a natural offshoot of Jean Violet's Franco-German activities. To describe it as a 'forum' is strictly accurate. There were no members in a formal sense. It was an informal group of broadly like-minded people, who met twice a year, once in America, once in Europe. Usually, some distinguished figure was invited to speak. Among the guest speakers at times when I was present were Strauss, Henry Kissinger (for whom I interpreted), Zbigniew Brzezinski, David Rockefeller, and Giulio Andreotti.

Within the wider Cercle, a smaller gathering called the Pinay Group met on occasion to discuss possible action. In 1980, Violet, who had serious health problems, asked me to take over the Pinay Cercle. In practice, I mostly shared the burden with a leading German member of the Cercle, Franz-Josef Bach, who had run Adenauer's secretariat and later served as ambassador in Tehran.

In Pinay's day, the old man himself presided over the meetings, but the chairmanship of each session was shared out among others, including Pesenti, Sir Peter Tennant, and myself. On my initiative, Julian Amery, MP (later Lord Amery), took over the presidency. I retired from the Cercle in 1985, having decided that it was making excessive demands on my staff and office time.

Some outsiders have jumped to the wrong conclusion that the Pinay Cercle was the same as my 'secret' organisation. One of them was a CIA veteran whom I had known since my FWF days. There was in fact some minor overlapping, but the functions of The 61, which I have been describing, were quite different. Some members of The 61's 'Politburo' also attended the Cercle meetings; others did not. Most members of the Cercle were unaware of the existence of The 61. Many on The 61's networks had no connection with the Cercle.

For all these reasons, the Langemann 'revelations' were deeply misleading. Hans von Machtenberg's indiscretion was nevertheless considered unacceptable, and The 61's directorate decided to sever relations with him. I was personally very sorry over this rift, as I held Hans in high esteem.

An example of the damage done. On the last day of October 1984, I addressed the Belgian Atlantic Association in Liège. When I sat down, the first questioner from the floor was a local leader of the *Ecologiste* Party (the Belgian equivalent of the German *Grüne*). As soon as he started speaking, it was clear that he was reading a French translation of the passages about me in the *Spiegel* article based on the Langemann papers. It was also clear from the *way* he was reading that until the translation reached him he had never heard of me.

The audience, mainly members of the Atlantic Association, was heavily on my side, and hostile voices were raised. Within minutes, the speaker was physically evicted from the hall.

I speculated at the time that the fact that a French translation of the

Spiegel article had been circulated in advance of my arrival indicated a KGB involvement. In conversation with me, some years later, a senior KGB defector confirmed this interpretation. The choice of a 'Green' to attack me was not coincidental: the KGB residencies had standing orders to penetrate and influence Green and ecological groups. I could hardly complain. After all, this *was* a secret war.

BETWEEN 1980 AND 1985, we had a Czechoslovak network, run from Geneva and filtered through Czech-born Josef Josten in London. Although the Czech network was not professional, and much of it was low-grade, it did provide useful nuggets about significant links with Gaddafi in Libya, with Palestinian terrorists, and with 'peace' agitators, notably in West Germany.

Josten was a determined fighter against the Communist regime in his own country. Twice he took refuge in Britain: in 1938 when the Nazis marched in, and ten years later, when the Communists took over in the bloodless Prague coup. He died in 1987, aged seventy.

A man of great courage and determination, Josef Josten had survived an attempt by the StB to poison him, which had forced him to spend weeks in hospital. The incident, as he had recounted it to me, was another example of the techniques used by the satellite secret services. A Czech 'friend' of his had sent him word, indirectly, of his intention to defect to the West. Could they meet in a Geneva hotel? They did, and sat down at a table in mid-afternoon. The 'friend' ordered tea for two, then excused himself. He never came back, and Josten drank the poison the false defector had slipped into his tea.

This was not the only attempt to assassinate Josten. His compatriot Josef Frolik, an StB man who defected to the US in 1974, has described an earlier assassination plot, hatched while he was serving in London.[4]

Josef Josten was an original, impossible to categorise or pigeon-hole. All intelligence agencies, whether official or private, attract such characters. Unlike run-of-the-mill career bureaucrats, they are irreplaceable.

NOTES

1 See Melvin J. Lasky, 'Ulrike Meinhof and the Baader-Meinhof Gang' in *Encounter*, June 1975; also Hans Josef Horchem, 'West Germany's Red Army Anarchists', *Conflict Studies* No. 46, ISC, June 1974; the same author's *Die Verlorene Revolution: Terrorismus in Deutschland* (BusseSeewald, Herford, 1988); and Jillian Becker, *Hitler's Children: The Story of the Baader-Meinhof Gang* (Michael Joseph, London, 1977).

2 'Victory for Strauss' (English in the original) in *Der Spiegel*, No. 37, 1982.

3 See David Teacher in *Lobster* (an occasional 'investigative' review published in Hull) No. 18 (October 1989).

4 See Josef Frolik, *The Frolik Defection* (Leo Cooper, London, 1975), pp. 65 et seq.

XVI

Poland, Canada, and other crises

NOT SURPRISINGLY, the German network was highly professional. One of its major intelligence coups enabled The 61 to play a hitherto unrevealed part in the great Polish crisis of 1980–82. When Lech Walesa created his Solidarity trade union federation in 1980, Brezhnev was still in power in the Kremlin. He and his colleagues could not ignore the situation: the emergence of an independent centre of workers' power in a 'workers' State' was intolerable, for it threatened their own title to permanent power, and the legitimacy of every segment of their empire.

In our bulletin of December/January (1980/81), we declared that Walesa's challenge, if he got away with it, 'would (and may yet be) *the beginning of the end of the Soviet empire*'. Eight years on, the prediction was fulfilled.

The Soviets and their Polish satellites faced an insoluble dilemma. If they intervened militarily, as they did in 1956 in Poland and Hungary, and in Czechoslovakia in 1968, they risked losing the technological transfers from the West made possible by 'détente'. If they did not, the situation might get out of hand.

They tried other methods first. The head of Poland's secret police, Stanislaw Kania, took over as First Secretary of the ruling United Workers' Party. In February 1981, the Polish Defence Minister, General Wojciech Jaruzelski, was appointed Prime Minister.

In March 1981, disturbing intelligence reached us through our German network. There were two separate reports, each reinforcing the other. The first came from a well-placed source in East Berlin. The gist of it was that during the night of 28 March a state of emergency would be proclaimed and units of the East German *Volksarmee* forces would cross the border during the early hours of 29 March.

The second report emanated from 'an Iron Curtain ambassador in a West European capital', who let it be known that the Warsaw Pact forces already in Poland on military manoeuvres would be ordered that weekend to 'sort out' the situation. Von Machtenberg declined, for his own security reasons, to tell us which Iron Curtain country the ambassador represented, and which West European capital he was stationed in. My guess was that the country was Czechoslovakia and the capital was Bonn. The point of the proposed move was to avoid the impression that an invasion was taking place; while the East German move would be presented as a cautionary one.

Von Machtenberg had telephoned both reports to me, and I immediately passed them on to the appropriate authorities. They were relayed to 10 Downing Street, the White House, and the Elysée. Albertini, who had alerted the latter, also, with my encouragement, passed the intelligence on to the Vatican (always a factor in any crisis affecting Catholic Poland, birthplace of Pope John-Paul II). Dire warnings were issued from the White House and we were given to understand that the 'hot line' to the Kremlin was used. The Pope also reacted, with a statement that if the Soviets invaded Poland, he would go there himself to face them. The Soviets cancelled their invasion plans. I received a personal letter from Dick Allen, the National Security Adviser, thanking me for the information we had provided.

The men in the Kremlin were clearly in a quandary over the Polish crisis. Invasion now seemed too dangerous; yet the bullying and arrests of Solidarity members by the secret police did not seem to be working either. At the end of 1981, we learned that the arrests had been carried out on the basis of meticulously compiled lists of anti-Communist 'trouble-makers' in the trade union movement. These lists had been prepared under the direction of the KGB.

Years later, the senior KGB defector Oleg Gordievsky confirmed our own intelligence. All available Polish-speaking KGB officers were sent not only to the Warsaw *rezidentsiya*, but also to the Soviet consulates in Gdansk, Cracow, Poznan, and Szeczin.[1] In October 1981, Kania was judged to have failed, and his job as First Secretary of the Party was taken over by General Jaruzelski. The KGB thereupon scored a splendid disinformation victory by briefing correspondents in Moscow. As they put it, Jaruzelski was a kind of Polish caudillo who was taking over because the Party had lost control. A number of the correspondents fell for this ploy, which was still being peddled years after the event.

In reality, the key decisions were still in Moscow's hands. Jaruzelski was a *political* general. As a young officer, he and other members of Stalin's Lublin Committee had camped on the Vistula while the Nazis were massacring the Polish rebels in Warsaw. He had risen to the key post of head of the Central Political Department of the armed forces. Moreover, the Polish forces were indirectly controlled by the Warsaw Pact organisation, based of course in Warsaw and under the command of the Soviet Marshal V. H. Kulikov.

Our view that the so-called coup was a Soviet deception was later confirmed by Gordievsky who (through his co-writer Christopher Andrew) said: 'The KGB's candidate to lead the coup was General Wojciech Jaruzelski.'[2]

And still the situation continued to deteriorate. On 11 December 1981, Jaruzelski proclaimed martial law. President Reagan revealed, at his press conference on 23 December, that the proclamation had been *drafted and printed* in Moscow.[3]

Allied reactions to these events were disjointed and feeble. The US State Department sent one of its top officials, Lawrence Eagleburger, on a pulse-taking tour of West European capitals, where he encountered indecision verging on apathy. In a radio interview[4], Lord Carrington played down the Soviet role and said there was no hurry for action.

In Paris, President Mitterrand's government issued strong statements but did nothing. The worst behaviour came from West Germany. Chancellor Schmidt chose the moment of Poland's agony to meet the Communist leader, Erich Honecker, in East Germany, still under Soviet occupation. On 27 December, the Foreign Minister, Hans-Dietrich Genscher, publicly opposed US sanctions and declared that neither the West nor the East should intervene. The East had already done so, of course.

President Reagan halted American shipments of grain to Poland, and imposed restrictions on Polish shipping in US waters. He also banned exports of computers to the Soviet Union, but grain shipments continued: the mid-West farming lobby had to be placated.

Mrs Thatcher felt that she had to do *something*, and pressured the BBC World Service to increase the hours of broadcasting in Polish by forty-five minutes a day. But behind the scenes, she acted energetically to stiffen the backbone of the Foreign Office and the Foreign Secretary. On Saturday,

2 January 1982, she received me at Chequers, where I briefed her on the Soviet involvement in the Polish crisis.

The Joint Intelligence Committee (JIC), dominated by the appeasement-minded Foreign Office, had prepared a report concluding that there was no hard evidence of Soviet involvement. I convinced her that this assessment simply ignored the very real evidence available.

On the Monday, two days later, she summoned the Chairman of the JIC and asked him why the Committee had ignored the absolutely clear contrary evidence. The outcome was that, within forty-eight hours, a new assessment emphasising the reality of Soviet intervention was delivered to Mrs Thatcher. Less than a fortnight later, the North Atlantic Council met in Brussels and issued an unusually strong communiqué condemning the Soviet role in the Polish military takeover.

That same evening, Monday, 4 January 1982, my Czech dissident friend Josef Josten had organised a mass 'Rally for Poland' in the Albert Hall. The speakers included Denis Healey, Labour's Deputy Leader, Frank Chapple, the ex-Communist electricians' leader, and myself. All three of us received ovations, but if measured by the duration, Chapple was the clear winner. Healey, however, stole a march on both of us by providing a copy of his speech for *The Times*, which duly printed it; other speakers were not covered because the newspaper had not sent a reporter to the occasion – a lesson in public relations.

In terms of results, my visit to Chequers was undoubtedly more effective than the Rally. Indeed, a substantial eating of words followed. In the House of Lords on 19 January, Lord Carrington declared that there was no doubt about the extent to which Russia was 'directly and indirectly involved in Poland's military clamp-down'. He called for strong and concerted economic measures against the USSR. Schmidt and Genscher also reversed their previous exoneration of the Soviet Union.

Sad to add, only token measures followed: strong words had to suffice.

The French External Relations Minister, Claude Cheysson, took a strong line in public, but France went on to sign a twenty-five-year contract for the purchase of eight billion cubic metres of Soviet gas a year.

OF ALL THE Allied leaders, by far the most negatively supportive of the Soviet side in the Polish crisis was Canada's long-serving Prime Minister, Pierre Trudeau. At his news conference on 12 December 1980, he commented on statements by Joseph Luns, NATO's secretary-general, and others, which threatened economic, political, and other responses to any Soviet intervention. Trudeau put his reaction in these words: 'I think we should steer miles away from any threat of intervention.'[5]

A French Canadian lawyer, Trudeau dominated Canadian politics as Prime Minister from 1968 to 1984, with a brief interval out of office in 1979–80. A former editor of the *Toronto Sun*, Peter Worthington, who had learned about Soviet Communism on the spot as a correspondent in Moscow, saw Trudeau as a man

> ... comfortable with Socialist/Marxist tyrants and their fellow-travellers. Not just infatuation with Mao-Brezhnev, Castro.... He wouldn't go to Chile after Allende's Marxist regime was overthrown, but he rushed to Cuba when Castro's mercenaries were rampaging in Angola contrary to the wishes of the people.[6]

ONE DAY in December 1971, a former senior officer of the counter-espionage division of the Royal Canadian Mounted Police ('the Mounties') sought me out. A tall man in his sixties, he had lately retired after a series of medical problems. At that time, French-speaking Quebec province – the Prime Minister Pierre Trudeau's native home – was in a turmoil of violence. The officer briefed me about the situation and I invited him to write a *Conflict Study* on it. The outcome, in February 1972, was 'Quebec: The Challenge from Within', by 'a Canadian correspondent' (*Conflict Studies*, No. 20).

It was an eye-opener. On 5 October 1970, the British Trade Commissioner in Montreal, James Cross, had been kidnapped by armed terrorists of the FLQ (*Front de Libération du Québec*). Five days later, the FLQ had seized Pierre Laporte, Quebec's Minister of Labour and Immigration. The lucky one was James Cross, who was released; Laporte was killed by his kidnappers.

The most interesting point about these terrorist acts was that the leaders of the FLQ were not native-born Quebecois: one was a Belgian immigrant named George Schoetters; another was an ex-Hungarian called François Schirm.

Behind the FLQ was a political front, the FLP (*Front de Libération Populaire*). Two years back, in 1968, two members of the FLP had been delegates at a conference hosted by the Canadian Peace Congress, a Soviet-backed front organisation in which the Moscow-line Communist Party of Canada played a leading role. It does not follow from this that the Soviet International Department (the ultimate controlling body of such offshoots) necessarily opted for the kind of direct action (kidnapping and murder) used by the FLQ in 1970. After all, Moscow had invested much time, effort and money in building up a Trade Mission and consulate in Montreal, the future of which could have been jeopardised by such violent action. As in so many other situations, the Soviet subversive apparatus kept its options open.

On 3 December 1970, James Cross was delivered unhurt, and the terrorists, under Cuban auspices, were allowed to fly out to Castro's island. There is no suggestion that Trudeau was personally involved in these machinations, although his personal support for the Cuban dictator must have caused him embarrassment. What this curious case demonstrated, however, was that the RCMP lacked effective powers to intervene in Quebec.

Nevertheless, there were complaints that the RCMP had exceeded its legal powers. Indeed, some of its officers were convicted of illegal telephone-tapping, acts of provocation, and breaking and entering.

The security crisis of 1970 in Quebec was not of course the first example of Soviet subversive interest in Canada. In 1945–6, the defection of Igor Gouzenko, a cipher clerk in the Soviet embassy in Ottawa, was given world coverage. Gouzenko had helped to unmask five espionage rings operating in Canada. He had revealed the existence of a network of 'sleeper' agents in Canada which had been built up from the 1920s.

When a fire broke out in the Soviet embassy in Ottawa in 1958, Soviet officials had prevented local firemen from doing their job. Gouzenko's explanation was that the first Soviet priority was the need to remove incriminating records about their networks in Canada.

Twenty years later, in February 1978, thirteen members of the Soviet embassy were expelled after the uncovering of a major intelligence operation led by one Igor Vartanian, who operated under diplomatic cover as a First Secretary dealing with sporting and cultural affairs. From April 1977, Soviet agents led by Vartanian had been suborning a member of the RCMP with a view to penetrating its security service. The RCMP man had reported these overtures. Later, acting on instructions, he had received more than $30,000 in cash on seven different occasions.

The Gouzenko and the FLQ cases pre-dated, of course, the creation of The 61. By the time the Vartanian case had surfaced, however, The 61 was functional, and we had built up a small but effective network of sources in Canada. For a full analysis of Soviet subversive activities in

Canada at that time, against the background of a major constitutional crisis over the separatist claims in Quebec, I turned to Major-General Rowland Mans, whose distinguished career had included three years as the British Army instructor at the Canadian Staff College. The outcome was a penetrating report, 'Canada's Constitutional Crisis: Separatism and Subversion' (*Conflict Studies*, No. 98, August 1978). The relevance of the Mans report to one of the major themes of this book is epitomised in the following passage:

> Canada is the latest of the Western powers to be seized by a suicidal desire to destroy its intelligence and security services. The Watergate affair was the excuse for powerful elements in and outside the United States to emasculate the Central Intelligence Agency (CIA) and the Federal Bureau of Investigation (FBI).... At the same time the Russians were having similar successes in penetrating and denigrating other Western intelligence agencies, particularly those in Italy, West Germany and Holland. The Canadian security service was to be the next in line.

Against this troubled background, the government went ahead with the creation of a new Canadian Security Intelligence Service. It was a protracted process, in which – without the knowledge of the Canadian authorities – The 61 was peripherally involved. One of our main Canadian contacts sent me a copy of the Canadian Security Bill in the summer of 1983. In a letter to my Canadian contact, dated 2 August 1983, I drew his attention to a potential problem in clauses defining domestic subversion. In their drafting, the Canadian lawyers had fallen into the same trap as Lord Denning (see Ch. XI) in that they assumed that subversion was a necessarily unlawful activity. The way I put it was as follows:

> ... The drafting team, it seems to me, has shirked the admittedly difficult problem of defining domestic subversion.... [paragraph 2(d)] rightly does not limit the definition of 'threats to the security of Canada' to 'covert unlawful acts', but includes activities 'directed towards or intended ultimately to lead to the destruction or overthrow of the constitutionally established system of government'. It therefore implicitly recognises the fact that *lawful* activities may be subversive, e.g., when the ultimate programme of any totalitarian group, whether Marxist-Leninist or 'Fascist', involves the liquidation of the present system and its replacement by permanent one-party rule. However, 14 (3) prohibits investigation of 'the affairs or activities of any person or group

of persons solely on the basis of the participation by that person or group in lawful advocacy, protest or dissent'.

The great majority of the activities of subversive groups are bound to be perfectly legal, or 'lawful' in any of our democracies. This does not necessarily mean that they are not subversive. If the proposed Security Service is precluded from keeping a watch on such subversive groups, subversion will flourish unchecked. It seems to me vital that this contradiction should be resolved. If it is not, it is going to lead to endless difficulties, and possibly make a large area of the activities of the Service inoperable.

When the final text of the Act was sent to me, I saw that the mind-set of the legal drafters had prevailed; as it usually does! The official definition of 'domestic threats to the security of Canada' (under Article 2, [d]), covered 'activities directed toward undermining by covert unlawful acts, or directed toward or intended ultimately to lead to the destruction or overthrow by violence of, the constitutionally established system of government in Canada. . . .'

The 1980s brought to light a sensational spy case rivalling the Gouzenko affair in importance; and a curious example of what might be termed perfectly lawful subversion. The star performer in the espionage case was a Canadian academic, Professor Hugh Hambleton, who was arrested in London in 1982 and jailed for ten years. The Professor had been recruited as early as 1947 at a cocktail party in Ottawa. He had served in NATO and had been passing classified material to his KGB minders for three decades.

An example of 'lawful' subversion was uncovered in 1987 by the Canadian Development Institute (CDI) of Ottawa, a non-partisan research organisation devoted, in its own words, to 'looking at government policies – in a practical, down-to-earth way'. A detailed research paper presented in November 1988 established that the Soviet-controlled Communist Party of Canada had penetrated, and ultimately controlled, the powerful countrywide tenants' organisation, the Toronto-based Federation of Metro Tenants' Associations (FMTA).

Since the Communist Party of Canada was in fact a legal organisation, there was no question of unlawful activity. However, as the report revealed: the FMTA had 'created a self-fulfilling prophecy in Ontario: in Marxist parlance, this is called the "Market Failure" Strategy'. Their method was to cripple the private market economy through constantly tightening rent controls. Having thus 'demonstrated' that the market did not work, this became the basis for a full government takeover. The report went on to note that new construction had collapsed and public-funded housing already accounted for 90 per cent of what was left. One of the informants of the Canadian Development Institute, a 'landlord of very modest means', had been virtually dispossessed by a rent review appeal board tribunal. One of the two officials presiding over the tribunal was a leading activist in the Communist Party. The rent review tribunal had forced this landlord to sell his small property, which was the only source of his small income.

Rightly, in terms of news value, the Gouzenko and Hambleton cases attracted far wider coverage. The penetration of the tenants' organisation, however, had to be seen as part of a worldwide network of manipulation ultimately controlled by the International Department in Moscow.

Further evidence was assembled from 1986 on by the Mackenzie Institute for the Study of Terrorism, Revolution and Propaganda, whose Director was Maurice Tugwell, lately retired as a brigadier in the British Army, and a participant in ISC study groups. A Mackenzie Institute report by Andrew Kavchak, published in 1989, documented the problems faced by the Canadian Security Intelligence Service (CSIS). Not to my surprise, the CSIS had run into many problems, arising partly from the inadequate definition of subversion in the original Bill and enshrined in the Act. In a 1986 working paper, *Crimes Against the State*, the law reform commission of Canada had reported that Canadian national security laws were inadequate: 'poorly arranged, resulting in overlapping and inconsistent provisions, excessively complex and detailed, and uncertain as to scope and meaning. The CSIS had had to operate against a background of public hostility, especially from the Canadian media'.[7]

Clearly, however, in Canada as elsewhere, the problem of subversion must be assumed to have been drastically reduced by the collapse of the Soviet Union and its satellite empire.

CARLO PERONI (as I shall call him) was a fair-skinned Neapolitan of middle height. He worked for a top-secret section of the *Carabinieri* and was sent to me by one of my ex-CIA friends, Ted Somers.[8] He was quick-thinking and fast-talking, even in English. He had no false modesty and told me once that the two most intelligent men in Italy were Giulio Andreotti and himself. Although I had met Andreotti twice, at Cercle gatherings, I never got a chance to ask him whether he agreed with Peroni's assessment.

In Italian politics, Andreotti was the ultimate chameleon, ready at all times to strike a deal that would bring him back to high office, preferably as Prime Minister, but ready also to settle for major but lesser office as Minister for Defence or Foreign Affairs. The intelligence world was wary of him, if only because, as Defence Minister in 1974, he had ordered the burning of 41,000 documents, thought to be mainly files of individuals and groups involved in subversion. In so doing, he was thought to have virtually destroyed Italy's counter-subversive capacity.

In October that year, a right-wing plot to poison Rome's water supply with stolen radioactive material was uncovered. The aim had been to provoke left-wing demonstrations that would give the armed forces a pretext to seize power. The plot was said to involve a former head of Italy's main external intelligence service, the *Servizio Informazione e Difesa* (SID).

In its counter-espionage capacity, the SID had been responsible for internal security. It was now stripped of this responsibility, which was transferred to a new *Servizio per l'Informazione e la Sicurezza* (SIS), a kind of inspectorate combining the resources of the Carabinieri and the *Guardia di Finanza* (GDF). Peroni's top-secret missions apparently arose from these new arrangements.

Peroni would turn up without warning, sometimes catching me, sometimes not. I tried to make him see the advantage of precise diary commitments, from his point of view as well as mine, but without much success. On one occasion I was about to close my office at 6.30 p.m. after waiting for him for two hours, when he turned up. His excuse, which I believed, was that he had been kept waiting by the head of Gaddafi's intelligence service. He explained that London was the most convenient place for them to meet, well away from Italy and Libya.

My Italian friend was a bundle of energy. Peroni, according to Somers, was the man who had provided the FBI with the vital evidence that enabled them to have the Mafia-connected Vatican banker Michele Sindona jailed for fraud.

The complications of Italy's subterranean activities in the late 1970s and into the 1980s almost defy analysis. Drugs and terrorism (of the neo-Fascist Right as well as of the extreme Left) were part of the mosaic. The Sicilian Mafia and the Neapolitan Camorra were involved in the running of both drugs and arms, for their own purposes, which sometimes overlapped with the activities of terrorist groups, such as the left-wing *Brigate Rosse* (Red Brigades) and *Lotta Continua* (On-Going

Struggle). Other elements were the Masonic lodge, P-2, the KGB and its Bulgarian subsidiary, the DS (*Durzhavna Sigurnost*), and the Vatican's bank, the *Istituto per le Opere di Religione* (IOR).

Some or all of these elements were involved in two incidents in which the innocent target was a pope.

How and why did the outspokenly anti-Communist Pope John-Paul I die suddenly in his room in the Vatican on the night of 28–29 September 1978, only a month after ascending the throne of Saint Peter? The hierarchy disallowed a post-mortem, on the ground that the Vatican Constitution made no provision for it. In June 1980, The 61 examined the hypothesis that John-Paul I had been assassinated by the KGB, on the basis of intelligence reaching us from sources in Rome and inside the Vatican.

The evidence was admittedly circumstantial, but it strained coincidence. On 5 September 1978, John-Paul had received Patriarch Pimen of Moscow, long notorious for his close KGB connection. With him was Metropolitan Nikodim of Leningrad. From our Vatican sources, we learned that before the audience Nikodim had beseeched the Vatican authorities to arrange for him to have at least thirty seconds alone with the Pope – specifically, not in the presence of Pimen.

Nikodim was granted his wish, which turned out to be fatal. He died, allegedly of a heart attack, in the arms of the Pope. Speculation in the Vatican suggested that in the thirty seconds he had asked for Nikodim would have (just) enough time to whisper to the Pope the name of a key dignitary who was a KGB agent. His intention must have been known to the KGB, doubtless through the agent he had planned to name. Therefore, he must be removed. And so, too, must the Pope as soon as feasible.

Some years later, in an impressively detailed 'investigation into the murder of John Paul I', David Yallop inclined to the view that the Pope had died of an overdose of digitalis, which leaves no trace, suggesting death by a heart attack. He records the sudden death of Nikodim, and quotes the theory that the Russian drank a poisoned cup of coffee intended for the Pope.[9] He does not mention the possible KGB connection, to which our informant inclined; and indeed produces other motives, in the complex Vatican involvement with the Mafia.

The high probability that the attempted assassination of that Pope's successor was a KGB operation suggests that there was a Soviet hand in the deaths of both John-Paul I and Nikodim.

*   *   *

THE ATTEMPT on the life of John-Paul II naturally attracted far more international attention. John-Paul I's successor was a Pole who had stood up to the Communist regime Stalin had imposed on his country. He was a charismatic figure who was spending much of his time carrying the Catholic gospel around the world.

Who had given the order to kill the Pope to the young Turkish terrorist Mehemet Ali Agca on 13 May 1981? When first arrested that day, Agca said he was a Communist. Later, he revealed he was a member of the extreme right-wing Turkish organisation, the Grey Wolves. Thereafter, he clammed up for more than a year. His interrogation was resumed in November 1982, when he revealed a Bulgarian connection.

His detailed confession was recorded by Judge Ilario Martella, the man in charge of the re-opened inquiry. He named two Bulgarians: Sergei Ivanov Antonov, thirty-five, an employee in the Rome office of Bulgarian Airlines; and Teodar Soyanov Ayvazov, a cashier.

At this point, as Peroni explained to me on one of his lightning trips to London, the plot thickened further. A link emerged between the attempt to kill the Pope and the kidnapping of the American General James Lee Dozier by the Red Brigades in mid-December 1981. In a brilliant joint operation between the Italian police and the CIA, Dozier was freed at the end of January 1982.

The Brigades terrorist, Antonio Savasta, was arrested during the raid on the flat in Padua where Dozier was being held. Interrogated by the Assistant Procurator, Domenico Sica, Savasta revealed the involvement of an Italian trade unionist, Luigi Scricciolo, with Bulgarian intelligence. A cousin of his, Loris Scricciolo, was a member of the clandestine 'Rome column' of the Red Brigades. Through Loris, Luigi obtained the record of the interrogation of Dozier by his kidnappers.

Luigi Scricciolo was in touch with Antonov, the man named by Agca. Scricciolo had come under Italian surveillance in 1977, after he had worked for the Bulgarians for a year.

More ramifications. In his trade union capacity, Scricciolo was in charge of foreign relations for the Socialist *Unione Italiana dei Lavoratori* (UIL: Italian Union of Workers). As such, he had established friendly relations with the Polish Solidarity leader, Lech Walesa. He posed as Walesa's best friend and provided the Bulgarians with a list of Solidarity's clandestine alternative leaders, which was duly passed on to the KGB. The leaders were then arrested.

Scricciolo organised Walesa's trip to Rome. One of Agca's most startling revelations was that he had an alternative plan to kill Walesa, should the attempt on the Pope fail. Of particular interest was the fact that although Scricciolo and Agca had never met, their stories matched.

The pieces of the jigsaw fell into place when Judge Martella, and two of his colleagues also engaged in judicial inquiries, decided to get together and exchange notes. The others were: Magistrate Carlo Palermo, in Trento, who was investigating the gigantic arms and drugs traffic passing through Bulgaria; and Judge Ferdinando Imposimato, who was looking into the contacts between Scricciolo and the Red Brigades and the Bulgarian secret service. At this point, the full story of the Bulgarian connection began to emerge.

As always, when drugs and terrorism are concerned, the Western services, and especially the Americans, were reluctant to make an issue of the KGB connection – in this case, the known fact that the Bulgarian DS was controlled by the KGB – for fear of jeopardising relations with the Soviet Union. The key man in Rome was Ivan Tomov Donchev, Secretary of the Bulgarian embassy, to whom Scricciolo reported. Donchev was hurriedly recalled to Sofia when Scricciolo was arrested on 4 February 1982. In Sofia, the key man was the Soviet ambassador, Nikita Tolubeyev, a close associate of the then head of the KGB, Chebrikov. Tolubeyev had taken up his post in Bulgaria in 1979, after serving as Soviet ambassador in Cuba.

The 61 provided the above details to its restricted readership in *Notes and Analysis* of January and March 1983.[10] In March, Peroni had come back to London. He was pressed for time. We met in the Grosvenor Hotel, Park Lane, and I noted his latest intelligence. The connecting thread was the heroin traffic from Bulgaria. The heroin, delivered to the Red Brigades, enabled the terrorists to buy arms from the Mafia and the Camorra.

The knowledge that the facts of the Bulgarian connection were now available to the judicial investigators caused the Bulgarians and their Soviet masters to 'go easy' on aid to the Red Brigades. Thereupon, the Sicilian and Neapolitan gangs attempted to bypass the Brigades and buy their heroin directly from the Bulgarians.

The outcome of this change of pattern was dramatic. The Red Brigades collapsed, at least for a time. Simultaneously, and not by coincidence, there was a spectacular increase in criminal, as distinct from political, kidnappings aimed at increasing the purchasing power of organised crime, whose profits on the American market were already enormous.

This was only one of the ways in which the Mafia and Camorra were acquiring a political dimension. A marked increase in gangland killings in 1982 was due in part to a new Italian police tactic of betraying individual gang leaders to each other so that, in effect, the gangsters could do the work of the police. This stratagem was rudely halted, however, when the head of the Carabinieri, General Carlo dalla Chiesa, was murdered in Palermo in September 1982.

AN EARLIER ITALIAN demarche of ours had ended in utter frustration for The 61, because of a scarcely believable piece of bureaucratic behaviour by Scotland Yard. Jean Violet had asked me to see two Italian contacts of his, both senior officials of the Guardia de Finanza.

The date of their arrival could hardly have been worse timed, from my point of view, as they landed up on Monday, 10 December 1979, the day Barbara Rose and I (with the others) moved into our new offices in Grand Buildings, Trafalgar Square. They had brought with them a list of Red Brigades terrorists who had moved to London under cover of working for a language school. We were still unpacking, and the photocopier I had ordered had not yet been delivered.

I took the Italians to lunch at the RAC to meet a Special Branch contact of mine, Superintendent N. The Italians knew no English and the Superintendent knew no Italian, so my interpreting skills were stretched. After lunch, we took a cab to New Scotland Yard, where the Superintendent introduced the visitors to a senior Special Branch detective whose Italian was much better than mine. I left the quartet in possession of the list of terrorists, on a promise that it would be photocopied for me.

When I rang Scotland Yard next day, the Superintendent refused to give me the list on the ground that it was now an official document and therefore classified. I reminded him of his promise and of the fact that without me he would not have gained access to the list. To no avail: bureaucracy had triumphed.

I would not have been treated that way by SIS or the CIA. . . .

UNTIL THE DISASTROUS leak from Bavaria which eventually reached *Der Spiegel*, von Machtenberg's German network had provided us with high-grade professional intelligence. In 1981, through their friends in Bonn, the Soviets were doing their utmost to unseat Chancellor Helmut Schmidt and bring back his predecessor, Willy Brandt. The main tactic was to foment anti-Americanism in the Federal Republic, and thus strengthen the neutralist and nationalist wings of the Social Democratic Party (SPD).

Egon Bahr, architect of the original Ostpolitik, made a scathing attack on Schmidt's pro-American policy in an off-the-record chat with left-wing journalists, a verbatim report of which reached us from the German network. In part, Bahr said:

'Despite the opposition of the Christian Democrats, the Americans and others, Brandt has an outstanding chance of forming the next Federal government. All the charges against him – that he is a Communist, that the woman he is living with is an extreme left-wing Marxist . . . – are of no account. He represents the hopes of the young generation for détente and the resumption of a more positive Ostpolitik, both of which are being ruined by Schmidt and his partners in the FDP. If Schmidt does not change his policy, he will lose his job. We are always ready to provide an answer.'

A similar line was being taken by Herbert Wehner, leader of the SPD's parliamentary group, and a former Communist who worked for the Comintern many years earlier but gave no sign of having changed his views. The reports on the views of Bahr and Wehner were hardly secret intelligence. However, von Machtenberg gave us the real stuff: the text of a minute which President Mitterrand had dictated after a talk with Chancellor Schmidt at the Elysée. The text reached us in a German translation.

Here are some extracts:

My impression was that the German Chancellor feared for his position as head of the Government, although he did not say so directly. He hopes for further support from France in the question of the deployment of the US Pershing missiles on German soil and for explicit French support of the American weapons policy. Schmidt's worst problem in the internal confrontation is Brandt's attitude and his apparent aim of getting him out. . . . He appeared to believe that some of Brandt's advisers – the name Bahr cropped up several times as though casually – were playing the Soviet card. . . . I got the impression that Schmidt would be happy if I felt able to attempt to use my influence on Brandt to persuade him to slow down his public and internal party pressures against the Chancellor. . . . Schmidt presented this in a very delicate and dexterous way.

The fact that The 61's bulletin had got hold of this text became known to President Mitterrand, who was said to be infuriated and launched inquiries (which proved fruitless) on the source of the leak.

Over the next few months, however, Schmidt, increasingly under pressure from the Brandt-Bahr wing of his SPD, began to waver. For example, when he met the French Premier, Mauroy, in Bonn on 29 January 1982, a detailed report of what Schmidt said came to us. At that time, as we knew from other sources, including published ones, Schmidt's SPD was moving in the direction of neutralism, and Schmidt, whatever he may have thought of the trend, was evidently not strong enough to resist it. The Chancellor's main arguments to Mauroy were these:

1 The division of Europe into spheres of influence under the Yalta agreements of 1945 could not be set aside without danger of world war. The Federal government would reject any pressure from the United States to adopt a harder line towards the Eastern bloc, and would refuse to go along with any proposals for far-reaching economic sanctions.

2 The Ostpolitik [Willy Brandt's initiative] would continue, with special reference to the reunification imperatives of the East–West German General Treaty of November 1972.

3 The military power balance between East and West should not be prejudiced by America's striving for superiority. Otherwise, the Soviets would be bound to increase their pressure on the Federal Republic to disavow the 1979 NATO 'two-track' decision on the deployment of medium-range missiles.

4 Schmidt complained that the Reagan Administration was supporting the opposition Christian Democrats. Moreover, the Americans were putting pressure on West Germany to adopt an extreme policy towards Poland. This was out of the question, said Schmidt, because of Germany's historic guilt in relation to the Polish people.

5 Schmidt also complained of a failure to recognise the Federal Republic's special vulnerability. Nuclear weapons were to be stationed on German territory, and Germany would have no control over them. For Moscow, any Western decision to impose 'global sanctions' against the Soviet Union would come close to constituting a *casus belli*. American policy was 'highly demagogic', said Schmidt, since the economic consequences would be suffered by Europe, while the American economy would be unaffected.

At this stage of the great game, victory in the Cold War still seemed a distant and problematical prospect.

I N 1981–2, I had a number of lunch meetings with the Israeli ambassador in London, Shlomo Argov. An intellectually impressive man, Argov was a useful source until, on the evening of 3 June 1982, he was shot in the head while leaving the Dorchester Hotel. Gravely injured, he survived, but did not recover sufficiently to resume public life.

The assassination attempt was the work of a hit team of the anti-Arafat Abu Nidal terrorist gang. The assailants were caught and received lengthy jail sentences. Before the attempt on his life, Argov had given me a Mossad contact. Through that channel, some months later, photocopies of some thirty secret PLO documents came into our hands, together with English translations.

The documents had been seized by the Israelis in the recent fighting in Lebanon. They confirmed the role of the Soviet Union and other Communist countries, including China, in providing training facilities for the Palestinians. They also revealed, or confirmed, the key role of the PLO in coordinating the activities of other terrorist organisations.

Among the latter were the Italian Red Brigades, the West German Baader-Meinhof Gang,. the Turkish Liberation Army, and groups from India, Pakistan, and Ireland. In groups or as individuals, the terrorists had been given forty-five-day training courses at a PLO camp attached to the Shatila refugee camp in Beirut.

The documents also gave the names of Fatah officers and men who had attended training courses in the USSR, China and Vietnam, Hungary and Bulgaria, Cuba, Algeria, and Pakistan.

The Mossad connection had proved useful.

NOTES

1 *Gordievsky*, pp. 484 et seq.
2 *Gordievsky*, p. 486.
3 In his autobiography, *An American Life* (Hutchinson, London, 1990), Ronald Reagan says: 'The crackdown fell short of the military intervention we had warned against, but our intelligence experts established that the entire exercise had been ordered from, and orchestrated by, Moscow' (p. 303).
4 BBC Radio 4, 21 December 1981.
5 *Globe & Mail*, Toronto, 13 December 1980.
6 Peter Worthington, 'What makes Trudeau tick?', *Toronto Sun*, 10 February 1988.
7 For a discussion of such problems and of some relevant cases, see J. L. Granatstein and David Stafford, *Spy Wars: Espionage in Canada from Gouzenko to Glasnost* (McClelland & Stewart, Toronto, 1990).
8 Carlo Peroni and Ted Somers are not the real names of the very real men concerned.
9 David Yallop, *In God's Name* (Jonathan Cape, London, 1984), pp. 311–24.
10 For fuller accounts, see Claire Sterling, *The Time of the Assassins: The Inside Story of the Plot to Kill the Pope* (Angus & Robertson, 1983); and Paul Henze, *The Plot to Kill the Pope* (Croom Helm, 1984).

XVII

French connections

FIRST IN FRIENDLY cooperation with Antoine Bonnemaison, and later in countering de Gaulle's policies with Gabriel Decazes, my French connections were of long standing. Under President Pompidou, both Albertini's network and Jean Violet's Cercle had continued the modest London–Paris axis. Under President Giscard d'Estaing, I also liaised (by now under our private-sector agency) with the SDECE man in London.

One day, early in 1980, the long-time Director-General of the SDECE, Comte Alexandre de Marenches, sent an emissary to my Grand Buildings office to say he would be pleased to meet me on my next visit to Paris. I had been somewhat inhibited about meeting de Marenches because of his known antagonism towards Jean Violet. In the end, however, and with Violet's full approval, I contacted de Marenches, who invited me to lunch at his Paris headquarters, universally known as *La Piscine* (the Swimming-Pool).[1]

In the Anglo-Saxon intelligence communities, de Marenches was known as 'Fatty', which conveys the wrong image of his bulk, for though he weighed around 280 lbs, he was six feet three inches tall. On strategic issues we were in broad agreement. The Comte made fun of the Quai d'Orsay, mimicking the precious tones of his diplomatic colleagues inquiring after titled relatives at official receptions.

I raised the matter of the break with Violet, as delicately as I could, but de Marenches declined to discuss it and changed the subject.

Lunch was an ample occasion, of substance rather than delicacy with roast lamb, sauté potatoes, and an abundance of wine and desserts. Two others were present: Dr Yves Beccuau, whose title was 'Psychological Counsellor', and Michel Roussin, a Gendarmerie officer, a specialist in Oriental languages and scientific research, who was de Marenches's Chef de Cabinet.[2]

The Comte's hostility towards Violet came into the open some months later over the affair of the so-called 'sniffer planes'. A Belgian named Bonnassoli claimed to have invented a device enabling aircraft to 'sniff' oil deposits while in flight over untested land. On learning of this claim, Violet had persuaded ex-Premier Pinay to raise the matter with the State-owned French oil company, ELF-Aquitaine.

On one of my visits to Nice, where Violet was confined for health reasons, he had told me that he was in deep trouble, but without saying why. The story erupted into a major scandal in 1984 when it turned out that the 'sniffing' device simply did not do what its inventor had claimed it could.

The claim was, in fact, exposed as a fantasy and a fraud. When Violet finally went into detail with me, he said, in humility: *J'ai pensé avec mon coeur français.'* A revealing phrase: Jean Violet's 'French heart' commanded him to play his cards very close to his chest so that the potential benefits of the sniffer device would be reserved for France. The problem was that there were no benefits, only losses.

Clearly, ELF should have rigorously tested the device. Instead it only tested the invention after it had failed repeatedly. One of the failures unfortunately involved Sir James Goldsmith, who invested millions in Guatemala after learning from the French that the sniffer plane had revealed a rich oil deposit. In one of our talks, Jimmy told me he had given the French government an ultimatum: immediate reimbursement of the equivalent of the $14 million he had lost, or legal action. He got his reimbursement, paid within twenty-four hours into a New York bank.

De Marenches, called as a witness in a State commission of inquiry, used his privilege to vilify Jean Violet's character, in abusive terms. Moreover, he also attacked, though without naming them, his two predecessors as head of the SDECE, whom he dismissed as 'mediocrities', as well as his successor, Pierre Marion: 'An amateur who will soon find out through bitter experience that Intelligence is a world where there is no room for improvisation or for the uninitiated.'[3]

In effect, de Marenches was claiming that he alone had run the service properly over the past thirty years, thus, by implication, dismissing not only his immediate predecessors, Generals Jacquier and Guibaud, but also the third man back, General Grossin. He also declared that President Giscard's only interest in the SDECE was in countries where he or his family had financial interests.

As for Jean Violet, de Marenches described him as an 'Intelligence swindler who drew large sums without doing anything worthwhile in return'.

The three generals resisted whatever temptation they may have felt to trade insults with de Marenches (a mere colonel, by the way). But all three wrote to Jean Violet praising the quality of his work in the highest terms.

Pierre Marion defended himself in radio and television interviews, and in a revealing book of memoirs, published in 1991. One of his revelations was that he was astonished, on taking over the French intelligence service in 1981, to discover that under de Marenches, the SDECE had hardly any agents behind the Iron Curtain, very few in Latin America, and only one in South-East Asia. They were numerous in French-speaking Africa, in Europe and the Near East.[4] He found out later that most of the SDECE career men in friendly countries merely traded African snippets for whatever they could get from Allied services, such as the CIA or SIS.

In a privately circulated memo, Violet quoted the distinguished diplomat Jean François-Poncet, former Secretary-General of the Elysée and later Giscard's Foreign Minister. As such, François-Poncet was of course one of the main recipients of SDECE reports: 'Ninety-nine per cent of the output,' he declared, 'was utterly worthless.' (This, view incidentally, was also shared in Allied quarters).

The report of the parliamentary commission declined to comment on 'testimony which, on the evidence, emanates from internal settlements of accounts'.

The rapporteur of the commission of inquiry into the sniffer planes affair was a Communist deputy, Parfait Jans. It must be difficult to live up to a first name like that, but 'Perfect' Jans did his best. His report presented the affair as a dark right-wing plot involving the Vatican, Opus Dei, the P-2 Masonic Lodge, Franz Josef Strauss, and other assorted ingredients, with Jean Violet at the mysterious heart of it. After studying the evidence, I am satisfied that Maître Violet was in no way a party to the swindle, responsibility for which was in any case admitted by the inventor, Bonnassoli (p. 361 of the report). All he did was to draw attention to the apparent potential of the sniffer device; ELF-Aquitaine rushed into it without adequate testing. Violet had refused all payments, including travel expenses.

I can confirm, from my many years of association with Jean Violet, that he was a man of exemplary probity. He never once requested a fee, or expenses, for his many services. He had serious health problems, and once faced heavy bills for a major operation which should have been covered by a private insurance policy. The insurers were refusing payment on the ground that he had not filled in his application form in triplicate. In the light of his unrewarded services to The 61, I offered to meet the bills out of our funds (to which his own fund-raising had contributed substantially), but he declined the offer, characteristically, adding the words: 'I shall never forget this.' That is not the way swindlers behave.

HOW, THEN, IS one to evaluate the work and personality of Alexandre de Marenches? An outsize ego, certainly, ready to dismiss lesser mortals as worthless. A cultured man, with an inherited fortune, which made him largely independent of official inducements. An American mother, who made him fluent in her tongue. Many contacts in high places, including personal friendships with such as the Kings of Morocco and Saudi Arabia, and President Saddam Hussein of Iraq.

Undoubtedly his advice was valued and sought in high places, such as the Oval Office. His book, co-authored (perhaps surprisingly) with the left-wing French television journalist Catherine Ockrent, reveals a firm and wide command of strategic thought.[5] To complete the positive side, under his direction, the SDECE (whose personnel was largely military) carried out several highly successful operations of the kind which Britain's SAS does so well.

Two examples came to us in detail, in the early days of The 61: the relief of the Grand Mosque in Mecca, which had been taken over by terrorists, and the deposition of 'Emperor' Bokassa in Central Africa. For these, he deserves thanks and praise; but not for running an intelligence service that rarely produced high-grade intelligence.

AT THE CERCLE meeting in Washington in December 1980, Georges Albertini had brought along a quiet Frenchman named François de Grossouvre. This was an impressive example of his foresight. De Grossouvre, a physician, was the closest friend and confidant of the Socialist leader and presidential candidate François Mitterrand. For many years, de Grossouvre had carried out special missions for Mitterrand. By nature and training, he was self-effacing. He played no part in our debates, but listened carefully, taking notes.

Five months later, François Mitterrand narrowly defeated Valéry Giscard d'Estaing in France's presidential elections. One of his first actions was to appoint de Grossouvre as his coordinator of security and intelligence. Shortly after, having obtained his direct line from Albertini, I went to see him in his modest office in the Elysée Palace.

We had reacted with alarm to Mitterrand's victory, but de Grossouvre reassured me. I expressed concern over the new President's appointment of four Communists as ministers in his first government. De Grossouvre's comment has stuck in my mind. 'One thing you have to understand about François Mitterrand is that he has a visceral hatred [*une haine viscérale*] of the Communists.' He did not explain the nature of this hatred which, later history suggests, probably reflected less an opposition to their policies than of Mitterrand's perception of the Communists as the main obstacle to his authority.

Not for nothing was Mitterrand known as *le Florentin*, in reference to his interest in Machiavelli and Florentine history. In his long career, he had been everything from apparently extreme Right to apparently extreme Left.[6] At a Cercle meeting, Albertini had explained the new President's conversion to socialism by analogy with Pascal's advice to the non-believer: kneel down every night and pray that you will believe in God. Mitterrand, he said, knelt every night and prayed that he might believe in socialism. One morning, on waking up, he found he did.

In 1974, his Socialist Party had joined the French Communist Party (PCF) in an electoral alliance known as the Union of the Left, and with a Common Programme.[7] In 1975, Mitterrand had led a Socialist delegation to Moscow and signed a cooperation agreement with the CPSU with Mikhail Suslov, the Politburo's chief ideologist. In the 1974 presidential elections, Giscard had narrowly defeated Mitterrand, by a margin of less than 2 per cent. Now Mitterrand had turned the tables.

Although this was not apparent at the time, his strategy was to use the redoubtable PCF, discarding it when it had served its purpose. That purpose, initially, was to muster left-wing support across the board. In the longer term, Mitterrand's strategy was to strengthen his Socialist Party at the expense of the Communists. It worked. In 1984, the PCF left the coalition. By then the PCF had been virtually marginalised.

In the wider confrontation, the advent of Mitterrand did give cause for alarm. In January 1976, as The 61 knew from a confidential source,

Mitterrand had made a vehement attack on NATO during a closed meeting of West European Socialist and Social Democratic parties at Helsingor, Denmark. Among those present was Harold Wilson, still Prime Minister.

In office, however, Mitterrand staunchly supported the Alliance, and never wavered in his determination to maintain France's independent nuclear deterrent. The fact that France did have its *force de frappe*, as its creator General de Gaulle called it, made it relatively easy for Mitterrand to support the deployment of the US Pershing II and Cruise missiles in *other* countries, for there was never any question of siting them on French soil.

To keep the Left happy in the face of his commitment to a strong defence, Mitterrand chose to pay an easy price: support for the Communist guerrillas in Latin America and southern Africa. This appeased both the hard and the sentimental Left.

In our reports to the Prime Minister and to President Reagan, we drew attention to the fact that the French President's wife Danielle was now, in effect, the leader of the French effort to help the Cuban-sponsored left-wing rebels in El Salvador. Indeed, her personal boudoir in the Elysée had been turned into the headquarters of the campaign. Officially, Mitterrand had appointed Régis Debray, revolutionary of the 1960s and friend of the late 'Che' Guevara, as his adviser on Latin American affairs.

His choice as External Affairs Minister was Claude Cheysson, whom I had known in London where he had served in the French embassy, and had met again in Hanoi and Algiers. Cheysson, a former aide to Premier Pierre Mendès-France, had a very wide knowledge of foreign affairs.

He was outspokenly anti-Soviet but sentimentally committed to Third World causes. At a meeting of EEC Foreign Ministers on 24 June 1981, he wanted to name the USSR as the aggressor in a communiqué on Afghanistan, but was talked out of a specific condemnation by Lord Carrington: On such situations as El Salvador and South Africa, however, Cheysson was on the same side as the Communists.

A revealing sidelight on Mitterrand's dealings with the Communists came in an inside report that reached us of a lunch at the Elysée in March 1982. The President's guest was the PCF's leader, Georges Marchais. Also present were Pierre Bérégovoy, Secretary-General of the Presidency, and the senior Communist minister in the Mitterrand government, Charles Fiterman.

Mitterrand raised the question of the Communist Party's attitude towards the Polish crisis. While he understood that the PCF was bound to support the Soviet position, he wished it would do so more discreetly. A few days later, Marchais obliged, though obliquely, when he declared publicly that the Polish crisis was damaging to 'the cause of socialism'. It was not difficult for the faithful to decode this form of words.

At the lunch, Marchais mentioned that he planned to go to Cuba shortly, and offered to transmit whatever personal message Mitterrand might wish to send to Fidel Castro. Thanking him, Mitterrand said it would be useful if Castro could help him to take on the role of mediator between the United States and the Communist-supported movements in Central America.

In the event, Marchais's trip to Havana was treated as an official mission and the government met his expenses. Marchais duly transmitted Mitterrand's offer, although nothing came of it.

Despite these early gestures to the party of his 'visceral hatred', it is fair to underline that President Mitterrand *did* marginalise the Communists. By July 1984, when the Communists left the ruling coalition, the Socialists had replaced them as the dominant force on the Left. The collapse of Communism in Eastern Europe might have done this anyway, but in the French context Mitterrand, the pragmatic 'socialist', did what no conservative president could have done.[8]

NOTES

1 So called because it is situated opposite the public swimming-pool in the Tourelles *quartier* of Paris.

2 The best account of the French secret services I have read is: Roger Faligot, Pascal Krop, *La Piscine: Les services secrets français 1944–1984* (Seuil, Paris, 1985), in which the careers of these and others are described (see page 215).

3 See three articles by Pierre Darcourt in *Le Figaro* of 6–8 May 1983.

4 Pierre Marion, *La Mission Impossible* (Calmann-Levy, Paris, 1991), p. 22 et seq. This book throws a lurid light on the internecine feuds of the French secret services.

5 Ockrent, Marenches, *Dans le Secret des Princes* (Stock, Paris, 1986).

6 Specifically, in his student days, Mitterrand had joined the far-right monarchist *Action française*, in which he served as a '*camelot du roi*', as the news vendors of the movement's newspaper, *Action française*, were styled. After the occupation of France by the Nazis, he joined the collaborationist Vichy government, serving as '*chargé des prisonniers*' (a reference to French prisoners of war). Later, however, he served as a Resistance fighter. There is no mention of these early involvements in his entry in the *International Who's Who*.

7 Antoine Bonnemaison, 'The Social Conflict in France', *Conflict Studies* No. 55, ISC, March 1975.

8 See Brian Crozier, 'Communism: Why Prolong Its Death-Throes?' (Occasional Paper 46, Institute for European Defence and Strategic Studies, London, 1990).

XVIII

The KGB lawsuits

IN THE YEARS 1981–6, I was deeply involved in two major lawsuits, and to a lesser degree in a third one. The connecting link in all three cases was the KGB.

In the first of these, Rudolf Augstein, publisher of the West German news magazine *Der Spiegel*, sued the Anglo-French financier Sir James Goldsmith for alleged defamation. In the second, I was sued by Richard Barnet, a co-founder of the US-based Institute for Policy Studies (IPS). In both cases, the plaintiff 'discontinued' the action, but only after several years.

The third case was one of a number involving the Greek tabloid daily *Ethnos*. In these cases, the outcomes were mixed.

This may sound like a digression from the story of The 61. In fact, without The 61, the outcome of the first two cases would have been a costly defeat.

At the heart of Augstein's action against Goldsmith was the *'Spiegel* affair' of 1962, which had wrecked the chances of the Bavarian leader, Franz Josef Strauss, of succeeding the aged Konrad Adenauer as Federal Chancellor of West Germany. In an interview with Strauss in Goldsmith's news magazine *Now!* of 15 February 1980, I had referred to the KGB's role in the smear campaign which had halted Strauss's meteoric career.

Nearly a year later, in early January 1981, Sir James Goldsmith rang me to say that he had been invited to address the Media Committee of the Conservative Party in the House of Commons. He had written a draft, but

wanted to make a reference to the *Spiegel* affair, which had caught his
eye in my Strauss interview.

We met in his office to discuss the draft of his speech, which was
entitled 'Subversion in the Media'. It was our third meeting. Robert Moss
had introduced us just before the launch of *Now!* in words flattering to
me rather than to Sir James: 'The legendary Sir James Goldsmith meets
the legendary Brian Crozier.' With his great height, piercing blue eyes,
and dazzling smile, Sir James is a charismatic figure, and a gambler of
genius. Neither of us realised, that day, how big a gamble he was about
to take on my advice.

The key passage in his speech referred to the campaign in *Der Spiegel*
to discredit Strauss, and said that it had been 'orchestrated by the KGB'.
It attributed this information, correctly, to 'General Sejna, the high-ranking
Czech intelligence defector'. Goldsmith's speech was printed in *Now!* on
7 February 1981, and on 6 March Augstein issued a writ for libel,
demanding a retraction and apology, with costs and damages.

The *Spiegel* affair had begun in October 1962, when the news magazine
carried a sensational article giving details of a secret NATO exercise,
codenamed 'Fallex 62'. At that time, Strauss, who was the West German
Defence Minister, was on holiday. The popular version of what happened
next was untrue but widely believed. He was reported to have exploded
at this breach of official secrecy, and ordered the arrest of Rudolf Augstein
and several members of his staff, including the editor, Konrad Ahlers. In
a speech on 2 November, Strauss proclaimed his innocence, but hardly
anybody believed him. In fact, the orders to arrest Augstein and staff
members had been given by Chancellor Adenauer, who was apparently
happy that the blame should fall on Strauss. The Communist press in the
Soviet Union and East Germany took up the anti-Strauss refrain. On 26
November, the Chancellor, apparently responding to the popular outcry,
sacked Strauss, thereby destroying his chances of becoming Chancellor.

The following May, the Federal Supreme Court dropped all charges
against Augstein and his journalists. Paradoxically, it also decided that the
police action against *Der Spiegel* had been lawful. It also ruled that Strauss
and his Defence Ministry had not, as alleged, played a decisive part in
initiating the raid. Several years later, the full extent of Strauss's innocence
was revealed.

THE MAN WHO revealed the story behind the story, Major-General
Jan Sejna – who had defected from the Czechoslovak StB during 'the

Prague Spring' in 1968 – has told the tale of his defection in his book *We Will Bury You* (1982). After months of debriefing by the CIA, Sejna was given a chance to make his way in capitalist America, but did not prosper. He was then offered a senior post in the Defense Intelligence Agency (DIA), the Pentagon's more limited equivalent of the CIA.

The CIA had been less interested than Sejna had expected in two of his revelations: the part played by the KGB in the Cuban drugs traffic; and the secret story of the *Spiegel* affair.

In 1977, nine years after Sejna's defection, Dr Walter Hahn, the Austrian-born defence specialist, had a long session with Sejna, who gave him the details. Sejna had been present when the then Czech Minister of the Interior, Rudolf Barak, explained the plan for the *Spiegel* operation to the Czech Central Committee. In 1965, Sejna had also been present at a meeting of high-level Warsaw Pact officials in Prague where one of his colleagues bragged about the success of the operation against Strauss.

Two years after his meeting with Sejna, Hahn passed the details to our mutual friend William F. Buckley, who wrote an article headlined 'The Vindication of Strauss' in his magazine *National Review* on 8 February 1980. The core of Sejna's revelations was that the StB, on behalf of the KGB, had been given the job of obtaining secret NATO documents and passing them to *Der Spiegel* for publication, in the hope that this would precipitate a scandal affecting Strauss's career prospects.

The Augstein versus Goldsmith case dragged on for three and a half years. As a consultant to Sir James, my job was to find the key witnesses and prove our case. The contract was a personal one with me, but in reality it was a contract with The 61. Without it, no valid defence could have been made.

My first priority was to get hold of General Sejna. With President Reagan in power, and Jimmy Carter out of it, I had thought this would be easy. I was wrong.

Throughout the dark post-Watergate years, I had maintained close links with the DIA, which had been relatively unscathed by the events that had virtually destroyed the CIA. I tried a friend there on my next flight to Washington, DC, but drew an unexpected blank. 'The General's under wraps,' he told me.

This was discouraging news, and I knew I was going to have to try the indirect approach, through Bill Casey of the CIA. Unfortunately, he was abroad at the time. Instead, I had long talks with Walter Hahn and a friend of his, Joseph Douglass, who had spent months closeted with Sejna. Both of them gave me signed statements, but I knew that in an English court of law these would only count as secondary evidence.

One of my main problems in this and subsequent cases was the (to me) astonishing ignorance of international politics in our legal profession. This applied in particular to the man handling the case for Allen & Overy, the solicitors retained by Sir James Goldsmith. His name was Graeme Hall. He knew the law; I knew the background. In effect, I gave him a beginner's course, without which his knowledge of the law would not have sufficed to win the case.

On a later visit to Washington, I had a long talk with Bill Casey at his Langley office, and told him I was being blocked by the DIA's bureaucracy. This time, my luck was in. Bill was having breakfast the following morning with General James A. Williams, Director of the DIA.

Next evening, Casey's personal assistant rang me with a code name for Sejna and his unlisted number.

The General, a pale, thin little man with a high forehead and blond hair, spent a whole afternoon with me in my room at the Madison Hotel. He explained to me that, as Chief of Staff to the Czech Defence Minister and Assistant Secretary to the Defence Council, many secret papers crossed his desk. They had included instructions from the KGB to the StB to handle agents in West Germany charged with obtaining secret NATO documents. The intention was to use these papers to create a public scandal calculated to discredit Franz Josef Strauss. This was our first breakthrough, but there was very much more work ahead.

Without Sir James Goldsmith's money, and his unflinching determination to defeat the enemy, the exercise would simply have petered out. Halfway through the protracted process, Jimmy told me that if the case came to trial, he planned to launch a daily newspaper, 'for the duration', to give a verbatim account of the proceedings. He was prepared to spend £18 million on it.

Apart from Sejna, our key witness was a senior KGB defector, who had personal knowledge of the *Spiegel* affair. His name was Ilya Dzhirkvelov. He had defected to Britain some years earlier from a United Nations post in Geneva. With my long-standing MI-6 contacts, I thought there would be no problem about meeting him, but I was soon disillusioned. I was given to understand that MI-5 had vetoed my request.

My SIS friends did their best, but came back empty-handed. Fortunately, my grapevine included a dissident of many years who had promised to put me in touch with Dzhirkvelov if the official channels failed. Within half an hour, the contact was made and we met over lunch. Dzhirkvelov, a Georgian, was a powerfully built man of medium height, with grey hair and a pencil-line moustache.

Through his entire career until his defection in 1980, Ilya had been involved in disinformation work. Early in 1960, he recalled, he had been summoned to a top-level secret meeting of the International Department (ID) of the Soviet Central Committee. In the chair was the Comintern veteran and head of the ID, Boris Ponomarev.

He mentioned an operation to prevent politicians undesirable in Soviet eyes from coming to power. The only name he specifically mentioned was Franz Josef Strauss. Dzhirkvelov and others present were instructed to work out practical proposals. Later, Ilya had discussed the German situation with Khrushchev's son-in-law, Alexei Adzhubei, at that time editor of the government daily, *Izvestiya*. Dzhirkvelov was instructed by his KGB superior, General Agayants, in charge of disinformation, to tell West German journalists that the Soviets had proof that Strauss was linked with US intelligence. German journalists, all Social Democrats, were invited to the USSR and given VIP treatment. Dzhirkvelov, under instructions, told them that the Americans were paying large sums to Strauss, who was more interested in getting rich than in the future of Germany. At a later top-secret meeting, in 1963, Ponomarev told Dzhirkvelov and his colleagues that 'we successfully used *Der Spiegel* to undermine Strauss.'

That day, and in a later detailed statement, Dzhirkvelov mentioned corroborating evidence from a number of other Soviet colleagues. There could be no doubt, he said, that the anti-Strauss campaign in *Der Spiegel* was launched on material planted by the KGB.

THE CASE HAD been scheduled for hearing in May 1984, but was postponed until early October. Material, mostly from expert witnesses, had been pouring in. We were bracing ourselves for the encounter, when suddenly, in early September, the other side caved in. Augstein declared himself ready to drop the action, on condition that the defendants made it clear that he was not 'controlled by the KGB'. Indeed, Sir James Goldsmith had never said he was. At a final meeting with Sir James's counsel, Lord Rawlinson, in his cramped chambers in the Middle Temple, I edited an agreed statement to appear in full-page advertisements in Britain, the US and Germany. The newspapers carrying it were: in the UK, *The Times, Daily Telegraph,* and *Financial Times*; in the US, the *New York Times*, the *Wall Street Journal,* and the *Washington Post*; and in the German-speaking world, the *Frankfurter Allgemeine Zeitung* and *Die Welt*. (The statement was turned down by the *Guardian, Neue Zürcher Zeitung* and *Die Zeit*.)

At the foot of the advertisements came Sir James Goldsmith's personal declaration, headed 'A Victory for the West'. In it he placed the *Spiegel* affair in the wider context of many similar examples all over the world. He had 'sponsored a massive international research effort' to prove the existence of this worldwide activity of the KGB, as well as the truth of his charge about the manipulation of *Der Spiegel*. He added the required rider:

> It was never my intention to imply that *Der Spiegel* was at any time aware that it was being used by the KGB. Indeed the whole point of Soviet manipulation of the Western media is that the publications so used should be unaware of the source of the material fed to them.

He ended by describing the agreed statement of 8 October 1984 as 'a famous victory for the defence of the West against its main enemy, Soviet imperialism'.

The cost of Sir James Goldsmith's 'famous victory' was enormous. My own research contract, including special payments to researchers, ran to about £439,000. Payments to the UK law firm I estimated at about £200,000, and to a German law firm about £15,000.[1]

BY THE TIME the *Spiegel* case had ended, I was in the thick of a similar action, at the defending end. I had unwittingly brought this new battle upon myself, by writing a short letter to the *Spectator*.

A few words of background are needed. In its issue of 7 April 1984, the magazine had carried an enthusiastic review by Enoch Powell, MP, of a book by the American writer Richard Barnet, entitled *Allies: America, Europe and Japan since the War* (Simon and Schuster, New York; Jonathan Cape, London, 1983–4).

I share in the widespread admiration for Powell, but I do have reservations about his views, notably about his anti-American attitude. Although Richard Barnet is an American, his book was anti-American, in the sense that, in his account of East–West relations, he usually sided with the Soviets. I had known of Richard Barnet for years, not only through previous works but also because he was a co-founder of the left-wing think-tank, the Washington-based Institute for Policy Studies (IPS).

My letter appeared on 28 April 1984 and read as follows:

Sir: Mr Enoch Powell never ceases to puzzle. How can such erudition cohabit with such innocence? The most important point about *Allies: America, Europe and Japan*, upon which he heaps such praise, is that the author, Richard J. Barnet, is a co-founder and is still a mainstay of the Institute for Policy Studies, a major front for Cuban intelligence, itself controlled by the Soviet KGB. Are readers not entitled to be forewarned?

In mid-June, a letter came from Bindman and Partners, a firm of solicitors frequently associated with left-wing clients. The letter called on me to retract my allegations and pay damages to Barnet. As it happened, the peripatetic Sir James Goldsmith was at his Surrey home. I knew he had no love for the head of the legal firm who had written to me, Geoffrey Bindman, who had defended *Private Eye* in the writs Jimmy had issued against the satirical review.

It did not take Jimmy long to offer to see me through. Without him, I fear, I might well have had to apologise in the hope of limiting the damage. Instead, I wrote to Bindman defending what I had said, and refusing either to retract or to apologise.

The expected writ was served on me on an unfortunately chosen day – 16 August 1984, the day I was under the surgeon's knife at the Middlesex Hospital for the removal of a gangrenous gall bladder. One of my first visitors was Robert Moss, who brought me a weighty package of photocopies of the incriminating contents of a briefcase belonging to the late Orlando Letelier, who had been the ambassador in Washington of Salvador Allende's extreme Left regime in Chile. These documents were essential to my defence, for they proved two things: that Letelier had worked for Richard Barnet's IPS, and that he was also on Fidel Castro's payroll. Letelier had been murdered by agents of General Pinochet's secret service with a bomb left in his car.

Not long after my release from hospital, I had seen Dzhirkvelov, who said to me: 'In the KGB, before I left, we were always told: "Public Enemy number one is Brian Crozier."'

I thanked him for the compliment. 'Who was Public Enemy number two?'

He paused for a moment, trying to recall the name, then came out with it: 'Robert Moss.'

Had I needed any further proof of the KGB's animosity, there it was.

Some time later, in Washington, I was introduced to a plain-clothes police-man, unkempt as they often are to merge with the targeted background. Tall and gangling, he wore his hair long, with an untidy beard to match. His target, in fact, had been the IPS. He went there from time to time for informal poker evenings.

He remembered one evening very clearly, for I was the sole topic of conversation.

'Me?'

'Yeah. Brian Crozier. One of them kept on asking: "How can we finish that guy off?" One guy wanted to do a research project on everything you'd written, so as to prove you were an agent of influence of the CIA. They kept on mentioning a book on Chile.'

We both agreed that by 'finishing that guy off' nothing as drastic as murder was implied. The point was to silence me by ruining my reputation. The reference to a book on Chile rang a bell. The refer-ence was clearly to Robert Moss's book on the Allende regime (see Ch. VIII).

The hippy-looking detective went on to mention two former members of my staff as the main IPS sources on me.

In various ways, the IPS case was even tougher than the *Spiegel* case had been. The main problem was that the plaintiff was an American, as was the organisation in question: his Institute for Policy Studies. The CIA was under severe legal and constitutional restraints. The Watergate investigations had made it clear that the Agency had no mandate to inter-vene in home politics. Worse still, from my viewpoint, the FBI, after years of spying on the IPS, had been ordered to discontinue all such investigations. The IPS had successfully challenged its right to do so in a writ alleging 'illegal surveillance' by the Bureau.

Once again, I had no option but to appeal to Bill Casey for his guidance and help.

MY TARGETS WERE two key defectors from the Cuban DGI: Orlando Castro and Gerardo Jesus Peraza. Both men, in testimony before Congress, had revealed the complete control of the Cuban *Dirección General de Inteligencia* (DGI) by the KGB. Castro had written a book about his experiences, entitled *Spy for Fidel* (1971). I wrote from London to Bill in some detail, and had the letter delivered directly by a mutual friend. I made it clear that I was aware the IPS was an American institution and that therefore the CIA was forbidden by law from playing an official part in my case. There were, however, some legitimate foreign angles, such as the European branch of the IPS, the Transnational Institute in Amsterdam, and the well-known involvement of the IPS in Central America.

I flew to Washington shortly after writing, and Casey saw me in his office in the Old Executive Building adjoining the White House.

This time, I left Casey's office empty-handed. He had greeted me as cordially as always, in his friendly mumble. I had asked him for Peraza's address; I already had his Boston telephone number, from a man who had interpreted for the defector when he testified. The other Casey – the tough Irish New York lawyer – came to the surface. 'No, dammit, Brian. Look, I have a duty to protect these people. First, we'll ask him whether he wants to see you. If he does, we can set up a meeting for you.' Bill lectured me on the statutory limitations of the Agency's freedom of manoeuvre in this kind of situation (which I already knew), but he did give me the name of a senior member of the CIA's legal department.

Next morning, two CIA lawyers came to my hotel and agreed, after much argument, to contact Peraza for me. I had already given up on Orlando Castro, who had let it be known to the authorities that he never wanted to talk about his case again.

I wrote a friendly letter to Peraza in his own language and an Agency contact delivered it.

Nothing more happened on that visit, but when I was back in Washington some months later, Bill Casey told me that Peraza had refused to take delivery of my letter. A female Agency officer had dropped in on Peraza with the letter. On hearing what she wanted to see him about, he had made a scene, raising his voice and shouting expletives at her. Seizing my letter from her hand, he had torn it up unread and scattered the contents in the air. He then flung the door open and ordered her out. A day or two later, a male officer, suitably burly, had gone to see the Cuban. By that time, Peraza had calmed down. He merely said that he wanted nothing to do with the case.

I had put together an impressive team of helpers in America. Robert Moss was one of them, and he had already helped me with the Letelier documents. A British friend of his, long resident in the US, John Rees, had bulky files on the IPS, and provided much documentary material. Others who helped were Lee Edwards, a journalist and biographer of Ronald Reagan; David Martin, a former Congressional aide, and a Trotskyist in his youth (see Ch. IX); and Donald Jameson, who for many years had been the CIA's top specialist on the Soviet Union. Apart from his fluent Russian, he also spoke Spanish and had a special interest in Latin America. All of them provided me with interesting material. Another was the man who had interpreted for Peraza: a Greek by birth, brought up in Italy, and an excellent linguist. His name was Al Tarabochia. Tarabochia gave me a signed statement about the involvement of IPS personnel with the DGI.

John Rees had introduced me to a New York lawyer, Allan Altman. Warning me that New York lawyers charged exorbitant fees – such as $2000 for one letter – Jimmy Goldsmith gave me an initial 'legal' budget limited to $10,000.

During the first few months of 1986, the most interesting stuff I had seen since the case started came to me from a remarkable woman whom I shall call Harriet. During the post-Watergate years, she had in effect created a private-sector equivalent of the FBI, and had built up an impressive archive on the subversive Left, and terrorist groups in her country.

From her and from several other sources, I obtained documentary evidence that the IPS had been set up on an initial grant of $25,000 from the Sam Rubin Foundation. Rubin was that unusual phenomenon: a Communist millionaire. He had made a fortune out of his Fabergé Perfume company. He and his wife had been members of the Communist Party USA. Harriet also sent me official Internal Revenue tax returns recording grants to IPS personnel and affiliated organisations from the Louis M. Rabinowitz Foundation. The original Louis Rabinowitz had set up his foundation in 1944 to help Jewish causes. His son, Victor Rabinowitz, a New York lawyer, was Fidel Castro's chief legal representative in the United States, and indeed, as such under US law, he registered as a foreign agent.[2]

These documents alone appeared to me to confirm the Communist and Cuban antecedents of the IPS. David Martin put me in touch with an American ex-leftist, David Horowitz, who as a younger man had been one of the editors of *Ramparts* magazine: the publication that had first attempted to expose the CIA's connection with Forum World Features (see Ch. VI). At that time, Horowitz was a member of the Communist Party, and indeed he had been brought up in a Communist household. He sent me some interesting material about the Cuban involvements of Saul Landau, a senior fellow of the IPS.

From Al Tarabochia, I had received the passenger list of a Cuban

Airlines flight from Mexico City to Havana in July 1969. The passengers included a number of American citizens, among them Saul Landau and Bernadine Dohrn, who had been involved in the terrorist activities of the Weather Underground (with which Richard Barnet's co-founder of the IPS, Arthur Wascow, had close links). Saul Landau thereafter became an unconditional supporter of Fidel Castro.

By September 1986, I had enough material to write a 'Draft Speech for the Defence'. Alasdair Pepper of Peter Carter-Ruck and Partners submitted it to counsel, who pronounced it a 'substantial' document but repeated the pessimistic professional verdict: that I still lacked conclusive evidence admissible as such in an English court of law.

A complicating factor in this case was that my co-defendants, the *Spectator* and its proprietor at the time of my offending letter, Algy Cluff, had no interest in pursuing the case and wished to apologise for the letter. This of course was unacceptable to me, as an apology for my letter would amount to calling me a liar. I raised the point with Jimmy Goldsmith, who fully supported me, and said we should put the *Spectator* on formal warning that I would sue them if they went ahead.

Cluff had lunched me to explain why he wanted to opt out. He was one of the defendants in another libel case, which at that moment was coming to trial. It involved the well-known Greek journalist Taki, author of the entertaining column 'High Life'. The case attracted wide media coverage when it ended unfavourably for the defending side some weeks later, and Mr Cluff emerged from the ordeal poorer, it was reported, by some £300,000.

I expressed my sympathy, but also my determination not to capitulate. I told him I reserved the right to sue the *Spectator* for libel if their proposed apology for what I had written in effect accused me of lying.

Early in October 1986, I learned from Pepper that Cluff and the *Spectator* had indeed decided to publish a letter of apology. I wrote to Cluff to protest, repeating that an apology from his side would amount to calling me a liar and thus seriously impugn my professional integrity.

On Geoffrey Bindman's advice, Algy Cluff was determined to go ahead. Bindman had advised the High Court Queen's Bench Division accordingly. I therefore, through Peter Carter-Ruck's firm, appealed against the High Court decision, thereby (or so Alasdair Pepper assured me) creating legal history.

Judgement on my appeal was given on Thursday, 11 December 1986, in the Court of Appeal in the Law Courts. I listened in amazement to the lengthy judgement read out by Lord Justice Ralph Gibson. My warning letter to Algy Cluff, and those from my lawyers, had had some effect, in that the proposed apology from the *Spectator* did not mention me by name. Yet the judgement delivered in open court mentioned me repeatedly – fourteen times, thus nullifying any advantage I might have gained from the *Spectator*'s reticence.

Judge Gibson described me as 'a journalist of distinction and a writer on international affairs'. But, he said, 'none of the parties was famous or notorious'. This included me. Therefore, he 'did not think that a statement made in open court in November 1986 [a reference to the agreement to settle the case against the *Spectator*] would have the slightest effect on a trial taking place in March to May or June 1987. Potential jurors would be unaffected. Any publicity resulting from such a statement would have passed out of their minds long before the trial.'

This seemed to me to imply that there was one justice for celebrities and another for the merely 'distinguished'. I was not Jeffrey Archer or Joan Collins.

In its issue of 30 December 1986, *The Times* carried a Law Report totalling forty-five column inches on the proceedings of the Court of Appeal.

That day, Pepper wrote to me, drawing my attention to the fact that the *Spectator* would not be mentioning my name in its agreed apology.

Some weeks later, Bindman rejected a proposal from our side for a straight withdrawal on both sides, each to pay its own expenses. Pepper put an alternative proposal to me: that I should offer to pay a portion of the other side's expenses – £10,000, say. I would make it clear in a confidential covering letter that I was doing this strictly for financial reasons, and was not admitting liability. I rejected this proposal, and wrote to Jimmy. His support continued, unwavering. In a terse note from Paris on 13 May 1987, he said: 'I agree with everything you say. If anything, they should pay your costs. I can see no reason for being soft.'

The lawyers, however, still insisted on a 'smoking gun' witness on my side.

And now, after the months and years of this war of nerves, I received a letter dated 27 May from the New York law firm, who had learned of a witness with first-hand knowledge of a Cuban–IPS connection. The man was Arturo Cruz, Jr, formerly the Coordinator of Intelligence for Nicaragua's Sandinista government with the Cuban DGI. At last, the 'smoking gun'! There was only one snag. Cruz had come into the news because of the Iran Contra hearings then in progress. The media had revelled in the news that he had been the 'boyfriend' of Fawn Hall, the glamorous and loyal secretary to Colonel 'Ollie' North, a key witness from the White House. He was willing to give evidence for me, but not until his involvement in the inquiry was concluded.

Some weeks later, Alasdair Pepper wrote to say that Allan Altman had indeed talked with Arturo Cruz, who apparently knew Saul Landau, and from first-hand knowledge was aware that he and his IPS colleagues were helping Sandinista intelligence, which was closely connected with the Cuban DGI. Pepper's letter ended with a PS:

> Since dictating this letter, I have heard from Barnet's solicitors that they are prepared to withdraw the action with no order as to costs. Great news. My congratulations to you.

A long letter from Bindman and Partners, dated 7 July 1987, confirmed the good news, which was made official by a court order dated 11 August. It was all over and, once again, we had won by default.

TO ETHNOS MEANS 'The Nation' in Greek. It is also the title of a sensational, and sensationally successful, tabloid newspaper launched in Athens in September 1981. Both in its news coverage and in editorial opinion, *Ethnos* favoured the Soviet interest to an extraordinary degree.

Whether allegations that the KGB controlled the newspaper were true or false has not been proved in a court of law. It can be shown, however, that the KGB did have an interest in *Ethnos*. The allegations sparked a number of legal actions, in two of which I was involved. So, too, was Sir James Goldsmith. For one Greek investigative journalist, the affair had meant years of trauma and battle.

Paul Anastasi, who sometimes writes as 'Paul Anast', was born in Cyprus but had spent most of his life in Greece. He graduated from Southampton and London and was bilingual. Settling in Greece, he became the Athens correspondent of the *New York Times* and the London *Daily Telegraph*. Anastasi spent fourteen months investigating the *Ethnos* affair and wrote a book entitled *Take the Nation in Your Hands*. In so doing, he was in effect challenging a powerful figure in Greek public life: George Bobolas, the publisher of *Ethnos*. The book became a bestseller, and a pirated edition sold 15,000 copies.

Some background is needed. Recent Greek politics had been dominated by one name: Papandreou. The veteran politician George Papand-reou, aged seventy-five, was elected to power in February 1964. His son Andreas, born in 1919, renounced his US acquired citizenship and came home to join his father's Cabinet. Though not himself a Communist, Andreas appointed a number of fellow-travellers of the Greek Communist Party (KKE) to positions in the Greek Central Intelligence Service. Papand-reou senior freed many jailed Communists or sympathisers.

During the seven-year rule of the Greek colonels, Andreas Papandreou went into voluntary exile again. Back in Athens when the military regime collapsed in 1974, he founded the Pan-Hellenic Socialist Movement (PASOK). He was elected to power with a comfortable majority in October 1981. One month earlier, *To Ethnos* was launched.

From the start, the new tabloid combined crime and scandal stories with anti-American material. On 28 July 1983, *Ethnos* published a tran-script of a telephone conversation between Paul Anastasi and his lawyer, which it described as a dialogue 'between Anastasi and a CIA agent'. A protracted period of trial and counter-trial followed. Anastasi was found guilty of criminal libel and defamation on 16 December 1983 and sen-tenced to two years' jail. At the last minute, his two key witnesses had opted out. One was Yannis Yannikos, a Communist who had initiated a deal with Bobolas and had been prepared to produce details of a deal between Bobolas and the Soviet authorities.

His son, Christos, however, did turn up in court. But the son's evidence was second-hand; hence the verdict of guilty. Anastasi appealed immedi-ately and was not jailed.

At the appeal hearing in May 1984, Yannikos changed his mind and gave evidence, referring to dealings with an identified KGB man, Vassily Sitnikov. Anastasi's sentence was reduced from two years to one, and on a further appeal the sentence was ruled invalid on a technicality. In further legal actions, Bobolas was found guilty of defaming Anastasi and insulting the authorities. Later, he was found guilty of illegal telephone-tapping.

These actions had virtually ruined Paul Anastasi. He had heard on the BBC's World Service of Sir James Goldsmith's offer of a major prize for investigative journalists exposing Soviet disinformation, and wrote to my office for further information. I discussed the matter with Sir James and advised that in the event of further litigation the KGB defector Ilya Dzhirk-velov should be brought in. In my office, Ilya had disclosed that before defecting he had been working closely with the KGB disinformation specialist, Vassily Sitnikov. They had even discussed a plan to set up a daily newspaper in Athens.

At this point, Sir James Goldsmith's Parisian news magazine, *L'Express*, became a target for Bobolas. So did *The Economist*, because of a story published in its confidential bulletin, *Foreign Report*.

L'Express carried an article by a former member of the Greek Communist Party, Ilios Yannakakis. The article described what he called a Soviet effort to 'Finlandise' Greece, and quoted from Paul Anastasi's book.

Ethnos replied in standard fashion, by vilifying Yannakakis. Bobolas issued a writ for defamation against Yannakakis and *L'Express*. At that time, Jimmy Goldsmith was in New York, and I became involved in the correspondence between him and his trusted senior employee at *L'Express*, the Managing Director, Tom Sebestyen. After a series of hearings and appeals, the case against Yannakakis was dropped on 7 March 1986.

BECAUSE OF ENGLAND'S eccentric libel laws, the battle between *Ethnos* and *The Economist* was more formidable. As it happened, I was in Jimmy Goldsmith's favourite club in Curzon Street, having tea with him and Dzhirkvelov, when we learned that Bobolas was suing *The Economist*. The news came through a telephone call from the then editor of *The Economist*, Andrew Knight, seeking Goldsmith's advice. The offending article had appeared in *Foreign Report* in April 1982. It said that *To Ethnos* had been started with a Soviet subsidy of $1.8 million, and claimed that the newspaper was running at a loss which was being met by the Russians. Goldsmith suggested that Knight should discuss the matter with me.

Knight came to my Regent Street office on a hot afternoon in July 1985. I offered to introduce him to Dzhirkvelov. The affair had come at a bad time for Knight, who was about to accept an offer from the Canadian magnate, Conrad Black, to be Chief Executive of the *Daily Telegraph*, which Black had bought. Three days later, on 11 July, Knight returned, to meet Dzhirkvelov in my presence. He then bowed out of the affair, and his Foreign Editor (and my former colleague) Brian Beedham took over, and also met Dzhirkvelov in my office.

At a subsequent meeting with one of the partners of Allen & Overy who were handling *The Economist*'s defence, Dzhirkvelov identified the Soviet officials who had conducted the original negotiations with Bobolas.

The Economist had ammunition of its own. In June 1982, *Ethnos* had published an article alleging that *Foreign Report* was controlled and financed by the CIA. So, *The Economist* counter-sued.

The two lawsuits came to trial before the Queen's Bench Division in London in February 1987, and ended some weeks later with a hung jury. *The Economist* declared itself ready to accept a majority verdict, but *Ethnos* was not. By then, *The Economist*'s costs were approaching £1 million. The Executive Editor, Dudley Fishburn, was against a retrial. He conferred with Bobolas in neutral Switzerland and reached a compromise settlement. Each side apologised to the other and withdrew its allegations.

In its issue of 18 April 1987, *The Economist* presented a full account of the trial. The paper had analysed all the commentaries in *Ethnos* during its first six months. During that time, *Ethnos* had carried seventy-one articles, only five of which had been written by Greeks. The remaining sixty-six articles had been contributed either by one or other of the KGB or other Soviet officials, or by two Western Communists. *The Economist*, therefore, did not propose to retract its general line, which was that *Ethnos* was 'a Soviet mouthpiece'.

In the end, Paul Anastasi emerged as the real victor in these protracted proceedings. Not only had he stood up to the personal and corporate wealth of George Bobolas and his Soviet allies, but he had also – and rightly, in my view – earned his £50,000 award from Sir James Goldsmith.

NOTES

1 Some years later, indirect confirmation of our allegations about the role of *Der Spiegel* in KGB operations came to light. In December 1990, the magazine's East Berlin bureau chief, Diethelm Schroeder, was officially exposed as an agent of the former East German security service, the Stasi. (*Der Spiegel* itself carried a detailed account in its issue dated 17 December 1990, covered in *The Times* of the 18th under the byline of Anne McElvoy in Berlin, headed '*Spiegel* exposes reporter as spy'.) As a consequence, the KGB was for many years able to use the magazine to disseminate disinformation. For a fuller account of these developments, see my article, '*Der Spiegel*: Confirmation from the East', in James Goldsmith, *Counter Culture*, Vol. 5 (1992). This is the fifth volume of Sir James's privately published collected speeches and writings, to which he invited me to contribute.

2 In correspondence on my behalf, a senior American associate of mine obtained confirmation from the US Department of Justice that Victor Rabinowitz was registered with the Department as a foreign agent for Cuba from 4 May 1964 to 10 September 1968. See also Steven Powell, *Covert Cadre: Inside the Institute for Policy Studies* (Green Hill, Ottawa, Illinois, 1987), note 15, p. 397; also, Lawrence V. Cott and Ruth I. Matthews, 'Left Bank – the Louis B. Rabinowitz Foundation', in the journal *Combat*, 15 June 1969.

XIX

Peace versus 'peace'
(1980s)

THE BEST THING The 61 ever did was to penetrate and defeat the Soviet 'peace' fronts and the Western campaign groups.

Ever since its creation in 1948, the World Peace Council (WPC) had been one of the most successful of the Soviet-controlled international fronts. In 1977 and 1978, it had conducted a major campaign against US plans to produce the so-called 'neutron bomb', which in fact was not a bomb but an enhanced radiation/diminished blast warhead with a purely defensive purpose: to halt a Soviet tank offensive, literally in its tracks, by killing the tank crews while leaving the environment intact and with minimal civilian casualties.

The Soviet campaign had yielded a spectacular success, when President Carter, ever the appeaser, announced in April 1978 that production of the neutron bomb would be deferred.

In a study published two months later by the ISC, a leading French strategic expert, General Pierre Gallois, first drew public attention to the new and acute danger to the NATO countries of the new Soviet SS-20 medium-range missiles, deployment of which had begun in 1977. He pointed out that these new, triple-headed, highly accurate missiles were capable of destroying all NATO's military targets in one surprise attack.[1]

Allied response to this new threat had been surprisingly slow off the mark.[2] The reasons for this were partly technical, partly emotional. The technical argument was that since the SS-20 could not reach the United States, it must therefore be classified as a 'tactical' not a 'strategic' missile. This made little sense, however, since a weapon capable of destroying all NATO's installations was clearly of strategic importance. Its range of 5000 kilometres (3125 miles) would have enabled the Soviet Union to strike at any target in Western Europe.

Western leaders were similarly slow to react. In a widely praised lecture to the IISS on 28 October 1977, Chancellor Helmut Schmidt of West Germany mentioned the need for West European parity with the Soviet Union in tactical as well as strategic nuclear weapons, but without being specific. A year later, his Foreign Minister, Hans-Dietrich Genscher, in an article published in NATO's internal bulletin (December 1978), complained of opposition to the modernisation of theatre nuclear weapons, but again failed to be specific. On 1 September 1979, Henry Kissinger, the former US Secretary of State and National Security Adviser, addressed a NATO audience in Brussels and contented himself with one passing reference to the SS-20. General Gallois's *Conflict Study* thus broke new ground by spelling out the high-risk problem of the SS-20.

The emotional element was that public opinion, as well as strategic studies, mainly dwelt on the terrible possibility of a war of annihilation between the superpowers. In comparison, the direct threat to Western Europe took second place.

In December 1979, at last, the NATO defence and foreign ministers met in Brussels to discuss the deployment of two new American missiles to counter the SS-20s: Cruise missiles and the Pershing II. The outcome was not a straight decision to deploy the counter-weapons, but a fudge known as the 'two-track decision'. The Allies decided to start deploying the new weapons, but not before the end of 1983, and then only if there had been no substantial progress in arms control talks between the US and the USSR by that time.

The WPC launched no fewer than three large-scale 'peace' campaigns. One was a repeat of the successful earlier offensive against the 'neutron bomb'. The others were against the deployment of the new counter-weapons in Europe, and (specifically for America) in favour of a 'nuclear freeze'.

President Carter's ban on production of the neutron warhead had been lifted by the Reagan Administration, and a prime objective of the Soviet propaganda apparatus was to secure a renewal of the ban. The campaign against deployment of the new counter-weapons was of course specifically aimed at maintaining the Soviet monopoly of medium-range guided missiles in the European theatre: in other words, to keep the SS-20s deployed and prevent any counter-deployment on the NATO side.

As for the nuclear freeze campaign, it was designed to maintain the Soviet superiority over the United States in intercontinental missiles.

Because of the self-destructive actions already described, the NATO allies were ill equipped to respond to these campaigns, and in fact showed no signs of responding for a dangerously long time. NATO's two-track resolution was indeed a self-inflicted trap, in that it played into the hands of the Soviet 'peace' campaigns, by encouraging negotiations with the Soviet Union, in preference to deployment of the Pershing II and Cruise missiles.

The long-term Allied plan – in the event of failure in the arms reduction talks with the USSR – was to deploy a grand total of 572 weapons: 464 Cruise missiles and 108 Pershing IIs. These were to be shared out among five countries: Britain, West Germany, Holland, Belgium, and Italy. Not surprisingly, these countries were the main Soviet targets in the new World Peace Council campaigns.

France was in a special position, having withdrawn from NATO's integrated command, and stuck with General de Gaulle's decision to rely on its own nuclear deterrent. The fact that there was never any question of deploying the new Western weapons on French soil enabled President Mitterrand to speak with some freedom in favour of their deployment – in countries other than France.

Over breakfast at Claridge's in London, I discussed the problem with a French visitor. We agreed that the best way to mobilise Mitterrand on this issue was to persuade him to invite General Gallois to brief him on the SS-20 danger. We both knew Pierre Gallois. I had translated his important *Conflict Study* analysing the SS-20 threat, and interpreted for him at Pinay Cercle meetings. Jean Violet gave him a 'genius' rating. Among his talents, as I found when I was his guest at dinner, was *trompe l'oeil* painting. Whenever one looked at the walls of his 8th arrondissement flat in the rue Rembrandt, one saw vases and books and statuettes, and only close study revealed which were real and which were painted.

More relevantly, for our purpose, he had a deep understanding of air strategy in the technological age, and a talent for persuasive exposition. He readily agreed to brief Mitterrand, who seized the opportunity to create a stir in Bonn. In the presidential plane on his way to the Federal Republic, François Mitterrand read the draft speech prepared for him by the Quai d'Orsay. The draft was so far from the Gallois briefing, so much softer, more tactful, more 'diplomatic', that he arrived in choleric mood.

With half an hour to spare, he borrowed a desk in Chancellor Kohl's office and wrote the speech *we* wanted him to deliver.

It was 20 January 1983. My informant, who spoke French, was sitting in the front row in the Bundestag. He watched the faces of Willy Brandt and the leftist duo, Egon Bahr and Herbert Wehner, turning red with rage as the meaning reached them through their earphones in 'simultaneous' translation.

Mitterrand began, appropriately, by recalling the wars between France and Germany, and praised both countries for outliving a barbarous dictatorship and reaching a close partnership for peace through the 1963 bilateral treaty.

After prolonged tensions, the two superpowers had started a dialogue for peace. 'But the balance of forces has not been truly maintained. One power has always outstripped the other.' Ever more weapons were being deployed in Europe. The Soviet Union had installed 'new mobile missiles with three warheads, with a range of 5000 kilometres and enhanced accuracy. A 5000-kilometre range, enough to reach Europe, not enough to reach the American continent.' Although he had not specifically mentioned the SS-20, Mitterrand's allusion was clear.

War could be avoided, he went on, only if the balance of forces was restored. Only thus could the Federal Republic's Ostpolitik be secured. It was essential to prevent any decoupling of the United States from its NATO allies.

He referred to the disarmament talks in Geneva and to the 1975 Final Act of Helsinki, the climax of the prolonged Conference on Security and Cooperation in Europe (CSCE). Détente could be ensured only by a balance of deterrence. It was not enough for the superpowers to agree on a balance of intercontinental missiles. France's own nuclear deterrent was, and would remain, independent, and France could do no more. It was essential to aim at a balance of medium-range nuclear weapons. Only thus could a potential aggressor be deterred, and war made impossible.

This was the message that shocked the Brandt–Bahr–Wehner trio: West Germany must stop opposing the deployment on its soil of the American counter-weapons in the medium range – the Pershing II and Cruise missiles. That evening, in Bonn, Mitterrand and Kohl took part in a televised dialogue. The Chancellor, referring to the forthcoming Bundestag elections in March, declared that if re-elected he would carry out the policy decided by his predecessor, Helmut Schmidt, which was also his own. If the East–West arms control talks failed, the Federal Republic would deploy the new American missiles.

IN THE ABSENCE of government reaction in any of the affected countries, it was left to private groups to counter the Soviet campaigns. At The 61, we took a decision to create new peace counter-groups wherever necessary, and to assist such groups where they already existed, both financially and with ideas. It was a considerable international coordinating effort which paid off in the end.

In the United States, with Carter still in the White House, a group of distinguished Americans had set up a highly effective pressure group called the 'Coalition for Peace through Strength'. Among them were personal friends of mine, including the late General Richard G. Stilwell and Richard Perle, both of whom were appointed by Reagan to high posts in the Pentagon, Perle as Deputy Defense Secretary and Stilwell as Assistant Defense Secretary in charge of administration.

In Britain, a small group of young men, one of them an American, set up a matching 'Coalition for Peace through Security'. They included Edward Leigh, a young barrister who went on to become an enthusiastically Thatcherite MP, and a gifted young man named Julian Lewis. Introduced to me by Norris McWhirter, Dr Lewis became The 61's leading activist in Britain, notably as the scourge of Monsignor Bruce Kent and the Campaign for Nuclear Disarmament (CND).

Another outstanding campaigner against CND was Paul Mercer, whose book *'Peace' of the Dead* (Policy Research Publications, London, 1986) was, and remains, an exhaustive and authoritative analysis of the CND and its affiliates. This book carried a foreword by Lord Chalfont, a former Labour Minister for Disarmament under Harold Wilson, who had seen the error of his affiliation with the increasingly penetrated Labour Party.

In a minor key, I was initially involved in setting up the Council for Arms Control, for which I raised a launching grant of £14,000 through intermediaries. Although the Council did useful work in producing authoritative reports and analyses, it was essentially passive and I stayed away from it. The Council was run by a former Foreign Office official, John Edmonds, and General Sir Hugh Beach played an important role in it (see Ch. IX).

Fortunately for our collective survival, there were intelligent enthusiasts in the NATO countries to counter the pacifists. By now, in the spring of 1981, The 61's budget was sufficient for general purposes, but not for the needs of the peace counter-groups. I naturally turned to the CIA, as the most likely source of funds, now that Reagan was President, with Bill Casey as his Director of Central Intelligence. I tried the normal channels, discussing the question with a young Agency man recently posted to the London station, and assigned to liaise with me. The new man was polite and appeared to be well motivated. I had not, however, allowed for the depressing legacy of Watergate and the Carter years. After several fruitless sessions, I decided to write directly to Casey:

29 May 81

Dear Bill

. . . Yesterday I had a further visit from your young man in London. This was the third visit, in each case to ask exactly the same questions. The questions are, however, by definition unanswerable. It is a typical chicken-and-egg situation. . . .

Nevertheless, I *have* made a start in two countries, using some of our own money. . . .

The trouble is that time is passing, while enormous resources are mustered and active on the other side. What a long way we have travelled, in the wrong direction, these past few years! Ten or fifteen years ago, few eyebrows would have been raised at the suggestion that a million dollars might be used, for a start, in a matter of this importance. Now, obstacles are raised in a matter of the equivalent of £50,000, which is chicken-feed in relation to a problem of this magnitude.

One thing I was able to give your young man in London was a detailed memo on the right psychological line. I just ask people to remember the track-record and give me the tools to do the job.

A month's silence followed. In mounting frustration, I wrote to the Prime Minister on 3 July 1981:

Dear Margaret

. . . Both SIS and CIA share my view that perhaps the most urgent challenge we face lies in the enormous Soviet 'peace' campaign, conducted through the World Peace Council and its many subsidiaries, the CND, the Socialist International, and related bodies. On the Western side, nothing is being done through official channels.

If the Soviet effort succeeds in making it psychologically impossible for the continental European members of NATO to deploy the new generation of

American nuclear missiles, then the missiles themselves will be worthless and the credibility of Trident and the French deterrent will be greatly reduced. . . .

Money (derisory amounts, really) is desperately needed. In Washington in March, I persuaded CIA, with Dick Allen's support, to put in an initial sum of £50,000, and I have had confirmation that in principle a favourable decision has been taken. But no money has reached me. I may soon find myself in the embarrassing situation of having persuaded people to go ahead, and with no money to give them.

Our friends tell me that as things stand in Whitehall, there is no way any public money could be provided for this purpose, although they are being very helpful in putting pressure on the Americans to live up to their promises. Apparently the new Information Department has no mandate on that kind of thing: we can have lots of papers (good ones) on Poland and Afghanistan, but nothing to counter the 'peace' campaign. Peter Blaker having been moved, one cannot turn to him.

Two days later, the young man brought me a letter from Bill Casey, dated 2 July. Its tone was almost effusively encouraging, but the message was negative. 'As always,' he wrote, 'I am impressed with both your analysis of the situation and the practical steps you have taken. We all share a concern that every effort should be expended to try to see that Soviet attempts to interfere with the Western alliance are countered. . . . The private sector must be associated with these activities to demonstrate that support comes from the people as well as the governments. Keep up the good work. . . .' By hand, he had added: 'I get a lot out of your reports which I read faithfully.'

The frustrating story nevertheless ended happily. Bill Casey did find a way to get the money to me: £50,000 that year, and $100,000 in 1982. On 31 December 1981, in a secret memorandum to the Prime Minister, I reported in detail on our activities during the year.

There was much to say. In the Netherlands, through long-established and more recent contacts, we were kept informed of the activities of proliferating groups. The one that was proving most useful in countering the Soviet-led campaign was the *Stichting Vrijheid, Vrede en Verdediging* (Freedom, Peace and Defence Foundation).

In Belgium, we decided to set up our own organisation, which our man in Brussels named the *Rassemblement pour la Paix dans la Liberté*

(Rally for Peace in Freedom). One of the highlights of this busy period was when a well-known general sought me out at an international meeting to tell me about the birth of the Rally, unaware that I had sponsored it. The Rally grew quickly and its influence spread not only through the Belgian Parliament, but into the schools, with the distribution of officially approved booklets on defence. In the Federal Republic, we liaised, through an intermediary, with the *Bonner Friedensforum* (the Bonn Peace Forum), largely composed of students alerted to the dangers of unconditional pacifism. Our funds contributed to the cost of posters and banners displayed during demonstrations.

Within the next year, we set up a link with a French organisation, created by the distinguished politician and former diplomat Philippe Malaud, who had been a minister in the governments of Presidents de Gaulle and Pompidou. The organisation styled itself the *Comité Français contre le Neutralisme*, and brought together some seventy-five well-known personalities from the worlds of politics, the media, and education.

In Britain, the energetic Julian Lewis and his young assistants wrote letters to the press, hired light aircraft trailing anti-CND slogans, organised counter-demonstrations, and challenged Bruce Kent and other speakers at CND rallies. Booklets, pamphlets, folders, posters were produced, all of them pithy and telling. One of the folders produced by the Coalition for Peace through Security gave the facts about Soviet military spending under the title 'Preventing Nuclear War'. One of the most effective folders was entitled '30 questions . . . and honest answers about CND'.

A Dutch friend did the basic research for a proposed pamphlet. I rewrote his rough draft, which was published under my name by Geoffrey Stewart-Smith's Foreign Affairs Publishing Company in 1980; the title was *The Price of Peace*. Three years later, an updated and enlarged version of it was published in Washington DC, by the influential Heritage Foundation.

The facts and the arguments were all there, but a more effective contribution to the counter-campaign was authored by the fearless Soviet dissident Vladimir Bukovsky, and published jointly by the Coalition for Peace through Security and the Committee for the Free World, with an effective introduction by Winston Churchill, MP. Bukovsky's pamphlet was entitled *The Peace Movement and the Soviet Union*. After surviving twelve years in Soviet prisons, labour camps and psychiatric hospitals, Bukovsky had no need to mince words. The public would take hard truths from him which, if expressed by others, might be suspect.

*   *   *

'YOU REALLY THINK this can be done, Brian?' In his Langley office, Bill Casey looked sceptical.

'Yes, Bill, I do.'

I had been telling him about a plan for a modest 'peace' demonstration in Moscow. Nothing spectacular: just a plan to send two young men to distribute peace leaflets in the Soviet capital. The leaflets would call for nuclear arms reduction measures by both the USSR and the USA, instead of unilateral disarmament by the West as called for by the World Peace Council and its international subsidiaries.

The whole exercise was planned and organised by the Russian anti-Soviet exile group, NTS, through their man in London, George Miller (see Ch. XX). What they lacked was the modest sum needed to send two daring young men to Moscow.

Casey looked pensive. 'How much money do you need?'

'Not much. Five thousand dollars should do.'

The DCI made up his mind. 'No problem. Our people in London will hand it over.'

There was no need for George Miller to know where the money came from, still less for the two volunteer 'peaceniks'. One was Harry Phibbs, at that time chairman of the Westminster Young Conservatives, and Peter Caddick-Adams, also a Young Conservative.

The preparations were thorough. Phibbs and Caddick-Adams spent eight evenings being briefed by George Miller in a safe house in London. He drilled his two candidates in what to look for in the unfamiliar Soviet environment, in the layout of Moscow, how to deal with the Metro and taxis, and, not least, on the methods used by the KGB, should either be arrested, and how to defend themselves. Each young man had been specifically warned of the danger of arrest and interrogation and had volunteered to go ahead in full awareness of the risks.

They travelled on the same flight but without 'recognising' each other, and stayed at different hotels. Phibbs had concealed his leaflets in knee-pads. He was stopped and detained for four hours at the airport and body-searched. The leaflets were confiscated. He was then taken to a hotel near the airport and held for another day and night. He was released and sent back to London, his mission unfulfilled.

Peter Caddick-Adams was luckier. He was not challenged at the airport. Next day, he was supposed to meet Harry in Pushkin Square, and realised something must have gone wrong when Harry failed to turn up. That day, he wrote and posted letters about his mission to various British and

American media representatives in Moscow. He also distributed many leaflets at five Metro stations, encountering friendly curiosity and no hostility.

Caddick-Adams had kept his leaflets in a double bottom in a travelling case. On the second day, his case was searched, but the remaining leaflets were not found. These, too, he handed out.

On his return, the two young men held a press conference on 10 September 1982. With one exception, all British national dailies covered the story. The exception was the *Guardian*. The CIA's minor involvement was not known to the two activists.

The operation was repeated in mid-September 1983. This time, the plan was to send Guy Roberts, a twenty-year-old student from Windsor, and the Rev. Basil Watson, an Anglican vicar from St Lawrence Jewry, well known for his anti-CND views. Roberts was to carry all the leaflets as he seemed less likely to be searched than Watson. They were to meet in Pushkin Square, where Roberts would hand half the leaflets to the vicar.

In the event, Roberts was on his own. Before the planned departure, the Korean Airlines plane on Flight 007 was shot down over Soviet territory, which caused Watson, understandably, to opt out because of the increased risk that he might be put on trial.

A front organisation, the Anglo-Russian Peace Campaign, was set up to 'sponsor' the trip. In Leningrad, Guy Roberts distributed several hundred leaflets to apparently enthusiastic citizens before being detained by the KGB, who later claimed that they had asked him in for 'a friendly talk'. Roberts came back to extensive media coverage.

As far as I know, the CIA was not involved in this second 'peace protest'.

SOME MONTHS AFTER the 'peace' campaigns had taken off in Western Europe, the Soviet International Department launched its nuclear freeze campaign in the US. John Barron, the noted American expert on the KGB, gathered the facts and presented them for the first time in October 1982.[3]

It all began at the 26th Congress of the Soviet Communist Party (CPSU) in February 1981, when Leonid Brezhnev issued a call for a nuclear freeze. As Major-General John Singlaub put it, commenting on Barron's revelations, Brezhnev's spell locked the West in a position of marked inferiority.[4]

Lee Edwards, biographer of Ronald Reagan, journalist and Republican Party activist, reported the facts to me in a detailed memorandum dated

25 October 1982. As Barron had said, within a month of Brezhnev's speech, the first national strategy conference of the American Nuclear Freeze Campaign convened at Georgetown University in Washington. There were two invited Soviet guests: Oleg Bogdanov, an ID specialist who flew over from Moscow, and Yuri Kapralov, who (Barron disclosed) was a KGB agent in the Soviet embassy.

Lee's memo listed no fewer than seventeen freeze campaign organisations already active in the US. He went on to propose a counter-campaign. One of his most effective moves was to invite a number of West European parliamentarians to Washington for a series of public appearances in June 1983. The list included two from West Germany, and one each from France, Belgium, Holland, and Italy.

IN BRITAIN, the peace counter-campaign merged with the general election of June 1983. In common with many others, I had assumed that the polling would not take place until October, but Mrs Thatcher took us by surprise. She led her party to a crushing victory over Labour (397 seats to 209).

At that time, the Labour Party, led by Michael Foot, was deeply committed to one-sided nuclear disarmament and to socialist policies indistinguishable from those advocated by the Communists. These policies were widely enough known to make Labour unelectable at that time. In other words, Mrs Thatcher would have won anyway. The 61 did, however, make its modest contribution to her party's victory, as I reported to her in a letter dated 15 June, five days after polling day.

In a series of articles in the *Daily Telegraph*, Douglas Eden had given precise details of the penetration of the Labour Party. He was an expert on the subject in his own right, but we supplied him with a good deal of his material from our files.

We had obtained a copy of Labour's proposals for a drastic overhaul of the secret services, in the form of a discussion document put together by a group of the Party's MPs chaired by Jo Richardson, a leading left-winger. That MI-5 in particular needed to be overhauled was not a proposition our group would have contested. In its day, the Shield committee had proposed to restore and strengthen its counter-subversion role. Not surprisingly, Labour's proposals were on quite different lines, calling for public debate on the activities of both MI-5 and MI-6 in Parliament, and for public scrutiny of their budgets.

I offered the story initially to *The Times*, which turned it down. I turned to the *Daily Express*, and presented the material to the then editor, Sir Larry Lamb, at a meeting in his Fleet Street office. By then, the Labour Party, without any publicity, had published its proposals in a pamphlet. On 21 May the *Daily Express* splashed the story under a dual byline: Chapman Pincher and Ted Daly.

Another 61 contribution to the attack on Labour came from the Coalition for Peace through Security. One of its bright young men, Tony Kerpel, a Tory councillor in the heavily left-wing London Borough of Camden, designed a highly effective poster, headed 'Guilty Men', the title of a book co-authored by Michael Foot and Mervyn Jones and published in 1957. The book had denounced the pre-war appeasement policy of Neville Chamberlain.

The poster showed the notorious picture of Chamberlain with his 'piece of paper, signed not only by Herr Hitler but myself', on his return from Munich in 1938. It also carried a picture of Michael Foot, with a piece of paper. There were two captions, one under each picture. The first one read: '1938, Neville Chamberlain'; the second, '1983, Michael Foot'. The wording at the foot of the poster read: 'Don't let appeasement cause another World War'. The poster was published by The Freedom Association. It was reproduced in the left-wing review *Tribune* (long associated with Michael Foot), with a protesting article. The picture and article attracted attention to the poster which it might not otherwise have received, and thus constituted an 'own goal'.

THE GREAT FINANCIER rang me at my office at 7.45 a.m. 'Brian,' he said, 'there was a very important dinner at Chequers last night. I want to tell you about it. Could you meet me at Heathrow an hour from now?'

We had twenty minutes together while he awaited the call for his Concorde flight to New York. He had come over for the dinner at the Prime Minister's urgent request; another tycoon had also crossed the Atlantic for the same reason. Sir Keith Joseph, at that time the Education Secretary, and Mrs Thatcher's long-time ideological soul-mate, was there too.

The dinner took place on 26 February 1985. The theme for discussion was neither the Soviet threat (Mikhail Gorbachev's ascent to the top, although widely expected, was still a month off), nor the state of the economy, nor a general election. It was an insidious domestic problem: the challenge to the government of the self-styled 'People's Republics' in the Greater London Council (GLC) and a number of municipal councils, including Liverpool, Sheffield, Glasgow, and certain London boroughs, including Lambeth, Camden, Haringey, and Brent.

At table, Mrs Thatcher explained the problem and asked the financiers to help. She had in mind full-page advertisements in the national newspapers, to tell the public what was going on, and to warn of the dangers presented by the misuse of local government funds on such matters as 'nuclear-free zones' and minor follies, such as gay and lesbian centres.

My friend commented that this would be a waste of money, as the impact of such advertisements was very short-lived. What was needed was a full counter-subversion programme, using the enemy's own methods. There was only one man capable of helping such a programme, with his existing organisation. And he named me. I would have to agree to a rapid expansion of my operations in the UK. He proposed a suitably substantial budget, to which he would make an equal contribution. The other tycoon present agreed to match the sum proposed, and two others, named but not present, would be expected to contribute.

At the dinner, Mrs Thatcher had mentioned that, as it happened, she would be seeing me at 10 Downing Street the following morning. That was why he had had to brief me at zero notice before returning to New York. Would I take this on? He knew the answer before I said 'of course'.

The call for Concorde came, and he left.

MY MEETING with the Prime Minister on 28 February started at 9 a.m. It was the first time I had met her in her office, not at Chequers. Her well-known adviser on foreign affairs, Charles Powell, was at the door of No. 10 to greet me. He started to enter the room with me, but to his surprise she told him she wanted to see me alone.

The reasons she gave for turning to the private sector for help were no less interesting than the problem itself. Her first thought had been to use the funds of the Department of the Environment, but the then Secretary of State, Patrick Jenkin, appeared to have no understanding of the problem, and adamantly refused to use his Department's funds.

I pointed out that in effect what I was being asked to do was the kind of work that could have been done, and which might have avoided the present situation, if our recommendations of some years earlier for the creation of a Counter-Subversion Executive (CSE) had been implemented. She let that pass without comment.

Mrs Thatcher mentioned that her biggest problem was unemployment. However, the biggest current challenge was the mineworkers' strike, and she informed me (in advance of the news) that the number of miners returning to work that day would bring the figure of miners back at work to more than 50 per cent. Arthur Scargill's strike was therefore defeated. She said she had often been discouraged but had always rallied round and had always been determined to go on to the end and not allow the government or herself to be defeated. She hoped this would be recognised – that she had shown the will to fight on where her predecessors had failed.

I said I thought that, among other things, she would go down in history as the Prime Minister who had broken the political power of the trades unions.

The inside story of the defeat of Scargill's challenge to Mrs Thatcher was not known to me at that time, and although passing references to it appeared in the press some years after the event, the full account that follows has not previously seen the light. A crucial role was played by David Hart – millionaire businessman, novelist, journalist, and political activist.[5] His name was well known to me, mainly from his concise and penetrating articles in *The Times*, but we did not meet until the summer of 1987.

Like me, though in different areas, Hart had been an unofficial adviser to Mrs Thatcher for some years. Doubtless there were others, in a category our late friend Charles Douglas-Home, then editor of *The Times*, called 'the Downing Street irregulars'.

David Hart, Old Etonian son of a Jewish banker, had resolved to find out for himself how the coalminers lived, much as Eric Blair, an Old Etonian of an earlier generation better known as George Orwell, had done in the 1930s. During the first two months of the strike, he had spent many days wandering around the coalfields talking to miners in both camps: those who *wanted* to strike and those who wanted to *work*. This was both a personal and a working assignment, for he was accredited to *The Times*, which carried several articles of his on the strike.

In May 1984, Hart began to hear of systematic intimidation by Scargill's National Union of Mineworkers (NUM) of working miners and their families. In search of evidence, he found it in a house in Shirebrook. The wife of a striking mineworker had been spat upon in a pub. Her car had been overturned in her driveway and a brick had been thrown at her front windows. Her crime? Their son had refused to join the strike. When Hart met her, he could see and hear for himself that her world was crumbling around her and she was heading for a nervous breakdown. Later on, he found other similar cases.

From the coalfields, David Hart reported regularly to Mrs Thatcher by telephone and in hand-delivered notes. One day he suggested to her that he should get together with Ian (later Sir Ian) MacGregor, the British-born American businessman appointed by the Prime Minister in 1983 as Chairman of the National Coal Board (later British Coal). Mrs Thatcher agreed, and a private meeting was arranged through David Hart's brother and the economist Lord (Ralph) Harris. The meeting-place was MacGregor's flat in Eaton Square. Also present was Tim Bell, MacGregor's adviser on public relations. David Hart gained MacGregor's confidence and the two remained firm friends after the coal strike.

Unlike the Prime Minister, at that time, and the Coal Board Chairman, Hart's view of the crisis was strategic. MacGregor, though a tough businessman, was not a political animal. His concern was to get the coal business going again. To that end, he was prepared for protracted negotiations and for a settlement that might be seen publicly as a defeat for the Coal Board, so long as the small print enabled business to resume.

In the early stages of the strike, the Prime Minister was very reluctant to get personally involved, for fear of the possible political consequences of a defeat. Some years earlier, Lord Carrington had advised capitulation in the event of a further coal strike (see Ch. X). For the first two or three months, she kept a low profile, and left it to Peter Walker, her Secretary for Energy to deal with MacGregor. Walker was a 'wet' in the Thatcherite parlance of the day.[6]

David Hart's strategy was simple. His aim was victory in what he rightly saw as a politically motivated strike designed to bring down the Thatcher government. He defined victory as a return to work by all the miners, *without a settlement*.

By August 1984, Hart had defined his strategy and was trying, with MacGregor and Bell, and certain working miners, to evolve suitable tactics. By September, he had persuaded Mrs Thatcher that the strategy made sense. Thereafter, he took many of the tactical decisions, carrying MacGregor with him, sometimes reluctantly, and reporting to the Prime Minister.

The tactics were as follows:

- To monitor the intentions of the NUM. This was achieved through indirect but reliable access to two members of the executive.
- To put pressure on Scargill's executive through legal actions by miners against their own union. These actions were very successful

and led to the sequestration of NUM funds, thus preventing the payment of pickets and the hiring of buses to take them to their picketing sites.[7]

- To encourage miners who wanted to work, and enable them to do so. To this end, Hart set up the National Working Miners' Committee (NWMC), which he financed initially. Later, it financed itself through newspaper advertisements drafted and placed by Hart.

  The first of these raised £80,000 from the general public in four days.

  The NWMC was more than a name: it was a legal entity, with a charter and its own accountants, and provided encouragement, security services, money and advice for miners who were working or wanted to work.

- To frustrate all attempts by Peter Walker and Ian MacGregor to negotiate a settlement. In this endeavour, Hart's greatest, though unwitting, ally was Scargill himself, whose aim was unconditional surrender by the government and the National Coal Board. In the final stages, however, Scargill's will began to weaken and Hart's efforts to frustrate the MacGregor–Walker line of seeking a settlement seemed in danger of foundering, though successful in the end.

Not unnaturally, Walker greatly resented Hart's 'interference'. On one occasion, in October 1984, he rang Hart at Claridge's and exclaimed: 'You can't run this strike from Claridge's.' Hart replied: 'I'm not doing too badly, so far.' Walker put the phone down.

Throughout the crisis, the Nottinghamshire miners were those most resistant to the NUM's directives. Towards the end of the crisis, they formed a break-away body, the Union of Democratic Mineworkers, with Roy Lynk as leader.[8] This, in effect, was the last nail in the coffin of the NUM.

The part played by David Hart in the coal strike crisis was of course not known to me at the time of my February 1985 meeting with Mrs Thatcher. At my last 'advisory' meeting with the Prime Minister, on 22 January 1988, I brought up the subject of Hart's role in the national coal strike. She looked pensive: 'I couldn't have done without him,' she said.

*   *   *

DURING THE FEBRUARY 1985 meeting I went on to brief Mrs Thatcher about our recent operations in the UK, specifically the work of the Coalition for Peace through Security, and in combating Marxist influences in education.

The most important point I tried to put across was that the biggest obstacle to our work, and indeed to any counter-subversion, was the total lack of cooperation, and indeed the obstructiveness, of the Security Service. The dissemination of intelligence on the home front had been discontinued in February 1974 by administrative, not political, decisions. As far as I knew, the material was still coming in but was not being disseminated, on orders from MI-5.

She asked whether I thought the present (and, at that time, outgoing) head of MI-5, Sir John Jones, was personally that obstructive. My reply was that the question answered itself since this was the state of affairs. I pointed out that MI-5 refused all contact with a former colleague who was now working in my organisation. Indeed, they had carried non-cooperation and non-recognition to the absurd extent of declining even to receive our reports.

She was listening intently, taking notes. I stressed that, in my view, it was absolutely essential, indeed indispensable, to restore the availability of MI-5 material to selected recipients. This, too, she noted, but she added that there was a real problem with leaks.

She complained about the rowdy and hostile leftists in the House of Commons and commented that they had no such problem in America. She was particularly incensed that her own 'triumph' in the United States (in particular, her speech to a joint session of Congress) had been greeted with loud laughter from the Labour benches. 'This was the weapon of ridicule,' she said indignantly. She complained that some Members on the Tory benches had joined with Labour laughter in a recent debate when references were made to Marxist influences within the local councils. 'So you see,' she went on, 'this is happening even on our own side.'

I called in my young London activists and we worked out a plan of action. The problem was complex. The core of it was the 'Free Two Pence' provision in the 1972 Local Government Act, which in effect allowed councils to spend 2p in the £ in any way they pleased. The Conservatives were in power at the time, with Edward Heath as Prime Minister. It had not occurred to anybody involved that the minority of Marxists in the councils would exploit this 'freedom' to further their minority aims.

We would therefore need to act on several fronts: penetration, legislation, influence, and publicity. We all agreed that a public and visible organisation would be needed, and various possible names were tossed around. The problem was to find a combination that yielded an easily pronounceable acronym. We settled for Campaign against Council Corruption (CAMACC).

Under Patrick Jenkin, an initiative had been taken to set up an 'independent' team of inquiry headed by David Widdicombe, QC, to investigate abuses. As Widdicombe was a Liberal, he was less likely than other possible candidates to be accused of left- or right-wing partisanship. It soon became clear to us, however, that the team would make recommendations falling far short of the required legislative constraints which we felt were necessary. The interim recommendations had focused almost exclusively on stopping 'party political' propaganda. This was no more than a timid step in the right direction, because the point at issue was not a matter of 'party' but of *ideology*. Most propaganda financed by the rates was not, on any strict construction of the term, party political. Indeed, it was doubtful whether the courts would be capable of defining a political party acceptably. For example, the Communist Party of Great Britain (CPGB), which was recognised as a political party, had far fewer overt members than CND, which denied that it was one.

In military terms, the 'nuclear-free zones' in various council areas were of no significance. The point was that £10 million or more had gone to CND and other like-minded bodies, thus building up further support for the 'peace' movement. The net effect was that the 'loony Left' councils, as they were increasingly called in the press, were spending millions to make the West safe for the Soviet SS-20s.

Much of the money was coming from the Greater London Council. In November 1984, the government had introduced the Local Government Bill, providing for the abolition of the GLC and of the Metropolitan County Councils (MCCs), mainly in the Midlands and the North. The bill became law at the end of July 1985, but there was firm evidence that the GLC would continue to hand enough money to leftist bodies to keep them in action after its own demise.

Our choice as Director of CAMACC, Tony Kerpel, was appointed a Special Adviser to Kenneth Baker, who had succeeded Jenkin as Secretary of State for the Environment. In Parliament, CAMACC's main activist was Edward Leigh, who had earlier played a leading role in our Coalition for

Peace through Security. The journalist Duncan Campbell attacked Leigh for having moved in with 'preemptive strikes against the government'[9] – which was one way of putting it.

CAMACC activists briefed various peers, and drafted speeches for them in relevant debates in the House of Lords. Letters and news coverage were secured in various national papers.

THE MUNICIPAL ELECTIONS of May 1981 provided a local microcosm of a possible future national coup by the Marxist-Leninist Left. The victors in the GLC elections were the Labour Party, led at that time by a moderate Social Democrat named Andrew McIntosh. Having led the winning faction, McIntosh was discarded and soon politically forgotten. The coup was led by Ken Livingstone, who took over as Leader of the GLC. A supporter of Sinn Fein, the political wing of the IRA, Livingstone was a man of considerable personal charm but a political extremist, who in the mid-1980s was for a time on close terms with Neil Kinnock. The Livingstone micro-coup was the basis of the plot of Frederick Forsyth's bestseller *The Fourth Protocol*.

ONE OF THE services provided by the Coalition for Peace through Security was the briefing of MPs of both Houses in preparation for debates on defence and foreign affairs. A major example was Lord Home's debate in the House of Lords in 1985. I normally left these briefings to Julian Lewis, but on this occasion I joined in. The organiser of it, Lord Orr-Ewing, had asked me to prepare a paper on Soviet involvement with the IRA, and to come along.

The theme of the debate was 'disarmament and subversion'. Unfortunately, there were two postponements, and on the appointed day – 23 April – several of the most important speakers were absent, as Orr-Ewing explained to me in his letter of thanks: Baroness Cox because of her promotion to the front bench; Lord Chalfont and Lord Chapple, both down with a nasty virus; and Lord Kimberley. There were enough good speakers left, however, to produce an effective debate, which absorbed much space in the national newspapers of 24 April. With the advantage of parliamentary privilege, Orr-Ewing was able to name James Lamond, a Labour MP, as British Vice-President of the World Peace Council, and various trade union leaders as members of the WPC's British offshoot, the British Peace Assembly.[10]

*   *   *

THE GRAND CLIMAX of our international peace counter-campaign came in September 1986, with the long-planned conference of the World Peace Council in Copenhagen. Our side, too, had done its planning. In the event, there were hilarious moments as well as drama: a climax for us, a messy anticlimax for the other side.

It was the first time for many years that the WPC had ventured to hold a conference in the West, away from the protective environment of satellite capitals, such as Prague or Sofia. One of our agents had penetrated the organising committee and actually sat on the platform. At the opening ceremony, two of our people – a tall young man and a tiny young woman – walked towards the platform, bearing an unfurled banner. As the crowd read the words, which those on the platform could not see, titters and shouts of shock or approval broke out. The banner read: 'Welcome to the KGB's peace conference!'

George Miller, of the Frankfurt-based anti-Soviet Russian exile organisation, the NTS, seized the microphone and started an anti-Soviet speech, until a determined woman, an East German Communist, wrested it from his hands.

Taking a leaf out of the enemy's book, The 61 had packed the hall with 'delegates' from imaginary peace groups, such as 'Welsh miners for Peace'. Leaflets exposing the hollowness of the Soviet commitment to 'peace' were distributed.

All this, and more, was viewed on television in millions of homes. The tables had been turned on the masters of disinformation.

By then, in any case, the Western side had won, for the decision to deploy the new US missiles – Cruise and Pershing II – in Britain, West Germany, Italy, Belgium, and the Netherlands had been taken.

NOTES

1 Pierre M. Gallois, 'Soviet Military Doctrine and European Defence; NATO's Obsolete Concepts' (*Conflict Studies*, No. 96, ISC, June 1978). General Gallois had served at Supreme Headquarters, Allied Powers Europe, where he had been responsible for defining and

implementing a new European defence strategy. For a full chronology of the successful Soviet campaign against the 'neutron bomb', see Bayard Stockton and Peter Janke, 'Nuclear Power: Protest and Violence' (*Conflict Studies*, No. 102, ISC, December 1978).

2 Thus the London-based International Institute for Strategic Studies (IISS) merely recorded, without comment, the deployment of twenty SS-20s in its annual, *The Military Balance* (1977–8), in a list of IRBMs (intermediate-range ballistic missiles). The following year, it gave the number deployed as 120, merely commenting (p. 4) that 'SS-20 deployment ... is not constrained by SALT' (Strategic Arms Limitation Talks). The Institute's analytical *Strategic Survey* for 1977 had nothing specific to say about the SS-20. The following year's edition went so far as to mention European anxiety over these new weapons 'which enhanced Soviet options for precise nuclear attacks on Western Europe' (p. 6).

3 *Reader's Digest* (US edition, October 1982). John Barron told the story in greater detail in his important book, *KGB Today: The Hidden Hand* (see Ch. IX, note 7), Ch. 6. See also Brian Crozier, 'The Great Nuclear Freeze Trap', *American Legion Magazine* (Indianapolis, January 1984).

4 *Washington Times*, 19 October 1982. President Carter relieved General Singlaub of his post as Chief of Staff of the US forces in South Korea in 1977 after Singlaub

had publicly criticised the President for his decision to withdraw all US forces stationed there over a period of four or five years. He was transferred to the post of Chief of Staff of the Army Forces Command.

5 In a short article in the *Spectator* (24 October 1992), David Hart mentions some essential points, but without going into details. He is, of course, my source for this account.

6 For a discussion of the 'wetness' of Peter Walker and other members of Mrs Thatcher's government, see Hugo Young, *One of Us* (Macmillan, London, 1989), p. 199.

7 In 1985, Scargill set up the International Mineworkers' Organisation (IMO), which was used by the Soviet All-Union Central Council of Trade Unions (AUCCTU) to help finance the NUM. The AUCCTU was run under the Soviet Communist Party's Central Committee. In June 1990, several Soviet miners' leaders came to my London office to give me details of this particular Active Measure. There is now documentary evidence that Gorbachev himself, with other senior Politburo members, signed a secret order, dated 4 February 1985, approving fund transfers to the IMO.

8 'The UDM was born largely as a result of the success of the National Working Miners' Committee, some of whose members and many of whose followers became official members' (Hart in the *Spectator*; see note 5 above).

9 *New Statesman*, 21 February 1986.

10 *The Times*, 24 April 1985.

XX
_____

Thatcher and Reagan in action

IN RETROSPECT, 1981 can be seen as a turning-point. In March, faced with the challenge of Lech Walesa's Solidarity, the Soviet leaders had contemplated military action, then pulled back at the brink (see Ch. XV). Already, in our bulletin of December 1980/January 1981, we had declared that if Walesa were allowed to get away with it, this could spell 'the beginning of the end of the Soviet empire'. Now, in our issue of May 1981, we urged Western leaders to 'consider contingency planning for the greatest contingency of all: *the collapse of the Soviet system*'.

We had reached this view independently on analysing the Polish crisis in the light of Moscow's decision not to use military force, but our view was strengthened by a series of reports that had been reaching us from the Russian exile group, the NTS. This source was regarded as suspect by SIS, partly because of an old dispute involving Philby and anti-Soviet operations that went wrong, with SIS blaming the NTS and the NTS blaming Philby. The Soviet General Andrei Vlasov, captured by the Nazis in 1942, had been given command of Soviet units of former prisoners of war. He surrendered to the Americans, who handed him over to Stalin, who had him executed. A tragic case: Vlasov was anti-Soviet, not pro-Nazi, but his gamble had gone wrong. After that, SIS banned all contacts with the NTS.

The London representative of the NTS, George Miller, a big bearded Russian, could have stepped out of a Tolstoy novel. I had known him for years and always found him straight and reliable. MI-6 had urged me to break with the NTS, and I had urged them to resume relations, as indeed had happened between the NTS and the CIA. The gap had not been bridged, but the reports of 1980/81 were in line with our own intelligence and analysis. Moreover, I had been impressed when the head of the KGB, Yuri Andropov, had singled out the NTS in a speech on 22 December 1967 as 'enemy number one'. In fact, the KGB had chosen an ingenious way of discrediting the NTS by spreading reports and rumours that it (the KGB) had penetrated the NTS. There may have been some truth in this, but the NTS operated in the USSR on the cell principle, so that penetration of one cell did not necessarily nullify other operations.

In the 1980/81 period, members of the Soviet nomenklatura had started taking advantage of meetings in the West to talk to Russian translators, known to them as NTS members.[1] The talks had been brutally frank, with a cynical recognition of the shortcomings of the system, of the unchallenged power of the KGB and of the prevailing confidence that the West (whether at government or at business level) would always be ready to help the Soviet Union to survive. This cynicism would underlie Mikhail Gorbachev's extraordinarily successful public relations exercise a few years later.

At that time, the 'passivist' approach to the Soviet threat prevailed. Neither President Reagan nor Prime Minister Thatcher was a 'passivist'; but Reagan had not yet got into his stride, and Carrington ran British foreign policy. Indeed, there was force in the passivist theory, as expressed with particular cogency by President Carter's adviser on Soviet affairs, Professor Marshall Shulman of Columbia University. The Professor had addressed the Cercle in Washington in December 1980, but had left without taking any questions.

Essentially, Shulman's argument was that the Soviet Union was heading for collapse anyway, and the best thing the West could do was 'nothing': just stand by and watch. The fact that Brezhnev had decided not to use military force certainly added weight to the passivist thesis, but, in my view, not enough. We were urging Reagan and Thatcher to study ways of assisting the coming collapse without risking a nuclear war. In particular, we asked: '. . . are there forces within the USSR which should be helped to take over when the time comes, to reduce the risks of an explosion inside the country which could intensify the risk of a nuclear exchange?'

We were about ten years early with our prognosis; for which we could either be praised for our foresight or criticised for jumping ahead too fast. Our analysis had been stimulated by several NTS reports over the previous year.

By mid-1982, the continuing passivity, and indeed the incoherence, of Western foreign policy were alarming. In July, I had a protracted telephone call from Sir William Stephenson, the Canadian more widely known as 'A Man Called Intrepid' from the biography of that name written by his near-namesake William Stevenson. At his end, the point of the call was for me to record his personal account of his relations with Churchill (which, by that time, had acquired many embellishments, I believe). But there was a more relevant point: he commissioned me to write a detailed analysis of 'The East–West Confrontation'. Having done this, I drew on it for a set of 'confidential' proposals for President Reagan.

On my next visit to Washington, in September, I handed the paper to Reagan's new National Security Adviser, Judge William Clark (see Ch. XIV). This was our first serious talk. Clark did indeed read my memo and, on his advice, so did the President. The title speaks for itself. I had called it 'The Case for a Roll-Back in the 1980s'. That term, 'roll-back', had often been on the lips of Eisenhower's Secretary of State, John Foster Dulles, stimulating false hopes that were dashed when the Soviets crushed the Hungarian uprising in 1956 and the US stood by and watched.

Dulles's non-existent roll-back had applied to Eastern Europe. I had nothing so dramatic in mind. I distinguished between tactical and strategic reverses. The Soviet Union had suffered numerous tactical reverses, but 'there is still no single instance of a country once lost to the West returning to the Western camp'. I gave several examples of important instances of tactical reverses achieved by the United States, mostly by the CIA, either alone or in concert with SIS: Iran in 1953, Guatemala in 1954, Lebanon in 1958, Laos in 1960, the Dominican Republic in 1965. In all these instances, except in the Lebanon, the object had been 'to forestall a Communist takeover, not to drive an existing Communist regime out of power, or to reverse an accomplished fact'.

The memorandum went on to suggest that certain Soviet colonies and outlying territories were highly vulnerable to low-risk counter-intervention: the Cuban-controlled island of Grenada in the Caribbean; the Cabinda enclave to the north of Angola, surrounded by Zairean territory, which provided the financial basis for the otherwise bankrupt government of Angola; and the Seychelles, where the recent failure by a group of Western mercenaries, with South African support, to overthrow the pro-Soviet government should not be regarded as final.

On a rising scale, I mentioned Nicaragua as a possible target for strategic reversal; and of course Cuba, where the risks were obviously much greater.

After a further visit to Washington, I wrote to Mrs Thatcher on 23 December 1982, mainly to report that I had had extensive talks in the White House and with the CIA. 'From the National Security Council I learned that my memo to the President [a copy of which I had sent her] had stimulated a great deal of discussion – still in progress – on the proposition that an attempt should be made to reverse Soviet advances in peripheral areas.'

In the event, the 'great deal of discussion' yielded one positive decision. On 25 October 1983, 1500 troops of the US 82nd Airborne Division and 400 Marines landed on Grenada. The stated intention of operation 'Urgent Fury', as it was styled, was to take control of communications networks and to guarantee the safety of several hundred American medical students.

Of the three relatively safe targets I had suggested, Grenada was undoubtedly the most important. There, as in other satellites, notably in South Yemen, Ethiopia, and Afghanistan, relatively moderate pro-Soviet leaders had been removed and executed, to be replaced by hardliners.[2]

The liberation of Grenada was the boldest thing President Reagan did in foreign affairs, just as the liberation of the Falklands was the boldest action by Mrs Thatcher. Curiously, he supported her, yet she opposed him.

The American force ran into unexpectedly strong resistance, especially from the Cubans on the island. In only two days, however, fighting had ended in St Georgia, the capital, although resistance dragged on elsewhere. The authors of the coup that had provoked the US operation, Bernard Coard and 'General of the Army' Hudson Austin, were seized; all 603 American medical students were evacuated.

On the day of the US landing, the Prime Minister had told the House of Commons that her government had 'communicated to the United States their very considerable doubts about the initiating action'. In the early hours, indeed, she had telephoned the President to try to get him to call off the landing, asking him to consider the propaganda value to the Soviet Union of US intervention in another country's affairs. She was criticised by some of her greatest admirers, including Lord Thomas in the upper House and Paul Johnson, the ex-Labour journalist turned Conservative.[3]

What was behind this breach of solidarity? The short answer was 'the Commonwealth'; but there was more to it than that. At the time of the

US landing, Mrs Thatcher was preparing for the forthcoming meeting of the Commonwealth leaders in New Delhi.

In April 1982, Grenada, alone among the members of the Caribbean Community (CARICOM), supported Argentina in the conflict with Britain over the Falklands. On 23 October 1983, two days before the American landing, the Caribbean leaders met in emergency session, and Jamaica and Dominica announced the breaking of diplomatic relations with Grenada and Grenada's suspension from membership of CARICOM, following the coup and the killing of the ousted Prime Minister, Maurice Bishop.

On the 26th, the day after the landing, Ms Eugenia Charles, Prime Minister of Dominica, and Chairman of the 'Organisation of East Caribbean States (OECS), told the UN Security Council that the British Governor of Grenada, Sir Paul Scoon, had appealed for help on 21 October.

Despite this, the Security Council passed a resolution deeply deploring the invasion as 'A fragrant violation of international law'. Although Britain abstained, Mrs Thatcher's government, in effect, had sided with the Soviet Union against Britain's closest ally.

On Saturday the 29th, two days after the collapse of Cuban resistance, I was the Prime Minister's guest at Chequers. The appointment had been made before the crisis, but Mrs Thatcher had not cancelled it. I spent two hours with her: the first hour alone, the second over tea with Denis Thatcher.

I tried in vain to explain my reasons for supporting President Reagan's action, but could not stem the flow of her indignation. 'That man! After all I've done for him, he didn't even consult me!' I tried to calm her down after each outburst. I would say: 'But, Margaret . . .' but I merely provoked a variation on the same theme, such as: 'He could at least have phoned me to ask me what I thought. Instead, he just went ahead without consulting me.'[4]

After about half an hour of diatribe, she did calm down, and listened absently while I put it to her that this was the first time since 1917 that the Soviets had been ousted from territory on which Communism had been imposed. She may have listened, but she gave no sign of hearing. There was presumably a good reason why Reagan did not consult Thatcher: he knew she would have tried to talk him out of his plan. The same thought must have occurred to her. Hell hath no fury . . .

In strategic terms, Grenada was far more significant than the Falklands, but this in no way invalidates Mrs Thatcher's triumph of leadership. In the eyes of the world, the Prime Minister's finest hour was undoubtedly 14 June 1982, when Argentina surrendered, a mere ten weeks after invading the Falklands. The military junta in Argentina, beset by problems largely of their own making, had thought they could get away with taking over the Malvinas, as they call the islands, and struck on 2 April.

Had any of the lady's male rivals been in charge at 10 Downing Street that day, General Galtieri and his colleagues would probably have pulled it off. The Iron Lady lived up to her Soviet-coined sobriquet and sent a massive expeditionary force 8000 miles to take on and defeat the invader. Nothing that I or anybody else may say can diminish this feat of boldness and leadership. And yet: some things do have to be said.

In terms of grand strategy and of the wider war that concerns us here, the Falklands War was an expensive sideshow. It brought enormous prestige to the Prime Minister and to the British lion whose tail had been tweaked once too often. It preserved, for a time, the rights of 2000 or so nominally British settlers and their half million sheep. It showed that Britain was still a major power on the world stage; although ironically, if the Argentinos had waited another year or two, the substantial naval cuts that had been decided would have enabled the invaders to hang on to their ill-gotten gains.

In domestic politics, too, the operation brought great success to the Prime Minister, for she acted in defiance of the defeatist conventional wisdom of the Foreign Office (see Ch. XII). MI-6 had correctly reported the Argentine build-up, but the FO thought the Argentinos were bluffing. So confident was the Foreign Secretary, Lord Carrington, that instead of dealing with the looming crisis he flew to Israel (as an unwelcome guest) to discuss the Palestine issue with Menachem Begin, who was not interested in his proposals. Returning on 5 April, the day the Royal Navy Task Force set off for the South Atlantic, Carrington did the honourable thing and resigned, accepting 'responsibility for a very great national humiliation'.

Mrs Thatcher was right to take up the Argentine challenge, just as she was right (as were previous prime ministers) to stand up for the rights of the 17,000 Gibraltarians in their little corner (twenty-two square miles) of imperial left-over. Let us keep a sense of perspective, however. In the same context, she was wrong to listen to the Foreign Office and negotiate away the rights of the 6.5 million inhabitants of Hong Kong to the totalist regime of China. But we come to Hong Kong later.

There was a little-publicised Soviet dimension to the Falklands crisis, to which The 61 drew attention in its bulletin. Our Czech network had reported a Soviet decision to launch a propaganda campaign to support Argentina. The themes would be that Britain was acting as an imperialist power; that American neutrality as a mediator between Britain and Argentina was a device to hide US support for Britain; and that the real interest of the British and Americans was in the large offshore oil deposits and not in the fate of the inhabitants or the sovereignty of the islands.

Henceforth, Argentina was to be described as an 'ally', and pejorative terms such as 'junta' or 'dictatorship' were to be avoided. There was an ironical side to these guidelines, as the Soviet Union had vilified the military regime during the terror campaign, in which it had played a significant, though indirect, role.

Despite this, the Argentinian government had given the Soviet Union an opening in January 1980 when it decided to ignore President Carter's call for an embargo on grain deliveries to the USSR, in the wake of the invasion of Afghanistan. Argentina's own invasion of the Falklands played into Soviet hands in various ways. Soviet spy ships and satellites started providing the Argentines with intelligence about the British Task Force on its way south.

Although I had exchanged a number of letters with President Reagan, I had not been granted an audience in the White House during his first term. Ed Hickey had promised me a meeting shortly after his second election victory in November 1984. On 19 December, I wrote to Reagan at some length about the arrangements reportedly made by the US embassy in Bonn for the President to receive the former Chancellor of the Federal Republic and chairman of the Social Democratic Party (SPD), Willy Brandt, on a visit to West Germany in early May 1985. The letter went on:

It seems to me, with all respect, that there are powerful arguments against your receiving Willy Brandt, and absolutely none in favour.

Since November 1980, Brandt has taken every possible opportunity to denounce you and your policies. In particular, he supports the Sandinistas in Nicaragua and has consistently denounced your Central American policy. He opposed the deployment of Pershing II and Cruise, without reservations.

Particularly indicative of his attitude was the occasion on 3 November 1984 when he addressed a public demonstration in Bonn to denounce your Central American policy. Standing beside him on the platform was Philip Agee, the CIA defector. He has of course turned the Socialist International into a tool of Soviet policy, with special reference to the undermining of NATO.... If you did receive Brandt, indeed if he were received at any high level in Washington, the only effect would be to increase his party's influence on other Socialist parties in Europe and elsewhere, inevitably to the detriment of the United States. Conversely, by receiving him you would, in my view, quite seriously tarnish your image internationally, and especially in Europe.

The research for this letter had been done by a former senior CIA officer who had long specialised in German and Soviet affairs. He had joined The 61 after being made redundant by President Carter's DCI, Admiral Turner, in his purge of specialists on Communism (see Ch. X).

I assume this letter provoked some debate within the National Security Council, for Reagan's reply was dated 6 February 1985. It read, in part:

> Dear Brian
> Ed Hickey has personally delivered your kind letter. Thank you very much for your warm words of praise on my reelection and for your comments about former German Chancellor Willy Brandt....
> Best regards
> Ronald Reagan

Some weeks later, the President went to the Federal Republic on his State visit. Ignoring the arrangements made earlier by the US embassy, he did not receive Willy Brandt. The snub, rightly seen as intentional, brought scathing criticism from Brandt's political friends, notably Denis Healey and Edward Heath.

In mid-May, Ed Hickey rang me from the White House with the good news that the President would see me on 29 May. The meeting took place at 9.45 a.m. in the Oval Office. I had been told that the standard time allowance for non-official visitors was ten minutes, but he gave me twenty. We were not alone. The others present were the National Security Adviser, 'Bud' McFarlane; his deputy, Admiral John Poindexter, both of whom I already knew; and his Chief of Staff, Donald Regan. McFarlane and Poindexter greeted me with friendly smiles, Regan with a scowl. They took no part in our conversation, which was conducted on a couch two or three yards away.

It was a conversation, not an interview, and I did most of the talking. I had prepared two documents, which I handed to him on leaving. He listened intently, and responded favourably to both my suggestions. One was a proposal for the announcement of a 'Reagan Doctrine for the Americas', which would bring the Monroe Doctrine of 1823 up to date. The essence of it would have been a declaration that the United States would not tolerate the imposition of further Communist regimes in the Americas.

Reagan responded to this proposal with spontaneous enthusiasm, and I went on to suggest that the State Department's handling of the Angola/ Namibia affair was potentially dangerous in that it looked as though it was heading for a vote on independence for Namibia while a considerable force of Cubans was still in Angola.

DESPITE THE PRESIDENT'S initial reaction, the idea of a Reagan Doctrine for the Americas was not followed through. As for Namibia, the problem in effect resolved itself when Fidel Castro, doubtless under Soviet pressure, withdrew most of the Cuban troops from Angola in 1988–9. South Africa withdrew its own troops from Namibia in late November 1989, three weeks after the first free elections in that country, now independent.

My other proposal, however, produced rapid results. My one-page memorandum was entitled 'The Principle of Equivalence'. The issue was 'equivalence' of diplomatic and other official representation between Western countries and the USSR, in view of the known fact that accreditation in the host country was widely used by the Soviets as a cover for espionage by KGB or GRU personnel.

In the case of the United Kingdom, a rough balance on the diplomatic side had in fact been achieved after the expulsion of the 105 spies in 1971, by the simple expedient of banning the replacement of expelled 'diplomats'. There was still considerable imbalance, however, if account was taken of other Soviet representatives, such as the Trade Mission, Aeroflot, etc.

The problem was much worse in the US, where Soviet diplomatic representation easily outnumbered US representation in the USSR: 'If total Soviet representation (including personnel without diplomatic status) was considered, the imbalance rises strikingly in favour of the USSR. If Soviet representation at the United Nations is added (about 800, of whom some 30 per cent have diplomatic status), the imbalance becomes almost grotesque.'

I suggested that the US should take the initiative in proposing uniform Allied policy in this field.

On 29 June, one month to the day after our talk in the White House, President Reagan delivered a nationwide radio address. After describing the problem of Soviet espionage, he went on:

> ...we need to reduce the size of the hostile intelligence threat we're up against in this country. Some 30 to 40 per cent of more than 2500 Soviet bloc officials in this country are known or suspected intelligence officers and all can be called upon by the KGB. We need to bring the number of their intelligence officers to a more manageable number. We need a balance between the size of the Soviet diplomatic presence in the United States and the US presence in the Soviet Union. The Soviets currently have a huge advantage. Now, we intend to take steps to accomplish this and we need to better control foreign intelligence agents working at the UN who have utilised that organisation as a spy nest.

I did not hear the good news of Reagan's broadcast for some time, because a copy of it had been sent to my old address in Grand Buildings. Returned to the White House, it was re-addressed to me by one of my most congenial contacts, Kenneth E. deGraffenreid, in his dual capacity as Special Assistant for National Security Affairs and Senior Director of Intelligence Programs (see Ch. XIV). I learned later that the question of equivalence had been discussed for some months by a committee of senior officials from the State Department, the CIA, and the NSC. My intervention, however, had apparently tipped the balance in favour of action.

In my view, action should have followed immediately after the President's radio address. In the event, expulsions of diplomats and other officials were not made for some months, until in early March 1986, 105 Soviet staff at the UN were told to leave. A further expulsion of fifty-five staff at the Soviet embassy in Washington and the consulate in San Francisco followed in October and November that year.

President Reagan was in a 'can't lose' situation. It was impossible for the Soviet side to retaliate on a numerically equal 'tit for tat' basis, for the very reason that Soviet personnel in the US heavily outnumbered American personnel in the Soviet Union. On 22 October, in a televised address in Moscow, Gorbachev gave vent to his frustration, describing the expulsions as 'wild and outrageous'. A mere ten US personnel were then expelled from the Soviet Union. Equivalence had been achieved, at last.

*   *   *

IN 1986–7, FURTHER NTS reports from agents in the USSR continued to reach The 61, along with detailed accounts of NTS talks with members of the Soviet nomenklatura on trips to the West. These reports supplemented our own intelligence from other sources. On this basis, we built up convincing evidence of a deepening economic crisis under the twin burdens of mismanagement and prohibitive military expenditure; food shortages; ethnic tensions; the deepening failure of the invasion of Afghanistan; and the semi-clandestine revival of religion and growth of a submerged opposition.

In late 1986, over lunch at the Madison Hotel in Washington, I briefed the future US ambassador to Moscow, Jack (John F.) Matlock. A Russian-speaking career diplomat, Matlock had succeeded Professor Pipes as a special adviser on Soviet affairs on the White House National Security Council. His knowledge of Russian and Soviet history was wide and deep, but he had not been informed of this special perception of a fast-crumbling situation. At the end of January 1987, Reagan appointed him to his new post in Moscow.

In December of that year, we distributed a further and detailed analysis of the situation inside the USSR, which showed the reality behind Gorbachev's façade.

1 In 1990, taking advantage of *glasnost*, the NTS had emerged as a Christian Democrat opposition party. It was allowed to hold meetings in Russia and a USSR-wide congress in Leningrad in November 1990. There was a brief return to the Stalinist past: Boris Miller, George's father, was deported to Helsinki by the KGB, which had stopped him in the street, confiscated his (British) passport, and axed down the front door of the friend's flat where he and his son were staying. His passport was returned at the airport. In 1992, with Gorbachev deposed and Boris Yeltsin as President, George Miller moved to Moscow where he opened an office as economic adviser to the Russian government. Times had changed.

2 See footnote, p. 16, Brian Crozier, ed., *The Grenada Documents* (Sherwood Press, London, 1987), with an introduction by Sir Alfred Sherman. This collection carries a detailed chronology, and a selection of texts of pacts with the USSR and Soviet bloc countries, covering military cooperation, training, ideology, propaganda, and security. Sherman's introduction benefits from his insights as a former Communist as well as his experience as a close adviser to Mrs Thatcher.

3 See *Hansard*, House of Lords debate, 1 November 1983, col. 475; also, Hugo Young, *One of Us*, op. cit., p. 350.

4 A different version of this incident is given by Edwin Meese III, in his calm, pro-Reagan but well-balanced account of his years in the White House, *With Reagan: The Inside Story* (Regnery Gateway, Washington, DC, 1992). Meese, who served as Counsellor to the President, and went on to be appointed Attorney-General, records that Reagan's 'closest international ally, Prime Minister Margaret Thatcher, opposed the action'. He goes on: 'Grenada was part of the British Commonwealth and had a British-appointed governor general, but the British were too far away to take any immediate measures. With this in mind, the President talked to Mrs Thatcher to brief her on the crisis and our impending action. For whatever reason, she was against it. The President was deeply disappointed, but he stood firm, telling her that we intended to go ahead' (p. 217). In the light of my conversation with the Prime Minister, I stick to my own version of the sequence of events. I have no doubt that the President did telephone Mrs Thatcher, but only after he had made his decision and given the marching orders.

XXI

'The 61' bows out (1986–7)

THE 61 WAS not a permanent organisation. It was an *ad hoc* attempt to cope with specific circumstances. By the beginning of 1986, after a long run of successes, we were in crisis.

The problems were both financial and personal. One of our major supporters, disillusioned with the West, cut his contribution by 75 per cent. A big European company, after a change of top management, dropped out. An American donor ran into problems over a new Tax Reform Bill in Congress. At my London headquarters, I made economies of staff and space, but the survival margin was shrinking. By mid-June, it was down to less that three months. Unless more money came in, or more economies were made, we would be forced to close down by late September. In the event, The 61 lasted another year.

The personal problem was simply one of time and work-load. The organisation had grown so fast, nationally and internationally, that by mid-1985 I was finding it increasingly difficult not only to guide and coordinate operations, but also to collate and analyse the ever-increasing flow of intelligence, and from it to distil the editorial content of the monthly bulletin, *Notes and Analysis*. My attempts to shed the editorial burden had failed, in part because it was clearly impossible to offer a long-term career prospect to any likely candidate, although I did interview one or two promising ones.

With the issue of January 1986, I discontinued *Notes and Analysis*. However, when material of exceptional interest reached me, I went on issuing an occasional bulletin simply entitled *Analysis*. Between April 1986 and April 1988, thirteen issues appeared.

Both nationally and internationally, the situation in 1986 was full of paradoxes. Within our group there was a broad consensus, on the following lines.

The major paradox was that the Soviet side was on the way to defeat, but might yet achieve victory by default. In that negative term 'by default' lay another side of the paradox: the fact that the West reacted only sporadically and in selected areas. There was no overall strategic vision. More precisely, President Reagan did have a strategic vision during his first term. During the second, the vision was blurred and undermined by a number of factors, among them: the 'Irangate affair' and its domestic political consequences, which included the departure of the Reaganites from the White House; the extraordinary success of Mikhail Gorbachev's international public relations operation; and the reassertion of traditional piecemeal diplomacy, especially in the State Department and the Foreign Office.

Nationally, in Britain, there was a parallel paradox. On the surface, everything was fine. Mrs Thatcher had defeated Scargill's protracted political coal strike, and it looked as though Rupert Murdoch, whose newspaper group was under siege at Wapping, would hold out against the militant trades unions. (His victory, and that of the anti-Communist electricians' union, did not come until September, and effectively marginalised the trades unions as a coercive force.)

There were signs that the Labour Party was changing its policies; or was it simply a change of image? And yet, behind the scenes, the Communist threat was in some ways greater than ever, if only because the public perception was that the threat no longer existed.

In *Analysis* and in a number of special strategic papers, the main recipients of which, as always, were the Prime Minister and the President, we tried to present affairs as they really were. Britain first. In countries with a mass Communist Party, such as Italy and France, the threat was clearly visible, whether or not it was politically possible to deal with it. In Britain, it was scattered and largely invisible, and thus easily ignored.

The various Communist groups (Trotskyists, crypto-Communists, Moscow-line, and Euro-Communists) were at loggerheads over tactics but agreed on the final goal of a Marxist-Leninist Britain. In a way, the fact that the Trotskyists aimed at a 'pure' Marxist-Leninist State, free from Moscow's Stalinist taint, was irrelevant. Even in the very unlikely event that they might achieve their goal, they lacked an international base. The only base that counted was the Soviet Union with its gigantic subversive apparatus and arms structure, and any Marxist-Leninist takeover, in any West European country, would itself be taken over by Moscow.

None of the groupings was capable, on its own, of staging a revolution, and none wished to ally itself with the others. However, the aggregate effect of their separate efforts was to make it very difficult for the Labour Party to modify its programme, even if the new leader, Neil Kinnock (in whom the commitment to socialism was still strong), so wished. Nor could a 'Livingstone-type' coup after a Labour victory be ruled out as impossible.

The most active of the Trotskyist groups was the Militant Tendency, which had achieved considerable success in capturing Labour Party organisations at constituency and municipal level. At this time, of course, The 61's CAMACC was in full counter-activity. Although Neil Kinnock had indeed taken action against the Militant group in Liverpool, and in particular against its leader, Derek Hatton, it was significant that he had acted on the basis not of ideological disagreement but of alleged breach of Labour rules. No effort was made to expel the two Labour MPs known to be supporters of Militant (David Nellist and Terry Fields).

The cryptos, essentially, were a group of Communists who, by agreement with Moscow and with the CPGB, were no longer card-carrying Party members. They operated in Parliament. Their status, according to a major Soviet defector with whom I discussed the matter some years later, was that of 'confidential contacts' of the Soviet embassy. One or two dealt directly with the Soviet International Department. They exerted a covert but at times decisive influence on Party policy.

As for the avowed Communists, there had been various splits, the most important one being between the mainstream, Moscow-line ones and the Euro-Communists. Surprisingly, the Euros had won, in that they had gained control of the Party apparatus; the 'losers' had kept the daily organ, the *Morning Star*, and were reorganising themselves as the Communist Campaign Group (CCG). All these moves, and many more, were rigorously documented in our reports.

To say such things publicly would have attracted the standard smear of 'McCarthyism', and our advice to all concerned was simply to quote the actual words of those involved. Among those words were those of Neil Kinnock. By publicly criticising the attitudes of the so-called 'loony Left', with particular reference to calls from Labour-controlled municipal councils for lesbian and 'gay' rights, he had managed to give the impression that he was in no way a political extremist. He had considerable personal charm and an oratorical gift (sometimes derided by critics in the nickname 'the Welsh windbag'). In doctrinal terms, however, he was still a committed socialist, emphatically not a social democrat.

Thus, in an inaugural lecture on 12 November 1985 to launch the Fabian Society's autumn series, Kinnock had denounced social democrats for wanting only 'social relief', whereas 'democratic socialists' like himself wanted 'social change'. His lecture appeared in pamphlet form in February 1986 as Fabian Society Tract No. 509, entitled *The Future of Socialism*.

By then, it already seemed unlikely that the SDP/Liberal Alliance, our social democratic experiment, was going to work. It followed that the only hope of saving the country from internal disruption, and possible takeover, lay in Margaret Thatcher and her Conservative Party, however confused and divided it often seemed. At times, indeed, the Tories could be seen as an obstacle to their own victory.

Partly for that reason, I asked for a meeting with the Prime Minister, which took place at 10 Downing Street on 28 February 1986. This time, her foreign policy adviser, Charles (later Sir Charles) Powell, was present, although the main themes I wanted to discuss with her were domestic. He took notes.

She was very friendly, but the conversation was less than satisfactory. I reminded her of the things we had been able to do in 1979 and 1983, which were found to have been useful. She agreed, and I told her of two important initiatives we had in mind: a campaign to expose the true extent of the Communist danger, of which there was widespread ignorance; and the continuing campaign against council corruption.

On CAMACC, I explained that, as we saw it, the real problem was within the Tory Party. I named William Waldegrave as one of the culprits. I dwelt on the uselessness of the Widdicombe Inquiry (see Ch. XIX), on which she agreed; and the weakness of the proposed legislation, which missed the point by concentrating on banning the use of council funds for 'party political' campaigns, whereas the real point was the money spent on non-party issues such as nuclear-free zones.

I raised the delicate matter of a book on socialism I was working on, which I thought might be useful to her Party at the next elections.

It had already had several lives. In its first incarnation, in 1984, it was a semi-satirical paperback, co-authored by the well-known free-market economist Arthur Seldon, and myself, with brilliantly apposite cartoons by Cummings of Express Newspapers. The title, deliberately low-key, was *Socialism Explained* (Sherwood, 1984).

Seldon, the long-time deputy to Ralph (later Lord) Harris, Director of the Institute for Economic Affairs, wrote the theoretical first section, in his punchy and original style. My second half examined the performance of socialism in the Soviet Union and Eastern Europe, in the Third World and in the major Western countries; and found it wanting. The lesson was that the bigger the dose of socialism, the worse the outcome.

A New York publisher, Louis Barron, spotting the book on his annual visit to the Frankfurt Book Fair, brought out a US edition, entitled *Socialism: the Grand Delusion*. The French anti-Marxist philosopher Jean-Marie Benoist (who died of cancer some years later at the tragically early age of forty-six) was enthused with the product, and solemnly 'pledged' to find a French publisher. So I translated my half of the work into French. By now, Cummings's cartoons had been outdated by the advent of Kinnock and the retirement of Michael Foot as the Labour leader. Arthur Seldon dropped out, and I started adding several more chapters (again, initially in French) outlining the history of socialist ideas in the nineteenth and twentieth centuries, from Owen to Marx and Engels, and on to a survey of the common ideological roots of Lenin, Mussolini and Hitler.

The proposed new title was *Socialism: Dream and Reality*. My partner in our Sherwood Press, Ken Watkins, who was enthusiastic about the whole exercise, had a plan to persuade the Conservative Party to buy, say, 10,000 copies of the book and use it as ammunition in the next general election. I thought this was a good idea, and was prepared to donate any royalties at least in part to Conservative funds, with an agreed proportion to The 61. I had discussed the project with Tom Arnold, at that time head of the Party's Research Department in Smith Square, and he had responded favourably.

I put the question to Mrs Thatcher, but her reaction was disappointing. The Party could not possibly *buy* the book, she said, but it could *display* it. I asked her if she would talk to Norman Tebbit, at that time Chairman of the Conservative Party, so that I could discuss various ideas with him, and she promised to do so.

The themes we discussed broadened to relations with our secret services. I confirmed that The 61's relations with MI-5 were non-existent. Not only did the Security Services deny us any contact but it even declined to receive our reports on domestic affairs. She found this incredible, and I commented that it was possible they were getting these indirectly. I suggested that it might be useful for me to meet the then Chairman of the Joint Intelligence Committee, Tony (Sir Anthony) Duff, and she offered to mention this to him. I believe she did, but nothing came of it.

As I rose to leave, Margaret said she would miss *Notes and Analysis*, which she found particularly useful so that she could draw attention to certain items. Charles Powell emphasised the same point. I explained my reasons for giving it up, but added that the occasional issues of *Analysis* would continue.

I made another point: the fact that we were able to operate in areas closed to our secret services. She found this difficult to understand. I explained that, for instance, SIS was not supposed to operate in France or West Germany because they were allies. We could. That was why we often got material they could not.

As I left, she gave me a warm smile and said: 'It's good to see you looking so well.'

NORMAN TEBBIT AND I had corresponded briefly, but I had never met him. Mrs Thatcher had indeed spoken to him, but his time-table was very crowded and our meeting was deferred until the afternoon of 22 May 1986, at Smith Square. With his dark, bony, saturnine features, Tebbit had a somewhat forbidding exterior. But his smile was warm and he listened carefully to some of the ideas I put to him. He confirmed, however, that it was out of the question for the Party to buy copies of *Socialism: Dream and Reality*. He did offer to talk to some of the Party's principal fund-raisers and suggest that they should help my organisation. Whether he did or not, nothing came of it.

The Labour Party's annual conference, at Blackpool in October 1986, confirmed our view that on international policy, even more than in domestic affairs, Neil Kinnock represented a very real threat to Western cohesion in the face of the Soviet threat. Both Kinnock and his wife Glenys were supporters of the unilateralist Campaign for Nuclear Disarmament (CND). At the conference, Kinnock committed Britain to a non-nuclear policy and said he would close down American bases in Britain within a year – a timetable he later extended, but without withdrawing the threat to order the Yanks to go home. He also declared that Britain would remain in NATO, with no apparent awareness that he was expressing contradictory propositions or merely offering a sop to the patriotic vote.

With Mrs Thatcher's approval, I liaised with Keith Joseph in certain psychological actions in the election year, 1987. We met either in the House of Commons or in Joseph's office as Secretary for Education.

One move, to which Keith Joseph attached particular importance, was to brief the television presenter David Frost for a proposed interview with Neil Kinnock. I had met Frost at Jimmy Goldsmith's home and, at Jimmy's request, had prepared a carefully detailed questionnaire for a proposed interview of Yuri Andropov. Unfortunately, Andropov died before the scheduled date for the interview.

Frost and I met for breakfast at the Connaught Hotel on 6 January 1987. I had prepared a detailed background paper on Neil Kinnock's views, activities, and personal relations in politics. The interview did not take place until 24 May, during the election campaign, but a number of the points I had suggested to Frost had survived the intervening months, and the interview made a considerable impact.

In March of that year, we had brought out a rather gloomy issue of *Analysis*, which contained an assessment of 'the end of Reaganism' during the President's second term, and a fresh and detailed account of 'the Communist takeover of Labour': essentially a factual guide to the problems Britain would face in the forthcoming general elections.

Some of our other actions during this critical period may be found controversial. Although never a partisan of the view that 'the end justifies the means' (which would make me a Leninist), I do believe in the value of covert action, so long as certain principles are respected: charges made and facts presented must be rigorously checked for accuracy; the people persuaded to express views or advocate action must believe in the cause they serve even if they are unaware of the identity of the initiator of the action chosen. Unawareness is sometimes essential, to protect those in the public eye and of course the initiator of the action, who may be hampered by premature publicity.

In my view, such covert action does not necessarily amount to 'dirty tricks', so long as the above requirements are respected. 'Tricks' are 'dirty' only if lies, slanderous or untrue allegations are involved. No such lies or allegations were made by The 61. To cause people to say things they know to be true, even if they had not thought of them, does not amount to 'dirty tricks'. I prefer to call it 'benign deception'.

In this context, one of our ploys was a booklet, the title of which had been suggested by Ken Watkins: *The Vision of St Kinnock*. It was a composite effort, although the final attribution was to Paul Mercer, one of the best of our activists. By the time the text was completed, in May, our funds were painfully low, but I persuaded a well-known City magnate, who had not previously helped our efforts, to meet the printing costs. The cover of the pamphlet, appropriately in red, carried a Cummings cartoon depicting a beatific Kinnock, complete with halo and dove of peace and bearing the word 'moderation' emerging from the cannon of the Labour Party.

The research had yielded many quotations from Kinnock, pacifist and neutralist in tone. The pictures showed him either playing the fool, or sharing a platform with such as Ken Livingstone, or in earnest conversation with Fidel Castro, or addressing a CND rally. We distributed it to hundreds of Conservative candidates who made good use of it in their speeches or election pamphlets.

On this exercise, and on the others, we had no help at all from the Conservative Party.

A highly effective operation during the 1987 election campaign was the provision to the Liberal Party of details, drawn from our files, of some 130 hard Left Labour MPs. The leader, David Steel, in an ingenious twist of his own, published the list, slightly reduced, and called it Labour's '101 damnations'. The echo of Walt Disney's 101 Dalmatians gave the ploy maximum publicity.

In many other ways, none of them publicly connected with my office, we influenced public opinion. Our exposure of 'loony Left' activities in the councils continued. We also produced several occasional issues of the *Monitoring Report*, an impressively researched survey of the political attitudes in the media, which showed, in my view beyond doubt, that there was a predominantly left-wing bias, especially in television. The first yearly report, at the end of 1986, attracted much press attention, most of it favourable.

For months in the run-up to the elections, we continued to provide factual material to politically compatible columnists, including Woodrow Wyatt (*News of the World* and *The Times*), Frank Chapple (*Daily Mail*), Bernard Levin, and Lord Chalfont.

On 12 June, Mrs Thatcher won her third consecutive term as Prime Minister. I wrote to her on the 14th to congratulate her and to report on our modest contribution to the election results. Essentially, I simply summarised the points described above.

I thought she should be told about the negative attitude in Smith Square. I referred to 'total non-cooperation' from Central Office in the matter of the Kinnock pamphlet:

We did get it into the hands of all Tory candidates. But no thanks to Central Office, which went so far as to refuse to give us the names and constituency addresses. As we had agreed to do the posting ourselves, I really thought that this was carrying the principle of disassociation to extreme and absurd lengths. I am not suggesting that you should issue a post-mortem rebuke, as we wish to maintain what had until then been a friendly and cooperative relationship, but I did think you should know this.

ALTHOUGH MRS THATCHER'S victory had removed the immediate extremist threat in Britain, there was less to rejoice about internationally. Our assessment of the coming collapse of Soviet Communism was being fulfilled, but the speed and degree of the deterioration in the USSR was hard to estimate. More and more, the West faced the paradox of a military superpower in a Third World economy. Relatively, the West was growing stronger as the enemy weakened, but there was neither unity nor unanimity in analysis or policy.

During his first term, President Reagan had given strong leadership, albeit at a high economic cost for his successors. 'Reaganomics' had worked, in the sense that lower taxes and general optimism had created jobs by the million. Strategically, Reagan had opted for vastly increased spending on defence, 'financed' by deficit budgeting. One of the major items was the Strategic Defence Initiative (SDI), misleadingly dubbed 'Star Wars': misleadingly, because its purpose was defensive, namely destruction of enemy nuclear missiles before they could hit their target.

There are, of course, divided views about the merits of SDI[1] and in general on high-cost military technology, the efficacy of which was stunningly demonstrated in the Gulf War in 1990–91. My own view is that it was the quantum leap into high-tech hardware, more than any other factor, that obliged the Soviet Union, for the first time, to negotiate an arms reduction treaty (as distinct from the earlier arms control treaties) with the US. Facing collapse, the Soviet economy was in no position to continue the arms race.

Another major initiative of Reagan's was less successful. The Reagan Doctrine of aid to anti-Communist resistance forces had worked only intermittently because of fluctuating Congressional attitudes, so that the Nicaraguan Contras, for example, had no certainty of continuous American support. El Salvador was another example. Indeed, there were a number of anomalies.

Three specific cases illustrate the problem: Afghanistan, Angola, and Mozambique. In all three countries, Communist governments were in power but they were challenged by anti-Communist resistance groups. With Bill Casey's full support, the CIA supplied advanced weaponry to the Afghan rebels, which enabled them not to defeat the Soviet-installed regime in Kabul but to achieve a military stalemate.

In strategic terms, Gorbachev's decision to withdraw the Soviet forces from Afghanistan was a major reverse comparable to the American decision to pull out of Vietnam in 1973. However, the agreements negotiated between the US Secretary of State, George Shultz, and his Soviet opposite number, Eduard Shevardnadze, in Geneva in May 1988 gave the Soviet side a fighting chance of turning defeat into victory. Under the agreements, the governments of Afghanistan and Pakistan pledged non-interference in each other's affairs, which in effect barred the use of Pakistani territory for further military supplies to the US-supported *mujahedin* guerrillas. There was nothing, however, to stop a continued flow of Soviet supplies to the puppet government in Kabul, across the vast frontier between the two countries. Despite this advantage, four years later, and after fourteen years of fighting, the Najibullah regime was toppled by the *mujahedin*.

In Angola, the absurd Clark Amendment ruled out US aid to Jonas Savimbi's UNITA guerrillas until its repeal in 1985. Thereafter, US arms deliveries enabled UNITA to fight their way to the negotiated settlement of May 1991. The subsequent shambles does not come into this story.

Essentially, the Mozambique problem was identical with that of Angola: two ex-Portuguese colonies, taken over by Communist forces with Soviet backing. In each case, there was an anti-Communist resistance: UNITA in Angola, RENAMO in Mozambique. Each, in the absence of other Western help (none for RENAMO, and very late for UNITA) received aid from South Africa. In Mozambique, however, the British involved themselves on the Communist side; and the Americans went along with them.

British instructors trained Mozambican government forces in Zimbabwe, and President Samora Machel was received in London on a State visit (as indeed was President Ceausescu of Romania). In my view, this policy was the outcome of Lord Carrington's role in the emergence of Zimbabwe and of the UK commitment to anti-South Africa policies in deference to the prevailing consensus in the Commonwealth.[2]

I discussed the Mozambique situation with high officials of the Foreign Office, on two occasions. The logic of the policy, as they expounded it, was the belief that Machel in particular was looking for a way to break out of his dependency on the Soviet Union.

The death of Machel in an air crash in October 1986 prompted me to write to both the President and the Prime Minister, in each case on 21 October. In both cases, I appealed to them to seize the opportunity of moving away from the 'ultimately insane State Department/Foreign Office policy' of support for the FRELIMO regime.

To President Reagan:

> There is a direct contradiction between the wise policy of aid to Savimbi, and the absurd antithesis of aiding the Communist ('Marxist') regime in Mozambique against much maligned resistance fighters who, if helped, could yield a pro-Western, and certainly an anti-Communist, government in Maputo.
>
> An exact parallel to the policy of helping the FRELIMO regime would be a policy of aid to the Soviet puppet regime in Kabul, against the Afghan resistance.
>
> The sophistries of the permanent officials should not be allowed to obscure the strategic realities.

I appealed to both Reagan and Thatcher to look at the relevant pages of *Notes and Analysis* of December 1985.

The Prime Minister replied immediately, on 23 October 1986:

> Thank you for your letter about Mozambique which I have read with interest. I believe President Machel was genuinely trying to draw Mozambique closer to the West and deserved our support in this. I find the prospects following his untimely death uncertain and worrying.

The President's reply was dated 17 November:

> Thank you very much for your letter of October 21 which has just reached my desk. Hence the late reply.
>
> Our help to the late Samora Machel was based on the belief that he was leaning toward the West and just possibly seeking a way out of his relationship with the Soviet Union. This had come to us through sources that seemed reliable. Those same sources indicated that the resistance fighters were not of the same caliber as the Savimbi forces.
>
> I shall try and find the 'Notes and Analysis – December '85' that you mentioned.

On policy toward Mozambique, however, officialdom prevailed. In May 1987, Machel's successor, President Joaquim Chissano, on a State visit to London, lunched with the Queen, talked with the Prime Minister, and was given promises of increased economic and military power.

The issue of *Notes and Analysis* to which I had referred both President and Prime Minister had carried a detailed account of the situation in Mozambique, and reproduced an interview by RENAMO's secretary-general and roving ambassador, Evo Fernandes.

There was a sordid and tragic sequel. I had had several visits in London from Fernandes. As with so many personalities in Mozambique, Fernandes was of Goanese Indian origin. A multilingual lawyer, he was a civilised and convincing advocate of the anti-Communist cause in Mozambique. On 17 April 1988, he was kidnapped from his home in Cascais, Portugal. His body was found four days later, riddled with bullets and with signs of torture.

By then, The 61 had been disbanded. However, our man in Lisbon, who had stayed in touch with me, sent me a detailed report on the case. Fernandes had been kidnapped by agents of section D-13 of FRELIMO's secret security service, the SNASP, trained by Cuban and East German specialists. The Anglo–US policy continued unchanged.

THAT ISSUE OF December 1985, the penultimate one of our original intelligence bulletins, also contained an inside account (after a personal briefing to me in the White House) of Reagan's private meetings with Mikhail Gorbachev, during their first summit at Geneva. In an earlier issue, we had argued that the President should use the proposed summit to warn Gorbachev, in strict secrecy, to call a halt to Soviet expansionism.

He had done just that. There had been hours of private talks with only two interpreters present; to the discomfiture of some 3500 journalists in Geneva for the story. In quietly confident mood, Reagan had taken care to be firm but not provocative. Although he refrained from actually warning Gorbachev to desist from further expansionism, he declared that any attempts by the Soviet Union to impose repressive regimes on local populations and to keep such regimes in power where they already existed were doomed to failure. He did warn Gorbachev that the US would provide assistance to guerrillas fighting to restore the freedom of their countries.

The widely reported second summit, in Iceland's capital, Reykjavik, in October 1986, was less successful. Reagan did stand up to Gorbachev's pressure to drop the SDI, but he came close to selling the pass by proposing a total ban on ballistic missiles. A zero/zero pact on the removal of missiles in Europe would have left the Soviet Union with total superiority in biological and chemical weapons and an overwhelming lead in conventional forces.

Over the previous two years, the President had been subjected to events and pressures which, in sum, considerably weakened his originally firm policy on the Soviet problem. Even before the first term had ended, 'passivism' was still strong in the Washington bureaucracy. In October 1984, on the eve of the presidential elections, one of our American team sent us the full text of an analytical paper by Herbert Meyer, Vice-Chairman of the National Intelligence Council and addressed to the DCI. Excerpts had appeared in the press.

I did not know Meyer at the time, but later had a number of meetings with him. A journalist and publisher, Meyer was in fact hawkish, but one would not have known it from the analysis, which must have been influenced by the prevailing consensus. Essentially, the theme was that the Soviet empire was now in the terminal phase of decay, and that the US should do nothing to try to weaken the regime still further, still less to bring it down.

Our information was that Meyer's line represented a growing consensus in the CIA, the State Department, and the White House itself. The realists had gone, among them Professor Richard Pipes, the erudite and uncompromising historian, who had served as the National Security Council's adviser on Soviet affairs, and had now returned to Harvard.

In the new and weakened White House, compromise and appeasement were the themes of the Chief of Staff, James Baker, and his deputy, Michael Deaver. The National Security Adviser, Robert 'Bud' McFarlane, had the right instincts but lacked the personality and self-assurance to assert his views against the tide of his consensual colleagues.

Reagan's second term was gravely weakened by the 'Iran Contra' affair, sometimes known as 'Irangate'.

The March 1987 issue of *Analysis* (referred to earlier) made a gloomy assessment, dissecting 'the end of Reaganism'. We described President Reagan's decision to appoint ex-Senator Howard Baker as White House Chief of Staff in succession to the discredited Donald Regan (castigated by the Tower Commission in a damning report) as a masterly stroke in domestic political terms. The real significance of it was that it represented the end of 'Reaganism' in international policy. The Reaganites, meaning political activists committed to fulfilling the Reagan Doctrine of aid to anti-Communist guerrillas, had virtually all, by now, left the White House, whether of their own volition (Pat Buchanan, 'Bud' McFarlane, who was recovering from a suicide attempt), or through dismissal (Colonel North, Donald Regan), or because they were eased out (Poindexter, Ken deGraffenreid). The main Congressional committees were now in the wrong hands, in the sense of standing up to Soviet imperialist expansionism.

The future of the Reagan Doctrine was thus in jeopardy. The illness and retirement of William Casey as Director of Central Intelligence had deprived Reagan of his most effective international activist. The appointment of Judge William Webster, until then head of the FBI, as his successor clearly heralded a new era of meticulous observation of the letter of the law – ideal for the avoidance of 'scandals' and Congressional opprobrium, but incompatible with true covert action.[3]

The aftermath of Watergate, Carterism, the Church Committee, and Congressional oversight, and the Freedom of Information and Privacy Acts, had forced Reagan to attempt to initiate covert operations (the only way of countering the far wider and more numerous Active Measures from the Soviet side) through the National Security staff who, however able and courageous, lacked the necessary professional training and the back-up that only the CIA could provide.

The alacrity with which the Administration had responded to Mikhail Gorbachev's offer of a deal on the dismantling of intermediate-range missiles (in practice, the SS-20s on the Soviet side and the Cruise missiles and Pershing IIs on the NATO side) clearly reflected the pressure Reagan felt to restore his waning popularity with a success in arms control. Therein lay dangers.

Our collective view of the Soviet new look under Gorbachev was that his reform programme (*perestroika* and *glasnost*), though a step in the right direction, was essentially cosmetic, with the weapons and the security apparatus intact. Active Measures (that is, the Cold War) were continuing in a more sophisticated form.

Gorbachev's overtures to Reagan brought the expected response from a weakened Reagan Administration, with the conclusion, in December 1987, of the INF Treaty eliminating intermediate- and shorter-range missiles. The Treaty attracted widespread praise, and some blame. The 61's own defence experts were highly critical of it. Our analysis, dated January 1988, and written by a leading American specialist, summarised his views as follows:

By signing the INF Treaty, President Reagan sacrificed his own arms control principles, repeatedly stated:

1 Significant reductions must be achieved;
2 Any treaty should affect both sides equally;
3 Any treaty should be 'verifiable';
4 Soviet compliance with earlier treaties should be seen to have been achieved.

One of the elements in this critical analysis of the treaty was a 'secret' State Department memorandum on 'Arms Control Compliance and Military Openness', which had been in our hands for some months, and which listed precise examples of Soviet evasions of previous arms control treaties.

The list was in itself a cause for satisfaction, in that it showed official recognition of the 'cheating' on the Soviet side to which we had consistently drawn attention. The conclusions drawn, however, were the opposite of those we advocated. Our view was that unless and until the Soviet side stopped cheating and proved it by untrammelled inspection and verification of existing agreements, the West (in practice, the United States) should suspend arms negotiations and offer no further concessions. The State Department's memorandum, however, put the onus on the American side to take the initiative to put forward compromise proposals acceptable to the Soviet side. We cited this conclusion as yet another example of what we called the 'diplomatic syndrome' (a variant of 'pactitis').

Although in the end Gorbachev had settled for an arms reduction treaty without securing his stated goal of a US commitment to abandon the SDI programme, the Soviet Active Measures apparatus was pursuing the same goal by different means.

The veteran US arms control negotiator, Paul Nitze, was a particular target. He was against the SDI and had been taking part in 'private' and unauthorised negotiations with the Soviets. According to a report in circulation, the President had personally rebuked Nitze in a confrontation in the Oval Office in late September 1987.[4]

We confirmed from our own sources that there had indeed been a confrontation, followed by a categorical order to Nitze from the new National Security Adviser, Frank Carlucci, to desist from further involvement in unofficial talks, which were still being held between American and Soviet scientists. Despite these strictures, Nitze continued to advise the US scientists who met their Soviet counterparts in Moscow towards the end of October.

These talks were indeed a Soviet Active Measure. The Soviet scientists were led by Academician Roald Sagdeev, Deputy Chairman of the Soviet Scientists' Committee for Peace – one of the new generation of 'professional' fronts launched by the Soviet International Department at a time when the major international fronts, especially the World Peace Council, had become widely discredited.

DURING THIS PERIOD of rapid change, intelligence kept coming in, albeit on a reduced scale. From various sources we had a rounded picture of the Soviet involvement in the international drugs trade – the ultimate taboo subject for Western governments, even more than terrorism; further depressing details about the turning of the German Social Democrats (SPD) in a pro-Soviet direction; and of the Soviet colonisation of Angola. Our last intelligence offering, in *Analysis*, was a detailed account of the unreported internal crisis in Fidel Castro's regime.

At the time, we kept the identity of our source secret, but the need for secrecy has lapsed. The man who brought this inside story to us, during two hours in my office, was a high-ranking officer of the DGI, Juan Benemelis, who had defected to the CIA from Angola. When he came to my office, he told me he had long wanted to meet me to ask where I had obtained the authentic details about the birth of the DGI, which I had described in the ISC *Conflict Study* of 1973 on the satellisation of Cuba.[5] My reply was evasive.

BETWEEN 1985 AND 1987, Castro had carried out a sweeping internal purge of the DGI, the ruling party, the armed services, and the media. The purpose was to preserve the 'purity' of his revolutionary regime against the contagion of Gorbachev and his reformist ideas.

By the time we distributed Benemelis's detailed revelations (April 1988), The 61 had ceased to exist. In the late summer of 1987, two considerations had influenced me. One was that my five-year lease was expiring; the other, that I had entered my seventieth year. Although I found new sources of funds after the crisis of 1986, I had lost my zest for fund-raising. I closed down five of my offices in the Linen Hall and paid off all The 61's agents, mainly in Britain, France, Belgium, Germany, Holland, Spain, Portugal, and the United States.

Much of the work went on, in other hands, and in separate segments. There were disputes and clashes of personality. Some took the end of a short era in their stride; others nursed resentments. The phenomenon of 'post-facto ingratitude' manifested itself; but so did the serenity of long-time friendships and the satisfaction of a job well done. I had no regrets. It was time to pull back and hand over.

NOTES

1 In the US, as in Britain and other Western countries, there was no shortage of either critics or defenders of the SDI. For detailed analyses of the pros and cons, see the files of *Strategic Review* (organ of the United States Strategic Institute) and *Global Affairs* (organ of the International Security Council), both published in Washington, DC.

2 See Brian Crozier, 'The Legacy of Carrington' in the *Salisbury Review*, London, September 1989.

3 For an account of White House in-fighting, see Constantine Menges, *Inside the National Security Council* (Simon & Schuster, 1988). For a hostile account of covert actions during Casey's terms as DCI, see Bob Woodward's *Veil: The Secret Wars of the CIA, 1981–1987* (Simon & Schuster, 1987).

4 Gregory A. Fossedal, in the *Copley News Service*, San Diego, 3 November 1987.

5 *Conflict Studies* No. 35, 'Soviet Pressures in the Caribbean: the Satellisation of Cuba' (ISC, London, 1973).

Epilogue

MIKHAIL GORBACHEV WAS in at the start of this memoir, and it is fitting that he should be in at the end. For he very nearly snatched victory out of the wreckage of the Soviet system. On course to the last, the West gave him every possible encouragement. Fortunately for us, and for humanity, the decay of the system had gone too far for the rescue operation to work. On 25 December 1991 – Christmas Day in the West but not in Orthodox Russia – Gorbachev resigned as President.

By then, the USSR had disintegrated into sovereign republics, known collectively as the 'Commonwealth of Independent States' or CIS. Boris Yeltsin, vilified by the KGB and snubbed by Western leaders, had taken over as President of Russia. The West had not won the long Cold War; the Soviet Union had lost it.

From the start, I was totally untouched by Gorbachev's charisma, and therefore immune to the infection of 'Gorbymania'. This was not, as I soon discovered, a recipe for popularity. Everything Gorbachev said and did, in fact, was in line with the teaching of Lenin, his earthly god. Nor did he hide the fact. In a little-noticed speech to Soviet media people in February 1987, he compared the situation as it then was with the total collapse that faced Lenin when the victorious Germans forced him to sign the Treaty of Brest-Litovsk in 1918. Lenin's Revolution had survived and prospered, and the ruling Party, by emulating his example, could overcome its difficulties. History could then resume its preordained course.[1] In his book, *Perestroika*, published that year, Gorbachev invoked Lenin many times, as he did in his speeches of that period, to justify his words and deeds. The book, in particular, provided an illuminating example of his own understanding of *glasnost* (which means 'publicity' in Russian but was, one assumes deliberately, mistranslated as 'openness'), in this passage on Stalin's collectivisation of agriculture:

> ... collectivisation was a great historic act, the most important social change since 1917. Yes, it proceeded painfully, not without serious excesses and blunders. But further progress for our country would have been impossible without it.[2]

The figure of 14.5 million deaths through famine or massacre is now officially admitted in Russia as the human cost of Stalin's collectivisation of agriculture. Gorbachev's 'not without serious excesses' does seem to narrow the scope of *glasnost*.

IT WAS NOT by happy accident that Gorbachev's first target in his prolonged public relations exercise was Mrs Margaret Thatcher, the 'Iron Lady' of Soviet propaganda as a result of an early speech drafted for her by my 'disciple' Robert Moss. If he could win over the Iron Lady, there would surely be no limit to his proselytising. He came to see her at Chequers in December 1984, some time before being promoted to General Secretary of the ruling CPSU. With him was his elegantly dressed wife Raisa. He was rewarded with Mrs Thatcher's famous words: 'A man I could do business with'.

Thereafter, all Western doors were open to him. President François Mitterrand of France and Chancellor Helmut Kohl of Germany were easy conquests. President Ronald Reagan, who coined the apt phrase 'evil empire', was a more resistant target, but he, too, yielded in the end.

By mid-1988, I was gathering material for a short book which I saw as a necessary corrective to the wave of adulation about the Soviet leader at that time sweeping the West. My prime discovery was that Gorbachev's first concern was not, as his speeches and his book had implied, the 'restructuring' of the Soviet economy and Party organisation, but of the entire apparatus of disinformation and other Active Measures. My aim was to present, in factual detail, the Soviet involvement – since Gorbachev's advent to supreme power – in 'peace' disinformation, including forgeries, in international terrorism and drugs-running, in penetration of the Western Churches, and in deliberate cheating in arms control negotiations.

The book was ready for submission to the publishing world in early 1989, and immediately began collecting rejection slips or letters. In all cases, and with variations only of wording and choice of adjectives, the reason given was that what I had written was out of tune with current trends and thinking. Indeed it was, and that was the point of the exercise.

In the end, I found a 'taker': The Claridge Press, Professor Roger Scruton's fearless mini-publishing venture.

By late 1989, the situation was changing with unprecedented speed, with the collapse of Communist rule in Poland, Hungary, Czechoslovakia, and East Germany. In the Soviet Union itself, the Party's Central Committee called a special plenum early in February 1990. On the 7th, it reached a decision, widely hailed as 'historic', to revise Article Six of the Constitution, enshrining the Party's 'leading role'. The Western media hailed this admittedly important news as a 'victory' for Gorbachev. In fact, it was a *crushing defeat* for him, as he had often said he would allow no such thing to happen. Two days later, I handed the revised proofs to Scruton. In the last three pages of the book, I had foreseen a hardline coup (which, of course, happened in August 1991), the collapse of Gorbachev, and the rise of Yeltsin.

This was manifestly not what the media wanted to hear. Negatively, *The Gorbachev Phenomenon: 'Peace' and the Secret War* broke new ground: for the first time in my writing life, not a single review appeared in the national press, although there was much praise for it in smaller and friendly publications, such as *Freedom Today, Soviet Analyst*, and even the *World Today*, the organ of Chatham House. The best review of all was written by George Bailey, a multilingual US Army interpreter and liaison officer during and after World War II, who had lately retired as Director of Radio Liberty in Munich. Bailey's review, however, never appeared. It had been commissioned by *Encounter*, which closed down in September 1990, the month before Bailey's piece was due to appear, after nearly forty years of its civilised defence of Western values.

During the entire period of 'the Gorbachev phenomenon', I was denied access to Britain's daily and Sunday national newspapers, with the single exception of the *Sunday Times*, apart from Letters to the Editor, that last refuge of obsessive eccentrics. I had to content myself with old and new outlets in New York, Washington, Paris, Madrid, and other places.[3]

Even the public humiliation inflicted on Gorbachev by the failed coup of August 1991 did not immediately end Gorbymania, although it did bring examples of the fickleness of high-level friendships. President

Mitterrand went on television on the 19th to say that he had been in touch with Gennady Yanayev, the initiator of the coup, whom he described as 'the new leader'. Two days later, he was back on the little screen, defensively acknowledging the role of Yeltsin. Three days on, the Elysée Palace flourished a message from Gorbachev, by then back in circulation, thanking the French President for convening a European summit.

Chancellor Kohl's first reaction was to assure the coup leaders that Germany would stick to its treaties. He made no mention of Boris Yeltsin. But shortly afterwards, Kohl and his Foreign Minister, Hans-Dietrich Genscher, were heaping praise on him.

On the Monday, Britain's Prime Minister, John Major, condemned the coup. While recognising Gorbachev's contribution 'over recent years', Major stopped short of calling for his reinstatement. Margaret Thatcher, by then out of power, called on the Soviet people to take to the streets in support of Yeltsin, but with the object of bringing Gorbachev back. The man who came back from his interrupted holiday was humbled and diminished. Moreover, he had learned nothing. His first concern, on 21 August, was to reaffirm his loyalty to the Party. He had clung to the belief that the Party could be reformed, and the system too. He had failed to realise that his own *glasnost* alone had made reforms impossible.

In contrast, Yeltsin's stature had grown, not only in the eyes of his countrymen but in the world at large. He had seized the moment, defying the Party and the Army, climbing one of the tanks surrounding the Russian 'White House' but refusing to fire or to storm the parliament building.

Two days after Gorbachev's return, before the Russian parliament, Yeltsin pointed his finger at Gorbachev and forced him to read the minutes of the meeting of the Council of Ministers on 19 August, when the state of emergency had been proclaimed, which revealed almost unanimous support for the coup. On the 23rd, Yeltsin obliged Gorbachev by his example to sign a decree suspending all activities by the CPSU.

The West's presidents and prime ministers were not the only political admirers of Gorbachev. Neil Kinnock, leader of Britain's opposition Labour Party, described Gorbachev's resignation as leader of the Soviet Communist Party in these words: 'I believe it will prove another act of greatness from a man who has made so many historic changes possible.'

On this note of bathos, Lenin's bloodstained legacy came to an end. Although Gorbachev struggled on, the Soviet Union disintegrated around him.

*   *   *

MIKHAIL GORBACHEV WILL undoubtedly be seen as an instrument of History. But the West's enthusiasm for his policies was misplaced. Was it really supposed that he *aimed* at the collapse of Communism, the disintegration of the satellite empire, the unravelling of the USSR? He had inherited a bankrupt system and State. He had recognised the situation in his Brest-Litovsk speech, and to some extent in his book. However, he had been blind to the causes of the great crisis. He had failed to see that the system was unreformable and the doctrine upon which it rested utterly discredited. The 'new thinking' which he continually invoked had been initiated by his mentor Yuri Andropov, who for fifteen years had run the KGB. It had been elaborated by his other mentor, Alexander Yakovlev. It was a very Leninist doctrine: the prize was to persuade the West that the Cold War was over and that it was to the advantage of the West to support him and ensure the survival of a changed Soviet system.

His slogan of a 'common European home' epitomised his political and strategic goal. A common European home implied the departure of the Americans, and the folding of NATO. Thereafter, in a new kind of 'peace', the rich capitalist West would meet the bills for the Soviet Union's recovery, and Lenin's forward march of History could resume. It almost worked. In the end, the dream collapsed under the weight of its own contradictions. If the West's leaders had had their way, there would still be a Soviet problem.

LENIN HAD DESCRIBED the capitalists of the Western world as 'deaf-mutes' who would connive at their own destruction, whether through greed or ignorance. With honourable exceptions, Lenin's estimation of the class enemy was correct. Throughout the Cold War, the Soviet International Department and all its fronts and subsidiaries had operated with relative freedom.

I have mentioned the difficulties I faced in raising funds for The 61 (see Ch. XIX). I now offer some more general observations. At no time did the 'capitalists' band together to defend their own freedom. In each of the Western countries, there were indeed privately funded groups which studied the phenomena of subversion, but their resources were relatively puny on the scale of the enormous means at the disposal of the Soviet Union.

There were, and indeed are still, legal and institutional impediments which made any concerted response by the 'capitalists' virtually impossible. The governments and institutions said (by the Marxists) to represent the capitalists had tied themselves into knots, thus making it difficult or even virtually impossible to defend themselves against the death threat that hung over them.

Let me illustrate this proposition. The general rule in Western societies is that visible (that is, declared) income is taxed. One legal way for capitalists to avoid taxes and put their money to non-profitable use is through tax-exempt institutions, known in Britain and the US as 'charities'. There's the rub. In general, the rule is that 'charities' may not involve themselves in politics. Much of course hinges on the definition of 'politics'. If the term is held to mean 'party politics', then some political activities are legally possible. However, to be concrete, at a time when Britain's Labour Party was being, not openly but visibly, taken over by Communists of various hues and labels, it became legally tricky to fight the trend and avoid charges of illegal use of 'charitable' funds.

An obvious source of funds on the necessary scale might be thought to be the banks, whose activity is central to the capitalist system. In the late 1970s and early 1980s, inflation and high interest rates sent the profits of the major banks soaring to colossal levels, measured each year in hundreds of millions of pounds for the big trading banks. A tiny fraction of this enormous wealth – say 0.5 per cent – would have been ample, not only to expose (passively) but to fight and defeat (actively) the subversive challenge which, if unchecked, would in time have destroyed the system that enabled Western banking to exist and prosper. One half per cent of, say, £600 million is £3 million. Such sums, multiplied by the number of contributing banks or companies, would easily have compensated for the vacuum of State institutions.

Instead, political timidity prevailed. The Western banks thought nothing of providing billions of dollars or pounds to sink without trace in the morass of Third World 'developing' countries. But modest sums to defend the system on which their survival depended caused agonising debates, mostly ending in zero or micro contributions.

As with all rules, there were honourable exceptions. There were big companies (very few of them) with discretionary non-accountable funds; though even with such companies, the bold spirits needed to exercise prudence in case they were thought to overstep the mark and might lose their privileges. There were a few (very few) friendly large, privately owned corporations; of which only a small percentage saw the need to act, and a smaller percentage still actually took action. During the Cold

War, capitalism, by and large, was a toothless tiger on its way to a jungle resting-place.

In the challenge I have described, all honour and credit go to the tiny number of very rich men of courage, who understood the challenge and saw the need to respond to it. They are among the unsung heroes of our time. But there were too few of them.

In a little-noticed speech during the 28th Party Congress in Moscow in July 1990, Gorbachev's Foreign Minister, Eduard Shevardnadze, gave the scarcely believable figure of *700 billion roubles* as the cost of 'ideological confrontation with the West' over the past two decades. One has to assume that 'ideological confrontation' was a euphemism for Active Measures and propaganda. At the admittedly artificial exchange rate at that time, the figure he gave yields the almost surrealistic average yearly figure of £35 billion for the conduct of the Cold War on the Soviet side.

I know of no easy way to calculate the global sums spent by the major Western countries to counter this massive and protracted effort, but it can be safely assumed that it would be a mere fraction of the Soviet total. Ironically, this vast expenditure contributed – along with the gigantic defence budgets – to the bankruptcy of the USSR.

In the face of Shevardnadze's revelation, even I have to admit that the Western advocates of inaction had a point.

NOTES

1 Yegor Yakovlev, *Openness, Democracy, Responsibility* (Novosti, Moscow, 1987), p. 10. See also Brian Crozier, *Communism: Why Prolong Its Death-Throes?* (Institute for European Defence and Strategic Studies, London, 1990).

2 Mikhail Gorbachev, *Perestroika: New Thinking for Our Country and the World* (Harper & Row, New York, 1987), p. 40.

3 On 1 September 1991, however, the London *Sunday Times* published a feature entitled 'The evil empire: heroes and villains – fellow-travellers and devoted foes in the West'. The author was Professor Norman Stone, the renowned Oxford historian and a regular *Sunday Times* columnist. The newspaper kindly included me in a portrait gallery headed 'They got it right', alongside Robert Conquest, Malcolm Muggeridge, Ronald Reagan, and George Orwell. In its gallery of those who 'got it wrong', the following were portrayed: Professors J. K. Galbraith, Fred Halliday, E. H. Carr, and Vic Allen; and Baroness Wootton, also an academic. A leader in the same issue observed that no member of the Left's intelligentsia had apologised for defending Communism, and added: 'For every Robert Conquest, Melvin Lasky, Frank Chapple or Brian Crozier who fought the good fight, there were a dozen Eric Hobsbawms, Ken Gills and Baroness Woottons anxious to appease, obfuscate or worse.'

Glossary of acronyms

AAP	Australian Associated Press
ANC	African National Congress (South Africa)
ASIO	Australian Security Intelligence Organisation
AUEW	Amalgamated Union of Engineering Workers (UK)
BfV	*Bundesamt für Verfassungsschutz*: Federal Office for the Protection of the Constitution (see LfV)
BND	*Bundesnachrichtendienst*: Federal Intelligence Service (West Germany)
CAMACC	Campaign against Council Corruption (UK)
CARICOM	Caribbean Community
CARSC	Current Affairs Research Services Centre (UK)
CBI	Confederation of British Industry
CCF	Congress for Cultural Freedom
CCG	Communist Campaign Group (UK)
CDI	Canadian Development Institute
CDU	*Christliche Demokratische Union* (Germany)
CSU	*Christliche Soziale Union* (Germany)
CIA	Central Intelligence Agency (USA)
CND	Campaign for Nuclear Disarmament (UK)
COHSE	Confederation of Health Service Employees (UK)
CPGB	Communist Party of Great Britain
CPS	Coalition for Peace through Security (UK)
CPSU	Communist Party of the Soviet Union
CSCE	Conference on Security and Cooperation in Europe (also known as 'the Helsinki Conference')
CSE	Counter-Subversion Executive (UK: a proposal never implemented)

DCI	Director of Central Intelligence (USA)
DDR	See GDR
DGI	*Dirección General de Inteligencia* (Cuban equivalent of KGB)
DIA	Defense Intelligence Agency (USA)
DS	*Durzhavna Sigurnost*: Security Service (Bulgaria)
EDC	European Defence Community (never created)
ETA	*Euzkadi ta Azkatasuna*: Freedom for the Basque Homeland
FBI	Federal Bureau of Investigation (USA)
FCO	See FO
FDP	*Freiheitliche Demokratische Partei*: Free Democratic Party of Germany (Liberals)
FDR	(President) F. D. Roosevelt (USA)
FMTA	Federation of Metro Tenants' Association (Toronto, Canada)
FO	Foreign Office (UK; also Foreign and Commonwealth Office (FCO))
FRELIMO	*Frente de Libertação de Moçambique*: Liberation Front of Mozambique (Marxist-Leninist ruling party)
FWF	Forum World Features (UK; CIA-supported)
GCHQ	Government Communications Headquarters (UK)
GDR	German Democratic Republic (*Deutsche Demokratische Republik* or DDR: East Germany)
GF	*Guardia di Finanza*: Inspectorate of Finance (Italy; see SIS)
GLC	Greater London Council (UK)
GRU	*Glavnoye Razvedyvatelnoye Upravleniye*: Chief Intelligence Directorate of Soviet General Staff; i.e. Soviet military intelligence
HUAC	House Un-American Activities Committee (USA)
HUMINT	Human intelligence
ID	International Department (of Soviet Communist Party's Central Committee)
IHT	*International Herald Tribune*
IISS	International Institute for Strategic Studies (UK)
INF	Intermediate-Range Nuclear Forces
INTERDOC	International Documentary Centre (Netherlands)
IOR	*Istituto per le Opere di Religione*: Institute for Religious Works (the Vatican's bank)
IPS	Institute for Policy Studies (US)
IRA	Irish Republican Army
IRD	Information Research Department (UK)
ISC	Institute for the Study of Conflict (UK)
JIC	Joint Intelligence Committee (UK)
KGB	*Komitet Gosudarstvennoy Bezopastnosti*: Committee of State Security (USSR)
LfV	*Landesamt für Verfassungsschutz*: Land Office for the Protection of the Constitution (regional branches of the BfV: q.v.)
MAPU	*Movimiento de Acción Popular Unificada*: Movement of Unified Popular Action (Salvador Allende's political grouping in Chile)

MCC	Metropolitan County Councils (UK)
MI-5	Security Service (UK)
MI-6	Secret Intelligence Service (UK)
MIR	*Movimiento de la Izquierda Revolucionaria*: Movement of the Revolutionary Left (Chile)
Mossad	Central Institute for Intelligence and Special Assignments (Israel)
MPLA	*Movimiento Popular para a Libertação de Angola*: People's Movement for the Liberation of Angola (Marxist-Leninist ruling party)
NAF	National Association for Freedom (UK: later, The Freedom Association or TFA)
NEC	National Executive Committee (of British Labour Party)
NKVD	Forerunner of KGB
NSA	National Security Agency (US equivalent of Britain's GCHQ: q.v.)
NSIC	National Strategy Information Center (US)
NTS	*Narodno-Trudovoy Soyuz Rossiyshikh Solidaristov*: Popular Labour Alliance of Russian Solidarists (Frankfurt-based anti-Soviet Russian émigré organisation)
NUM	National Union of Mineworkers (UK)
NUPE	National Union of Public Employees (UK)
OECS	Organisation of East Caribbean States
OID	Overseas Information Department (UK)
ONUC	See UNOC
OSS	Office of Strategic Services (USA; forerunner of CIA)
P-2	Masonic Lodge (Italy)
PASOK	Pan-Hellenic Socialist Movement (Greece)
PCF	*Parti Communiste Français* (France)
PLO	Palestine Liberation Organisation
RENAMO	See RNM
RNM	*Resistencia Nacional Moçambicana*: Mozambican National Resistance (also known as RENAMO)
RSL	Revolutionary Socialist League; also known as Militant (Trotskyist group, UK)
SAVAK	*Sazamane Etelaat va Amniate Kechvar*: Security and Intelligence Organisation (Iran)
SDA	Social Democratic Alliance (UK)
SDECE	*Service de Documentation Extérieure et de Contre-Espionnage*: External Documentation and Counter-Espionage Service (France)
SDI	Strategic Defense Initiative (US; misleadingly dubbed 'Star Wars')
SDP	Social Democratic Party (UK)
SEATO	South-East Asia Treaty Organisation
SED	*Sozialistische Einheitspartei Deutschlands*: Socialist Unity Party of (East) Germany
SID	*Servizio Informazione e Difesa*: Information and Defence Service (Italy)
SIGINT	Signals intelligence

SIS	Secret Intelligence Service: MI-6 (UK)
SIS	*Servizio per l'Informazione e la Sicurezza*: Information and Security Service (Italy; combining *Carabinieri* and *Guardia di Finanza*)
SMERSH	*Smert Shpionam* (Death to Spies: KGB department handling 'wet jobs', i.e. murders of selected people)
SNASP	*Serviço Nacional de Seguridade Pública*: Mozambique's National Public Security Service
SOE	Special Operations Executive (UK, during World War II)
SPD	*Sozialdemokratische Partei Deutschlands*: Social Democratic Party of Germany
STASI	*Staatssicherheitsdienst*: State Security Service (East Germany)
StB	*Statni tajna Bezpecnost*: State Security Service (Czechoslovakia)
TGWU	Transport and General Workers' Union (UK)
UNITA	*União Nacional para a Independencia total de Angola*: National Union for the Total Independence of Angola
UNOC	United Nations Operation Congo (alternatively, ONUC: *Opération Nations Unies Congo*)
WFTU	World Federation of Trades Unions (Soviet International front)
WPC	World Peace Council (Soviet International front)

Index